BUSINESS STUDIES

FOR AS I REVISION GUIDE

Edited by
Ian Marcousé

Andrew Hammond
Marie Brewer

Acknowledgements

Every year hundreds of teachers put themselves forward to mark AS and A Level examinations. From these, dozens become team leaders and some become senior team leaders. From these ranks of examiners come the insights that are reflected in this book. Each summer the three of us are part of this important process. We would like to acknowledge the contribution made by examiners to the A Level system and to our understanding of the advice and support students need when the exams are looming.

Marie Brewer, Andrew Hammond and Ian Marcousé

Orders: please contact Bookpoint Ltd, 130 Milton Park, Abingdon, Oxon OX14 4SB. Telephone: (44) 01235 827720. Fax: (44) 01235 400454. Lines are open from 9.00–6.00, Monday to Saturday, with a 24 hour message answering service. You can also order through our website www.hodderheadline.co.uk.

British Library Cataloguing in Publication Data
A catalogue record for this title is available from the British Library

ISBN 0 340 81106 4

First published 2004
Impression number   10 9 8 7 6 5 4 3 2 1
Year   2008 2007 2006 2005 2004

Cover artwork by Jacey.
Typeset by Phoenix Photosetting, Chatham, Kent.
Printed in Spain for Hodder & Stoughton Educational, a division of Hodder Headline, 338 Euston Road, London NW1 3BH

CONTENTS

iv

INTRODUCTION

This revision book is written to help push every reader's AS results up by at least one grade. It does this by focusing the AS subject content on the exam skills sought by examiners. The writing style is analytic, but applied to the context of real businesses, just as the examiners want. Every chapter points out key evaluative themes within the syllabus. As knowledge of the syllabus counts for only one third of the marks at AS level, revision must do more than re-hash facts and definitions. This Revision Guide teaches the reader to develop all the exam skills needed for success.

Each Unit within the book covers a different section of the AS specification. All the key concepts are explained, with the more difficult ones getting longer, fuller explanations. The content is full of references to real firms, and application is further enhanced by dedicated sections in each Unit. There are also questions to test yourself in every Unit. The answers are set out at the back of the book, to provide immediate feedback on how your revision is going.

There are three other features to help build grades:

- At the end of each section (Marketing, Finance and so on) is a final unit containing many questions, including exam-style papers; again, answers are at the back to help you study for yourself.

- Towards the end of the book are four articles providing advice on exam technique; you should read these with care.

- Revision checklists, one for each exam unit, prompt you to consider carefully whether you know everything you should.

The authors

Ian Marcousé has devised the format of the book and edited all the text and questions. Ian is the AS/A2 Chief Examiner for a major exam board and a leading author. He is also the founding editor of *Business Review* magazine and teaches at Lambeth College, London.

Marie Brewer is an experienced author and a Senior Examiner for a major exam board.

Andrew Hammond is an experienced author, a regular contributor to Business Review, and a Senior Examiner on AS Unit 2 for a major exam board. He is also Head of Business Studies at Darrick Wood School, Bromley.

MARKETING – INTRODUCTION AND OVERVIEW

What?

Marketing is the business activity that links the producer to the customer. In order to sell to the customer the business needs to have knowledge about the market. With good market knowledge a business can achieve its objectives. It can have the right products in the right place at the right time and promoted in the right way.

Market knowledge has five parts:
- Knowing how big the market is;
- Understanding the competitors;
- Understanding existing customers;
- Understanding the attitudes of buyers of rival products;
- Knowing the key outlets and how the products get to the market.

The most important aspect of this process is understanding customer tastes, attitudes and behaviour.

Which?

Market knowledge should be easy for a *small business* with close day-to-day contact with its customers. However, knowledge is not the same as understanding. The owner needs to know how customers will react to changes in the product or prices. Selling to customers is an ever-changing activity; as tastes change, so does the level of competition.

Large firms have more customers and often more products. They may operate in more than one market and be faced with many different competitors. Their marketing will therefore need to be more carefully managed. It will require time, money and expertise.

Successful large businesses have effective marketing departments that:
- take advantage of the firm's strengths;
- are ahead of the market;
- understand customer psychology.

How?

Having good market knowledge gives the firm the background in which to begin the process of selling to the customer. Businesses need to decide what they are trying to achieve: their *marketing objective*. Without a clear *marketing objective* the firm will have no focus for its activities. Once a firm has set an objective it can then develop a *marketing strategy* to enable it to reach the objective.

Examples of marketing objectives and strategies
- *Marketing objective*: Increasing our share of the instant coffee market from 16 to 20%.
- *Marketing strategy*: Reduce the price of the product and increase sales through discount supermarkets.

- *Marketing objective*: Increase sales of holidays to affluent over 50s.
- *Marketing strategy*: Launch a separate brochure with different resorts and features, backed by an advertising campaign targeted at this group.

Market research is the key to gaining market knowledge.

Other marketing tools such as product portfolio or product life cycle analysis can be used to further understand the market. Promotional tools such as advertising and point of sale displays can then be used to inform and persuade the customer.

But

Marketing is a complex and ever-changing activity. Marketing needs to be a continuous process. Businesses need to ensure that marketing activity gives value for money. The return should be greater than the cost.

Firms need to know:
- What does our marketing activity cost?
- Can we afford it?
- What do we get in return?

This requires that the firm monitors the marketing activity. Especially in large firms the marketing budget can be very high (Unilever spends over £3000 million each year!). The firm needs to be sure that this is money well spent.

The marketing function should not operate in isolation from the rest of the business. The whole of the company must work together if marketing expenditure is to be effective. Finance is needed to fund a marketing programme and production and distribution must be ready to deal with any increases in sales.

A marketing objective of increasing sales will only work if the production department can produce sufficient items. An advertising campaign that increases sales needs to be backed up by a distribution system that ensures that the product is available in the shops.

Application of marketing

All businesses need to have some marketing activity. The marketing needs to be tailored to the individual business in the context of its market place.

In 2002 the Multiple Sclerosis Society won a prize for the effectiveness of its new, large marketing campaign. It was based on a new visual image for the Society and the launch of an interactive web site. After several years of low growth in donations there was a 30% increase in income. The direct marketing campaign was three times more successful than in previous years. Another success was to influence government policy to secure a commitment to £50 million for new medicines each year. The total cost of the campaign was £4 million but it generated a surplus of around £5 million. Mike Johnston, a judge from the Chartered Institute of Marketing, said:

> The Society's approach demonstrates innovative thinking, careful strategic planning and successful implementation. Achieving growth in today's competitive markets requires excellence in marketing knowledge and skills as well as application and understanding of business priorities.

All businesses need to understand their markets. It is at least as important for a new small business as it is for a large multinational firm. Charities are not normally thought of as businesses that need to 'do marketing'. This example shows that marketing can be effective in all types of organisation. Some people might criticise a charity for using £4 million of donations to fund an advertising campaign, but the result was extra money for the Society to continue its work.

Is marketing ethical?

There are many people who think that persuading customers to buy products is unethical, particularly when targeted at vulnerable groups (e.g. positioning sweets at supermarket checkout tills or persuading customers in developing countries to buy cigarettes). The firms would argue that the justification for trying to sell their products is that this is necessary to keep staff in a job and provide a return to their shareholders. They would also argue that it is up to the customer to decide to buy or not to buy. In an exam, it is well worth considering whether a firm's marketing approach is ethical. Examiners do *not* assume that businesses always do the right thing.

E Exam insight

When asked about marketing, students often concentrate on one aspect of marketing such as advertising or one of the marketing tools such as the four Ps. Take care to relate the answer to the particular aspect of marketing that is being dealt with in the case study or asked for in the answer. Remember that marketing is about understanding the market and successfully developing a strategy to sell the product.

S Student howlers

'Only large companies need marketing.'
'Advertising is what sells products.'

Is the amount of money spent on marketing worthwhile?

There is an argument which says that consumers would be better served if businesses spent less on advertising and more on improving the product or service and reducing prices to customers. In defence to this, marketing experts would say that marketing is looking to improve the product for the customer by finding out what the customer wants. In addition, advertising means that the customer is aware of the product and is also aware of competitive products so is in a better position to make a choice.

T Test yourself

1. What is meant by market knowledge? (2)
2. Why do businesses need market knowledge? (3)
3. Why does marketing need to be integrated with the other business activities? (4)
4. What is a marketing objective? (2)
5. Outline an appropriate marketing strategy for Cadbury's, if it wishes to increase the market share of its 'Crunchie' brand. (6)
6. Is it ethical to aim advertising for crisps and fizzy drinks at young children? Explain your answer. (8)

MARKETING OBJECTIVES AND DECISION MAKING

What?

Marketing objectives are the marketing targets that must be achieved for the company to attain its overall goals. Marketing decisions are based on these objectives.

Who?

In most businesses marketing objectives follow from Boardroom decisions about the direction that the company as a whole should take. This company 'vision' should clearly show what the company wants to achieve in the future. It should be easy to understand. The former president of Sony wanted everyone to have access to 'personal portable sound'. The result was the Walkman and subsequently personal CD and MiniDisc players. Firms may also have specific business objectives such as expansion, moving into a new market or profit building.

The marketing contribution to these company aims will be to achieve the *marketing objectives*.

How?

The purpose of objectives is to set out what the business wants to achieve. Marketing objectives set the targets on which the marketing activity will focus.

Marketing objectives should be SMART:
- **S**pecific: They should have a clearly defined goal that all staff know and understand.
- **M**easurable: If the objective is measurable (e.g. increase sales by 5%) it will be possible to check that the marketing effort is being effective.
- **A**chievable: The objectives should be challenging but achievable. The objective should be supported by a budget that allows the targets to be achieved. It should also recognise market conditions. In a highly competitive market, rivals will react to any aggressive marketing strategies. This will make it harder to achieve the objectives.
- **R**elevant: The objectives should make good business sense.
- **T**argets.

All marketing objectives need to be based on a sound understanding of the market. Therefore they rely on effective market research.

Which?

Small businesses are unlikely to have formalised marketing objectives. The owners are likely to have dreams and plans, but may never have written them down. Larger companies are more likely to have marketing departments and to have a more formalised marketing process.

Service industries are no different from manufacturers or retailers. The setting of marketing objectives will often depend on the size or sophistication of the firm.

What sort of marketing objectives are there?

There are three main types of marketing objective: increasing product differentiation, growth and innovation.

Increasing product differentiation
A product that is different from its rivals is easier to sell. Making the product distinct is essential in a crowded market. Firms will try to make their product stand out by:
- developing a unique selling point, or a unique sales image; at the time of writing, Renault have done this by using Thierry Henri to promote their cars' 'va-va-voom';
- using different distribution channels;
- reinforcing sales to a particular type of person or group.

Growth
Most businesses focus on growth. They see increased sales as the way to increase profit. This needs to be properly managed or it could damage the firm. A firm whose products are too available may lose their exclusive brand image.

Innovation
In some business areas such as technology (e.g. electronics, cars and medicines) and fashion (e.g. clothing, music, entertainment) innovation is the key to success. Innovation adds value. Being the first into the market will give the firm major advantages. It may for instance be able to take advantage of skimming pricing.

Why not?

Problems in achieving marketing objectives can be because of problems within the business (internal constraints) or outside the business (external constraints), as shown in the following examples.

Internal constraints

1. *Financial*: The budget needs to be sufficient to achieve the objective. If a firm wishes to increase its market share it must find the funds for a major marketing campaign.
2. *Personnel constraints*: Marketing requires expertise. If the business wants to expand into overseas markets it needs people who can operate in those countries.

External constraints

1. *Competition*: Firms may have very well thought out marketing objectives and campaigns but if the competitor reacts to the strategy then it could well fail. A price reduction to increase market share could result in a price war.
2. *The economy*: Changes in taxation or interest rates may affect consumer spending and confidence. As the economy moves into a boom or a recession the medium- and long-term objectives may have to be adjusted.

Application

The marketing objectives of each firm need to be understood in the context of that particular firm. A firm may wish to increase its market share but if it has cash problems it may not have the resources to invest in strategies to achieve the objective. Firms in highly competitive markets will find it harder to achieve their objectives.

Vodafone's business objective is to become one of the world's top ten brands. It has a presence in 28 countries and over 100 million customers worldwide. Its marketing objectives are to:

- retain existing and attract new customers;
- continue to develop the Vodafone brand;
- introduce successful new technologies and services (Vodafone live! and mobile internet).

As part of the marketing strategy to achieve these objectives it has sponsorship deals with both Manchester United and the Ferrari Formula 1 team. Both offer Vodafone high exposure with worldwide television audiences. Vodafone's link with both of these teams gives them a unique selling point (USP).

How do firms make marketing decisions?

Marketing decisions follow from the marketing objectives. Once the marketing objectives have been set, market information must be gathered. With this vital background information the firm can come up with a suggested strategy. This should then be tested – perhaps by test marketing or market research. The results are then reviewed. If they show that the strategy would be successful it can be put into action.

However, the results may show that the objectives are not achievable. This will then lead to a review and possible change to the objectives. This ongoing process is known as the *marketing model*.

The most likely issues for evaluation will focus on how useful and relevant the marketing objectives are. It is generally agreed that having objectives helps firms to focus their marketing activity. They have an aim that can be developed into specific targets and activities. However, the objectives need to be realistic within the context of the particular firm.

K Key Terms

Constraints – factors that limit a firm's ability to achieve its objectives

Marketing model – a procedure for making marketing decisions in a scientific manner

Service industries – firms such as doctors, accountants, advertising agents; they provide a service rather than manufacturing a product

Vision – a view of what the company wants to do in the future

E Exam insight

Be careful not to confuse marketing objectives and marketing strategies. Marketing objectives are what you want to achieve; marketing strategy is how you plan to achieve it.

S Student howlers

'Marketing objectives are about capturing market share.'
'Firms can only reach their objectives if they have good targets.'

T Test yourself

1. Why do firms need marketing objectives? (3)
2. What are the three main types of marketing objective? (3)
3. What is product differentiation? (2)
4. What internal and external constraints might cause a business to fail to achieve its objectives? (4)
5. Why is market information necessary in setting objectives? (3)

ANALYSING THE MARKET

What is a market?

A market is a place where buyers and sellers meet. When a business talks about the market it is talking about its customers and the factors such as the economy and competition that affect customer behaviour. Successful marketing needs a complete understanding of the market.

What more?

Which market is the firm in?

The business must decide which market it is operating in. Above all else, it must decide whether it wishes to view its market narrowly or broadly. News International (Rupert Murdoch's company) started as a newspaper business, but decided that it was in the broader media communications business. It therefore started a TV station (Sky) and bought into American TV and cinema with Fox.

Other businesses keep a tight focus, such as Manchester United, which hasn't even made much effort in women's football, let alone other sports such as rugby or ice hockey. Manchester United sees itself as a football business, not a sports business.

How?

A firm must break the market down, to really investigate it.

Market size

The business needs to know the size of its market. Without this information it cannot measure its share and its competitors' share of the sales. Market size can be measured by volume or value.

- *Volume* gives the *quantity*, which may be in units such as number of cars sold, by weight such as tonnes of wheat or by volume such as litres of petrol.
- *Value* is a measure of *how much customers spend on the product*. It will be quantity sold multiplied by the price per unit. The market by value for petrol will be the total number of litres sold multiplied by the price per litre.

Consumer usage and attitudes

Firms need to understand why customers behave in the way they do. They need to understand why

customers are buying their products and just as importantly why they are not.

Businesses use many different methods to gather information about customer attitudes.

- The most common is by quantitative research such as surveys. These may be used on an ongoing basis or after a particular marketing activity such as an advertising campaign.
- The simplest method is to get feedback from staff who deal with customers. This is particularly useful in service industries and in situations where the customer meets the sales person directly, such as when buying a car.
- Another method is to hold customer group discussions run by psychologists. Customers will be encouraged to talk about their 'relationship' with the product. This will give the company an insight into customer buying habits and attitudes. This can be useful for product development.

What tools are available?

Consumer profiles

These give a picture of the customer. They categorise the customer perhaps by age or geographical location. This picture of the customer will enable the firm to focus on a *target market*. A consumer profile may show the customer to be a male between 20 and 30 years old with an interest in sport. Clearly advertising at sports stadiums will be more effective than advertising in shopping malls. Customer profiles are also helpful when setting quotas for market research.

Market mapping

This shows where the product or brand sits in the market compared to other products. The product is mapped against other similar products using set criteria and can be shown in a diagram.

What is market share?

Market share shows the percentage of a particular market held by any one company or product. For many firms the main aim is to be the market leader, in other words to have the largest market share. This will help the firm by:

- giving them more shelf space as most distributors will want to stock the brand leaders;
- reducing the necessity to discount the price to the retailers;
- allowing a better launch pad for new products.

How do firms use market share information?

It is used by businesses to measure their success. In any market, whether growing or declining, it is helpful for a firm to know how well they are doing compared to their competitors. It can also be used to measure the success of a marketing campaign.

Many marketing managers will concentrate on increasing or maintaining their market share. Continual measurement will allow companies to tailor their marketing budgets and activities.

What determines market growth?

For any business an estimate of future sales is essential for planning. Ideally a firm would like to operate in a market that is not only growing but where the value of sales is also increasing.

Key factors affecting market growth include:

- *Economic growth*: If the economy is growing then sales of most normal and luxury products will increase.
- *Social changes*: Influences such as the change in the size of family units or a lower birth rate or increased life span can all affect markets for different products.
- *Changes in fashion*: Obviously as tastes change so a market will develop or go into decline.

Application

Market information is essential for all firms. Whatever industry or sector the firm operates in, it needs to know about its market. Selling to industrial markets requires a slightly different approach for some businesses. The relationship between the supplier and the customer will often be closer. In some cases the supplier will work with the customer to produce goods specifically for the business.

In September 2003, Levi Jeans announced the closure of their North American production facilities. This was partly to save costs by shifting production to cheaper labour cost countries. It was also a result of falling demand for their product. Customer attitudes have changed and the once universally strong brand has faced increasing difficulty in selling its products to the youth market. This changing attitude has resulted in a smaller market share. Understanding what is happening in the market has enabled Levi to make changes in marketing and company strategy.

In October 2003, BBC News reported that the Japanese supermarket chain Aeon was to start stocking quarter-size cauliflowers and cabbages as part of a new dwarf vegetable range for single people. Two-thirds of all households in Tokyo are single persons. Company spokeswoman Naoko Ueda said:

Both these examples show how firms react to market changes.

There is little doubt that all firms need to understand their markets. Without this vital information any other marketing effort could be wasted. Understanding the market is perhaps the most important contribution that marketing makes to the profitability of the firm. The way each firm goes about gathering its market information will depend on the nature of the business. A firm with one product will need to do less research than a firm with multiple brands.

K Key Terms

Industrial markets – businesses selling to other businesses

Target market – the group of or types of customer that the firm wants for its product or brand

E Exam insight

When analysing the market for a product or service take care to note if the figures are units or value.

S Student howlers

'Having a large market is the most important thing for a business.'
'As long as the firm is successful there is no need to do market research.'

T Test yourself

1. How can firms measure the size of the market? (2)
2. Identify the narrow and the broader market that each of the following businesses are in:
   a) Saga Holidays;
   b) Volvic water;
   c) British Gas. (6)
3. Identify three factors that influence the growth of markets. (3)
4. What is the formula for calculating Maltesers' share of the chocolate market? (2)
5. What is meant by a consumer profile? How is this helpful to a business? (7)

MARKET RESEARCH

What?

Market research is the process of gathering information about customers, competitors and distributors within a firm's target market.

- *Quantitative research* gathers statistical information about customers and the market.
- *Qualitative research* looks at <u>why</u> consumers behave in certain ways.

Which?

All businesses will benefit from understanding their market. A small local firm such as a hairdresser or butcher will have direct knowledge of their customers and competitors so may not need to conduct any formal research. If they wish to expand or to introduce new products, market research will be helpful in avoiding costly mistakes.

Large multinational firms with a wide portfolio of products will need to be constantly researching their markets. They may have a wealth of information about existing products and markets but they may still want to do research to see what would happen if the product was modified or if the price was changed.

Businesses supplying other firms may have less need of market research if they are providing products or services to customer specifications.

How?

Researchers gather information either by using information that already exists (secondary or desk research) or by going out into the market to gather first-hand information (primary or field research).

Secondary research

This uses data that already exist. It is available from many sources such as:

- *Trade journals*: There are many specialist journals, such as *The Grocer* or *Caterer & Hotelkeeper*, which provide information for specific industry groups.
- *Market intelligence reports*: These are prepared by organisations such as Keynotes, Mintel and Retail Business (EIU). They collect a vast range of data on markets and give valuable analysis of trends that they sell to interested parties.

- *Government statistics*: Government departments collect and publish a wealth of statistics relating to population and economic activity.

Primary research

This is the process of gathering information directly from the market. Firms can talk to retailers or to customers directly. The retailer is in direct contact with the customer and can identify buying patterns and changes in customer behaviour. Talking directly to customers is useful for getting customer ideas.

For more extensive research firms may use market research agencies.

Qualitative research

For qualitative research two main approaches are used: group discussions and in-depth interviews.

Group discussions

These are sometimes called focus groups. Group members are asked to focus on a particular topic such as the taste or name of a product. This can help to:

- reveal problems or opportunities;
- tell the firm why customers are making certain choices;
- make decisions about taste or design.

In-depth interviews

These are usually conducted on a similar basis to group discussions but on a one-to-one basis so they avoid the problems of members of the group being influenced by others. They are however more expensive and the amount of information gathered is more limited.

Questionnaires

Questionnaires ask preset questions to a sample of people. They are widely used in market research. The information obtained is normally quantitative but they can also gather qualitative information.

Questionnaires need to be properly designed if they are to be of any value. If they are poorly designed they could lead the company to the wrong conclusions – an expensive waste of time and effort.

The key features of a good questionnaire are:

- Questions are focused on what the company is trying to find out.
- Questions do not lead towards a particular answer.
- Questions are clear and unambiguous.

- Questions will include basic demographic information, thus enabling a better analysis of the results.

Another important consideration with questionnaires is the response rate. Traditionally postal questionnaires have a low response, which may lead to biased results. Face-to-face questionnaires have a much higher response rate. However, this is an expensive way of carrying out a survey and the business will need to balance both cost and effectiveness.

Why is it important to get the sample right?

Questionnaires are based on samples. It would clearly be too expensive to ask the whole population. The art of sampling is to get a sample that represents the population that is being surveyed. There are three main elements to this.

1. *Sampling method.* This can affect the validity of the sample. There are two main sampling methods:
   — random sampling, which involves picking the sample at random (e.g. by picking every fiftieth person);
   — quota sampling, where the people used for the sample are chosen to represent the profile of the target market. If, for example, 20% of the target market is of the under-18 age group, then the sample will have 20% of under-18 year olds.

2. *Sample size.* The sample has to be large enough to ensure that it is valid. Generally samples of about 500–1000 are considered large enough to reflect opinions accurately. Firms will often use smaller samples because of the cost of conducting surveys on this scale.

3. *Statistical significance.* This is a mathematical measure that tells the firm how accurate the researchers feel the information from the survey is. They may say that the results have 95% confidence. This means that they are pretty sure that the result will be correct in 19 out of 20 cases.

Application

We are very aware of the market research that is often seen outside supermarkets or the questionnaire that comes through the post. These are often focused on consumer products. However, market research is relevant to all sorts of organisations.

Recently the England and Wales Cricket Board carried out some market research. Although cricket is a traditional UK sport, the attendance at cricket matches and club membership had declined. Cricket seemed to have lost its appeal, particularly with younger people.

The Board carried out research to learn how it could:

- increase interest in the game;
- encourage more people to play;
- encourage more people to watch matches.

As a result of this the Board has launched the '20-over' game that lasts around 3 hours. They have also introduced different marketing strategies and have added value to the game by including other attractions such as music at cricket grounds.

The extent to which companies, especially larger businesses, have come to rely on market research is often criticised. There is little doubt that an understanding of customer behaviour will help a business to produce products that the market wants. Like many other business tools, market research needs to be cost effective. Using market research is often seen as a scientific approach to marketing. However, some of the best marketing initiatives come from hunches or 'gut feel' initiatives.

K Key Terms

Multinational firms – firms that operate in many countries

Target market – the section of the population that the firm wants to sell to

E Exam insight

Remember that market research is not just about questionnaires.

When answering a question about market research, take care to focus your answer on the particular business. Ask yourself: What does the business need to know? Then think about how it should go about getting the information. A broad sweeping answer will not get you any application or analysis marks.

S Student howlers

'Questionnaires are the best sort of market research.'
'Only large companies can afford to do market research.'

T Test yourself

1. Explain the difference between primary and secondary research. (4)
2. What is the difference between quantitative and qualitative research? (4)
3. Identify two disadvantages of each of the two main sampling methods. (4)
4. Outline two factors affecting how large a sample size a firm would want to use. (4)
5. What do you need to do to design a good questionnaire? (4)

PRODUCT LIFE CYCLE AND PORTFOLIO ANALYSIS

What?

The product life cycle describes the pattern of sales of a product over its lifetime. Normally sales increase slowly after a product is launched. This is known as the introduction period. If the product becomes more widely accepted sales will rise. This is the growth phase. Eventually sales will level off as the market becomes saturated and demand for the product is satisfied. The product is now said to be at maturity. At some point sales will begin to decline. The diagram below shows the four main stages of the life cycle, plus the development stage. During this period the sales of the product are obviously zero. It is useful to include this stage when looking at the relationship between product life cycle and cash flow.

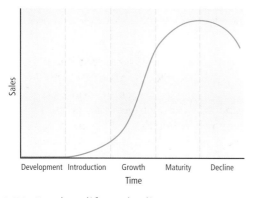

Fig. 1.5A: Product life cycle diagram

Why?

Each product or brand will have its own life cycle. Some are very long, such as manufactured cigarettes, which were 'born' in Britain in 1871 and enjoyed their sales peak in 1971. Sales today are about half the 1971 level. Other life cycles are short, such as toy or fashion crazes. The Pokemon craze lasted less than 2 years.

Firms need to have a good idea of whether a new brand's life is likely to be long or short before deciding on a marketing strategy. Pricing decisions, for example, may be very different – with a skimming approach adopted for short life-cycle products, but penetration seeming wiser for those expected to have a long life.

How useful?

Businesses need to understand not only *what* is happening to their sales pattern but also *why* change is taking place. The product life cycle is a useful tool but only if managers really understand their products. If sales are falling this may be the start of the decline stage, but it may just be a short-term event that is happening in the market such as increased competitive activity. Knowing why change is occurring will help the firm to devise an appropriate strategy.

What next?

Marketing support is often used to alter the product life cycle. A well-focused marketing campaign can boost the initial level of sales following a product launch. It can also help to speed up the growth of sales. The maturity stage is usually the most profitable stage of the life cycle, so firms try to extend this period using *extension strategies* such as
  • Selling the product to a new market segment;
  • Finding other uses for the product;
  • Changing the marketing mix.
Not all products go into decline. Maltesers enjoyed their best-ever sales year in 2003 – 70 years after product launch!

Cash flow and the product life cycle

When a business is developing a product, it will have expenses but no revenue. This can be seen on the diagram below as a negative cash flow. As the product is introduced, revenue will start to increase but cash flow may still be negative, as the business needs to spend money to promote the product. As sales grow the need for this marketing support may diminish and so cash flow will become positive. If the product needs support to maintain its maturity stage then cash flow may again dip.

What is a product portfolio?

Most firms have more than one product. The range of products that they sell is known as their product portfolio. Firms need to be aware of each product

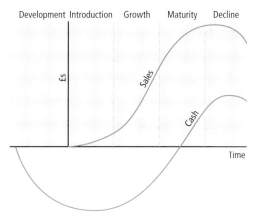

Fig. 1.5B: Product life cycle and cash flow diagram

within this portfolio. They need to understand what contribution each product is making to sales and profits. Firms clearly want the best mix of products. Portfolio analysis will help firms to choose which products are worth investing in and which may no longer deserve support.

How?

One tool that is useful in helping firms to analyse their portfolios is the Boston Matrix. This looks at a firm's brands in relation to two key factors:

1. What is the market (or sector) share?
2. What is the rate of growth within that market/sector.

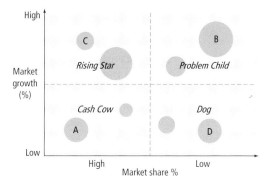

Fig. 1.5C: The Boston matrix

The results are then plotted on a diagram according to the market share and market growth for each brand.
  Products are classified in four ways

1. *Cash cow*. A cash cow product has a high market share with low to average growth in the market. These products provide a steady income to the business and their profit can be 'milked' to provide cash support for 'rising star' or 'problem child' products.

2. *Rising stars*: These products have a high market share in a growth market. Their future potential makes them obvious candidates for heavy marketing support.

3. *Problem child*: A product with a low market share in a growing market. Although the market may look inviting, these products have disappointed. The firm will need to decide if a new marketing strategy can save the product or if it will prove too expensive.

4. *Dogs*: These products have a low market share in a static or declining market. In most cases the costs of reviving these products outweigh the likely returns. They are therefore allowed to die when they fall below their break-even point.

Application

In 2001 Unilever announced a new strategy based on cutting down its portfolio. The firm is now focusing on 400 key brands and trimming more than 1000 brands. The 400 key brands – such as Magnum ice cream, Lipton tea and Dove – are global brands. They contribute almost 90% of the total revenue for the business. Advertising support will be shifted to these key brands and gradually withdrawn from the others. The company is hoping that this will increase revenue and cut costs. In 2003 Cadbury's introduced a very similar strategy for its chocolate products.

  Dell, the US computer firm, has managed to increase its share of the computer market even though the market has been very sluggish. It has done this by using an aggressive pricing policy. It has also launched a new range of digital music players and televisions in an attempt to break into the consumer electronics market. Dell has recognised that its core products, computers, are operating in a mature and saturated market.

Although there is agreement that it is useful for firms to gather knowledge about their product portfolio and the life cycle of individual products, it is important that managers understand what the information is telling them. They need to be able to make sensible and cost-effective decisions based on the information.

  In reality the information gathered will probably be more useful in understanding why something has happened rather than as a planning aid.

Themes for evaluation

T Test yourself

1. What are the five stages of a product's life cycle? (5)
2. What may explain why some products such as Coca-Cola never seem to go into decline? (4)
3. How can firms extend the life of their products? (3)
4. What is meant by a product portfolio? (2)
5. Outline two possible drawbacks to Unilever from the strategy it has recently adopted. (6)

NICHE VERSUS MASS MARKETING

What?

Niche marketing is tailoring a product to a small market. A niche market is a segment of a larger market. Many small firms start off by targeting small niches. As they are only able to sell to a small market, there are no cost savings from mass production. This means that niche products are generally sold at a higher price. Customers are willing to pay more for something they see as being different or exclusive. Niche products are likely to be less price sensitive, i.e. price elasticity will be tend to be low.

Mass marketing is selling products that have wide appeal. This may be on a national basis, such as the soft drink Irn Bru (mainly Scottish, but with reasonable sales in the rest of the UK). Or the mass market may be on a global scale. If you travel to the Far East or to South America, in all but the remotest areas you will be able to buy a McDonald's burger and wash it down with a can of Coca-Cola. These two companies have achieved what most businesses can only dream of: they have produced products that have global appeal and recognition.

How?

- *Mass production*: Mass marketing requires mass production. The product must be able to be produced in quantity and at a price that will appeal to a large number of consumers.
- *Efficient distribution*: If mass marketing is to succeed the product has to be available to a large and diverse group of customers. There needs to be a well-developed and efficient distribution system. The growth of supermarkets has brought many products to a mass market.
- *Effective promotion*: For mass marketing to work the product must have universal appeal. It is no good producing millions of a product if customers don't want it. Most successful mass marketers have backed their products with extensive promotional campaigns. Some take full advantage of the global market by using the same advertising campaign in all of the countries in which they trade – with occasional modifications for language or cultural reasons.

Application

The price of digital radio sets is expected to fall following the announcement that Japanese electronics group Sony is to enter the market. The cheapest digital radio sets cost about £99, but with the first mass producer applying its marketing muscle to the technology, the move towards more affordable sets will accelerate. Ian Dickens, chief executive of the Digital Radio Development Bureau, said Sony's entry into the market would elevate digital radio from a cottage industry product to a mass-market home entertainment appliance.

> "As Sony enters the market next year we expect to see competition among manufacturers increase, which in turn will lead to competition between retailers. All of which is good news for consumers."

Sony will not reveal the design or price of its first digital radio, but said it was a portable set that would be distributed across Europe, with particular emphasis on the UK, where 175,000 digital sets had been sold by May this year. Total digital radio sales are expected to reach 1 million by the end of next year (*The Guardian*, 12 September 2003).

This is a good example of how a product moves from a niche to a mass market. Here the entry of a mass producer will bring down the product's price, making it more affordable to a larger group of people.

Why?

When a business achieves a high level of sales it gains benefits. Its unit production costs should fall (economies of scale). This means that it can cut its prices. As sales increase, so will customer recognition. This makes it more likely that the brand will become established. Brand recognition is important for businesses as it gives the product many advantages. For example:

- It is easier to persuade retailers to stock the product.
- Smaller discounts need to be given to retailers.
- Customers are more likely to make repeat purchases and less likely to try out a competitor product.

What now?

Firms are increasingly aware of the risks in treating customers as one large group. Customers are more sophisticated and have more spending power. Globally the mass marketers have also recognised that while brand recognition is desirable they need to be more sensitive in their marketing campaigns in non-western countries. These campaigns are now often focused on the country's culture rather than trying to sell a western lifestyle.

E Exam insight

Mass marketing does not necessarily just mean high sales. It is about the product having wide appeal. Some firms achieve high sales by offering many niche products, such as BMW.

You should not assume that mass marketing is the aim of every firm. Many very successful businesses thrive on profitable niches – sometimes worldwide ones, such as Mercedes.

Application

Firms may use niche markets as an introduction to a market or as a way of introducing new products in an existing market. Some firms will stay and be successful in their niche markets. Decisions about mass marketing or niche marketing will depend on the particular firm and the marketing circumstances surrounding its products and its market place.

Standard Chartered has decided to turn its back on the mass market in Cameroon, and has announced a new policy of serving only the wealthy. Letters have gone out to its customers advising that the new minimum balance for personal accounts is £2200 and for business accounts £5500. For the vast majority of local people this is an impossible figure. The bank is effectively cutting off the mass market.

This move away from mass marketing is based on profitability. The company has recognised that because of the particular circumstances in this market they are better off targeting a smaller but more profitable group of customers.

A good example of niche market success is the Morgan car company. A family business, it produces fewer than 750 cars each year. The soft-top sports cars are considered by many to be old fashioned and even uncomfortable. Despite this, customers are prepared to wait, sometimes for up to 3 years, to own one. Demand always exceeds supply. It is difficult to know

why this company has remained successful. It is probably because the product remains exclusive as so few cars are produced.

K Key Terms

Economies of scale – cost savings due to an increase in the scale of production

Price elasticity of demand – a measure of how sensitive demand is to price changes

Price inelastic – the product is not very sensitive to changes in price; demand for a price-inelastic product will fall by a lower percentage than the price rise

Evaluation

There is no 'one best way' to market your products. In fashion-oriented sectors mass marketing can be a mistake, as success may lead to over-exposure. The fashion conscious may then find a new product or label to support. Yet Bill Gates did not become the world's richest man by niche marketing. His Microsoft company has a 90% share of the world market for personal computer operating systems. Mass marketing blew away the niche market operators. In exams, think carefully about the circumstances each business faces.

S Student howlers

'Mass marketing concentrates on cheap products.'
'Niche markets are only for expensive products such as designer clothes.'

T Test yourself

1. What is meant by mass marketing? (2)
2. How may customers benefit from mass marketing? (4)
3. Which products are best suited to a niche market? (4)
4. How might a large firm use niche marketing? (4)
5. Outline two reasons why Morgan cars should keep away from the mass market. (6)

MARKETING STRATEGY

What?

Strategy is the medium- to long-term plan to achieve company objectives.

Marketing strategy is a plan for future marketing activity. A good marketing strategy:
- finds the best fit between company objectives, available resources, customer requirements and the activities of competitors;
- looks to the future;
- is realistic.

Strategy is about what is possible, not just desirable. It must take into account market potential and company resources. The company needs to recognise its own limitations and potential.

Strategy is not the same as tactics. Strategy is an overall plan. Tactics are short-term responses to an opportunity or threat. The marketing strategy may be to increase sales by developing a new market segment. One of the tactics may be to undercut the price of a competitor's new brand.

Who?

Small businesses are less likely to have formal marketing strategies. Marketing strategy will vary from company to company, reflecting each firm's individual circumstances. Within the same industry, one company may be aiming to increase market share whereas another looks for cost reductions in order to compete on price.

How?

To develop a marketing strategy it is necessary to:

1. *Define overall company objectives.* These should take account of the external climate and the state of the business.

2. *Analyse the existing business and understand the market.* Sales may be increasing. This may be due to better products or to poor performance by a competitor. There are several tools that can be used, for example:
   a) *Statistical analysis* of past performance figures for sales, market share and contribution will identify trends that are useful for estimating future sales.
   b) *Market research* into understanding customer behaviour will help explain sales patterns and indicate future buying patterns.
   c) *SWOT analysis* is a tool used to audit the internal and external business environments. SWOT stands for Strengths, Weaknesses, Opportunities and Threats.
      - The *internal review* looks at what the business is doing well (strengths) and what it could do better (weaknesses).
      - The *external review* looks at the business environment. It will look at issues such as the state of the economy, what competitors are doing, what is happening to technology and at changes in population structure.

3. *Analyse available resources.* The strategy must be realistic and achievable. The company must have sufficient resources to carry out the strategy. This will include production, finance and human resources.

Which?

There are many possible strategies for a business and at any one time the business could be pursuing several different strategies. These should take advantage of the company strengths and the available market opportunities.

Marketing strategy should:
- be part of the overall business strategy;
- add value;
- be asset led – use the company's strengths;
- take advantage of market opportunities.

A good strategy will link together analysis of customer preferences to the company's strengths. This is known as *asset-led marketing*.

What type?

Strategies include market penetration, market development and product development.

Market penetration
This is about increasing market share by increasing sales. It is the most common and safest strategy. It

concentrates on existing markets and products. This may be by:

- finding new customers;
- taking customers from competitors;
- persuading existing customers to increase usage.

Market development

This is finding new markets for existing products. It is a more risky strategy as it involves dealing with new customers and markets. It may be done by:

- repositioning the product to target a different market segment;
- moving into new markets – many British retailers have opened up outlets abroad.

Product development

Companies continually develop their products. In some industries, such as electronics or pharmaceuticals, innovation is essential. Strategies may include:

- changing an existing product
- developing new products.

K Key Terms

Competitive differentiation – making your product or buying experience different from your competitors

Demography – the study of population

Diversification – when a company expands its activities outside its normal range; this may be done to reduce risk or to expand possible markets

Repositioning – changing the product or its promotion to appeal to a different market segment

When?

Marketing strategy needs to be constantly reviewed. An idea that looks good on paper will not necessarily work in action. There may need to be some testing of strategies, especially if they are risky. Market opportunities will be constantly changing. If the company is to be successful it needs to be responsive. The marketing strategy of one business does not exist in a vacuum. It may provoke responses from other players in the market.

Market research and monitoring are necessary to ensure that the actions are producing the desired results. Evaluation of results will feed back into the system and in turn contribute to the development of revised objectives and strategies.

E Exam insight

When asked to suggest a marketing strategy, take care that the suggestion is realistic for the business.

Application

In August 2003, Tati, the French cut-price chain, announced that it was facing liquidation. The chain, founded in 1948 by a Tunisian immigrant, enjoyed huge success for many years and had expanded worldwide. The store was based on the 'pile 'em high, sell 'em cheap' philosophy. Analysts consider that the reason for the failure was its inability to respond to what was happening in the market coupled with a poor marketing strategy. It was faced with competition from chains such as H&M and Zara who were offering better quality but affordable fashion goods. The firm chose to widen its range of products to include more household items and to continue to sell its range of cheap clothing. Clearly this strategy did not work.

Themes for evaluation

It would be nice to think that businesses carefully evaluate the marketing environment and then devise a strategy that fits in with overall company objectives. In reality, management, shareholders or even circumstances may impose the strategy. In some instances the only business objective may be survival. Strategy may then be reduced to crisis management. The other reality is that the business environment is not always clear and logical so it may be very difficult to generate realistic and effective strategies.

S Student howlers

'A good marketing strategy is to cut prices.'
'Manufactures do not need marketing strategies.'

T Test yourself

1. What is marketing strategy? (2)
2. What is the difference between marketing strategy and marketing tactics? (4)
3. What is meant by product differentiation? (2)
4. What is a SWOT analysis? (2)
5. Explain the difference between market development and product development? (5)

ELASTICITY OF DEMAND

Elasticity of demand shows the effect on demand of a change in a related factor such as the price of the product or the income of buyers. Using elasticity of demand enables a business to see what will happen to demand for their products when the other variables change.

What?

The most commonly used elasticity is *price elasticity of demand*. This tells the firm how demand for the product can be expected to change with changes in price. It gives the business an indication of how *sensitive* demand is to changes in price.

The formula used to calculate price elasticity of demand is:

$$\text{price elasticity} = \frac{\% \text{ change in quantity demanded}}{\% \text{ change in price}}$$

If the percentage change in demand is greater than the change in price, i.e. the price elasticity is greater than 1 (>1), then the product is said to be price elastic.

If the percentage change in demand is less than the change in price, i.e. the price elasticity is less than 1 (<1), then the product is said to be price inelastic.

Why are some products price elastic and others price inelastic?

Price elastic products tend:
- to be widely available;
- to be undifferentiated from other products;
- to have many acceptable alternatives (have *substitutes*);
- not to be classed as necessities.

They will include products such as sun and sand holidays, and retail petrol brands.

Price inelastic products tend:
- to be in short supply;
- to be necessities;
- to be branded;
- to be innovative.

They include basic products such as electricity but also designer/fashion clothes or distinctive cars such as the Mercedes Smart car.

How to change?

The ideal situation for a business is to have products that are price inelastic. They can make the products more inelastic by:
- differentiating them from other products in the market (ideally by adding a USP, a unique selling point) – this may be done by product development or a change in presentation such as packaging;
- encouraging brand loyalty (e.g. better quality or a good after-sales service);
- removing competition (e.g. taking over a rival firm).

E Exam insight

Percentage change is calculated as:

$$\frac{\text{change}}{\text{original figure}} \times 100$$

If sales were 100 units and increased to 120 then the percentage change would be:

$$\frac{20}{100} \times 100 = 20\%$$

If the price of the product was increased by 15% and the demand for the product fell by 30% then the price elasticity would be:

$$\frac{30\%}{15\%} = 2.$$

Every firm wants to predict the likely effect on sales of a change in the price of its products. If you know the elasticity and the percentage change in price you can calculate the percentage change in demand. You just alter the elasticity formula so that:

$$\% \text{ change in demand} = \% \text{ change in price} \times \text{price elasticity}.$$

Income elasticity of demand

If the annual increase in household income is greater than the level of inflation this is said to increase *real income*. This will mean that householders will have more spending power. The formula for calculating income elasticity of demand is:

$$\text{income elasticity of demand} = \frac{\%\ \text{change in quantity demanded}}{\%\ \text{change in real income}}$$

When real incomes rise it is generally expected that demand for goods will increase. This is true of 'normal' goods such as skirts or chocolate bars. However there are exceptions.

- *Normal goods*: Demand increases in line with income. Elasticity is positive and at or below one, e.g. +0.8.
- *Inferior goods*: Demand falls as income rises. Elasticity is negative, e.g. –0.5.
- *Luxury goods*: Demand increases more than income changes. Elasticity is positive and more than one, e.g. +2.

When there is a recession, i.e. a fall in real income, customers will tend to buy more inferior goods and the demand for luxury goods will fall sharply.

What for?

In order to plan and successfully market their products businesses need to know what factors affect demand and how sensitive demand is to those factors. Elasticity is one tool that will help to gauge possible reactions to changes in the other factors.

A business may want to raise prices. However, it needs to understand what effect this will have on sales and profitability. If the product is *price elastic* then revenue will fall if prices are raised.

Example:
A firm is selling 1000 items at £10 each. Currently revenue is £10,000 (£10 × 1000). If the price is increased by 20% to £12 and the price elasticity of demand is 2 then the demand for the product will fall by 40% to 600, i.e. percentage change in demand = 20% × 2 = 40%. Now revenue will be £7,200 (£12 × 600), i.e. it falls by £2,800.

Clearly for this firm a price rise means a loss of revenue so this strategy makes little sense. Management needs to consider other ways of raising income and in this case a price cut would actually increase revenue.

If the business knows the *income elasticity* of its products it will be able to forecast future sales based on future growth in household earnings.

Application

For a number of years many of the world's largest airlines operated a high price policy. They were able to rely on brand image, shortage of competition and business customers who were insensitive to price. In recent years that has all changed. More competition – especially from low priced, no-frills airlines – has meant that there are alternatives and, with more leisure travel, customers are more price sensitive. Business users have also woken up to the cost-cutting possibilities of the low cost airlines. As a result, many major airlines are now offering cut-priced seats. What the airlines have experienced is a change in the price elasticity of demand. An apparently price inelastic product has become elastic.

How valuable are elasticities?

Calculating and using elasticities can help in making business decisions, but must be treated with some caution. Like many business tools it is a guide and helps a business to gain an understanding of what is happening in the market place. For example, if a product is very price elastic then the firm may be able to work on ways in which to reduce the elasticity so that it has more flexibility and control over pricing policies.

Do businesses really use elasticities?

Elasticities are often thought to be a theoretical rather than a practical business tool. However, it is vital that businesses are at least aware of what the market reaction will be to changing prices or to an advertising campaign or to changes in the economy. Without this basic understanding the business could make costly marketing decisions.

S Student howlers

'When a product is price elastic demand will increase.'
'People will always buy luxury goods.'

T Test yourself

1. Explain the meaning of the term 'price elastic'. (3)
2. State the formula for calculating price elasticity of demand. (2)
3. A firm increases its price from £20 to £22 and the demand for its product falls from 120,000 to 102,000. Calculate the price elasticity of demand and state whether it is elastic or inelastic. (5)
4. Why would a firm not want to raise prices if its product was price elastic? (2)
5. For each of the following identify one example of:
   a) a price inelastic product;
   b) a price elastic product;
   c) a normal good;
   d) an inferior good. (4)
6. State two things that a firm can do to make its products more price inelastic. (2)
7. What is meant by real income? (2)

MARKETING MIX

What?

The marketing mix focuses attention on the elements needed to carry out a marketing strategy successfully. It consists of four factors: product, price, promotion and place.

How?

Marketing managers look at each of the ingredients in the mix. They decide what marketing actions need to be taken under each of the headings. If marketing activity is to be effective each ingredient needs to be considered individually and together. The mix must be properly blended and coordinated, to give a balance between cost and effectiveness. The ingredients need to work with each other. A good product poorly priced may fail. If the product is not available following an advertising campaign the expenditure is wasted.

Who?

Where one business is supplying another (*industrial markets*) the key factors may be price, reliability, quality and availability. The product may have exact specifications agreed with the customer. The image of the product/brand is unlikely to be significant.

The *consumer market* is more likely to be affected by psychological as well as real factors. Hence the use of quirky advertising campaigns and pricing at psychological points such as £9.99. In order to understand this market, businesses need to know who their customers are and to understand their buying habits.

Customers can be categorised by:
* spending power;
* age;
* gender.

The differences in customers and buying habits result in many 'markets within markets'. These are known as *market segments*. Each segment will require its own marketing mix.

But

In most cases the product is the vital ingredient. Marketing effort alone will rarely make a poor product succeed. However, a good product without good support may also fail. The ingredients need to work together to maximise results.

What?

The *product* is something that is offered to the market. Businesses need to understand what it means to the consumer. Products are not just physical things. They *do* something for the customer. They provide both *tangible* and *intangible* benefits. Tangible benefits are those that can be measured, such as the speed of a car; intangible benefits include psychological factors such as pleasure, satisfaction and happiness.

A product can be:
* a good such as a washing machine or shampoo;
* a service such as accountancy or hairdressing;
* a place such as a tourist destination;
* perhaps even a person such as a football player or pop star.

How?

Good marketing means developing products that 'fit' the market. They need to be designed correctly and then developed to keep pace with market changes. This means that effective market research is a vital part of a successful mix.

New products give competitive advantage. They bring new customers. When a new product is developed it should take account of market and customer requirements. Test marketing is useful. The product may be launched in a small area. This will test customer reactions. Many companies have panels that try out the goods before launch. Modifications can then be made before the final launch.

With *existing products* the business needs to monitor the product's performance. This will maintain its life cycle and ensure that competitors do not overtake it.

What are the key elements?

Promotion is about communication. It is about getting a message across to potential consumers. It should be:

- informative;
- persuasive;
- reassuring.

The importance of promotion will depend on:

- the competitiveness of the market – if no alternatives are available there will be less need to persuade the customer to buy;
- availability – if the product is in short supply there will be little need to promote it;
- how easily the product can be differentiated in the market – if the differences are obvious there may be less need for promotion;
- the stage of the product life cycle – a new product usually needs promotional support. If the product has been altered, promotion will tell customers of the change.

Businesses will use a mixture of promotional activities. This is known as the *promotional mix.*

What and where?

Place is about availability. It includes the physical place, availability and timing.

Where the product is sold is known as the *distribution channel.* There are three main channels of distribution:

- *Traditional*: Products go from the manufacturer to a wholesaler then to the retailer and then are purchased by the final customer.
- *Direct*: Sales are made directly to the final customer, perhaps via the firm's web site.
- *Modern*: This cuts out the wholesalers. Large stores such as supermarkets and department stores buy directly from the manufacturer.

The right place is where the customer is. Manufacturers need to get their products displayed in the right retail outlets. There is great competition for 'shelf space'.

Products also need to be available when the customer wants them. Getting the product to the customer at the right time is an important part of the marketing effort.

Application

Research by the Chartered Institute of Marketing has shown that TV advertising is the most effective form of promotion. A survey showed that about 75% of those questioned remembered a TV advert seen the previous day. The same number could not remember adverts on posters, mobile phones and the Internet.

This suggests that TV advertising is the best way to communicate with customers. But is it right for everyone? Certainly not for small businesses, as TV advertising is too expensive. Nor for industrial suppliers, where direct contact with the customer is the most effective way of getting the message across. Advertising has to be tailored to the particular circumstances of the business.

The marketing mix has been a part of the language of business since the 1950s. Many firms find it useful as a tool for looking at the whole marketing effort rather than just the promotional aspects. So which is the most important ingredient? Obviously a poor product rarely sells for long and it is often said that a good product sells itself. How important each factor is will depend on the business and its market. For this reason alone the marketing mix cannot be considered in isolation. For it to be useful it needs to be backed by good market analysis and clear marketing objectives and strategies.

K Key Terms

Above the line promotion – paid-for advertising through the media; all other forms of promotional activity are considered 'below the line'

Market segment – a smaller part of a larger market

Price elasticity of demand – a measure of how sensitive demand is to changes in price

E Exam insight

Avoid repeating general textbook knowledge about the four Ps. Focus on the aspects that are relevant for the particular business in the case study. Try to make specific points such as: 'This particular small business needs to boost product trial by having a wider promotional campaign, as customers lack awareness of the product'.

S Student howlers

'Advertising is the only way to sell a product.'
'Supermarkets have made it easier for firms to sell products.'

T Test yourself

1. What are the four ingredients of the marketing mix? (4)
2. Which of the four Ps might be the most important for a new small producer of healthy soft drinks? Briefly explain your answer. (4)
3. How might Volvo market its lorries to an industrial customer such as Tesco? (4)
4. What is meant by a market segment? (2)
5. Why might a business want to differentiate its product?
6. What are the three main channels of distribution?

PRICING

The price is the amount paid by the customer for a good or service. Pricing is a vital element in marketing strategy. It must fit in with the business objectives and the overall marketing mix.

Why?

Pricing is important because it is one of the main links between the customer (demand) and the producer (supply). As part of the marketing mix it plays a strong role in marketing the product. For most customers price is a fundamental part of the buying decision. The importance of price will depend on:

1. *Customer sensitivity to price.* Consumers have an idea of the correct price for a product. They balance price with other considerations such as:
   a) the features of the product such as its design and performance;
   b) the real or perceived quality of the product;
   c) their income.

2. *The level of competitive activity.* Customers have more choice in a competitive market. Businesses may use price to differentiate their product. They may also use price as part of their promotional activity. For some products such as branded goods the price is kept higher to reinforce the brand's value. In a *monopoly* the business is able to charge higher prices.

3. *The availability of the product.* If the product is readily available, consumers are more price conscious. Scarcity removes some of the barriers to price. This can be seen in the art world where huge prices are paid for paintings. Shortage of the product forces the price up.

Another why?

Pricing is also important because it determines business revenue. Unlike the other ingredients in the marketing mix it generates revenue:

Sales revenue = price per unit × number sold.

Getting the price right is therefore vital. Price has a direct influence on demand. If the price is not right the business could:

- *lose customers* – if the price is too high, sales may drop sharply and therefore revenue will be lost; this is true of price elastic products;
- *lose revenue* – if the price is too low revenue may be lost.

Pricing involves a balance between being competitive and being profitable.

E | Exam insight

Take care not to confuse price and cost. Price is what the customer pays and therefore what the business charges the customer for the goods or service. Costs are what the business pays for its raw materials etc.

When?

Businesses need to make pricing decisions when they launch a *new product*.

There are two main strategies for new products:

- *Skimming* is used when the product is innovative and there is no competition. The price can be set at a high level, thus allowing the firm to recoup the development costs.
- *Penetration pricing* is used when launching a product into an existing market. The price is set lower than that of competitors to gain market share.

Firms also need to manage prices throughout the product life. The *lowest price* a firm can charge is set by costs. These will be manufacturing or purchasing costs and costs such as distribution, administration and marketing. The market determines the *highest price* that can be charged.

Which?

There are several different pricing methods: cost-plus, contribution, competitive and predatory.

Cost-plus

This is a commonly used method among small firms. A mark-up is added to the average cost.

$$\text{Average cost} = \frac{\text{total cost (fixed + variable)}}{\text{number of units}}$$

This method ensures that some profit is made, as long as sales meet expectations. This is because all costs are accounted for in the price.

Contribution

As long as the selling price is above the variable costs, the business receives a contribution to covering its fixed costs. Therefore the business may charge high prices to those that can afford to pay more and lower prices to people who can afford less (or want the product less). This is the basis for *price discrimination*, as used in rail and air travel. A second class return Virgin Rail ticket from London to Manchester can cost between £20 and £180, depending on who is travelling and the time of day. Virgin Rail try to sell as many tickets as possible at £180, but know that students paying £20 are still making a contribution to fixed costs and profit. Price discrimination means charging different people different prices for the same product.

Competitive

This method sets the price in relation to competitors' prices, i.e. it is a 'price taker'.

Prices may be lower or the same as competitors', depending on the marketing strategy.

- *Set at the market level*: Used in highly competitive markets such as retail petrol. If Shell charges 2p per litre more than Esso, sales will suffer badly. Businesses want to avoid a price war that will lower returns, so all price at the market level.
- *Set in relation to the price leader*: For example, if Heinz Beans are priced at 52p per tin, HP will price at 48p. If the Heinz price rises, so will HP. The company knows it cannot price alongside Heinz, because HP sales would fall sharply.

Predatory

This means pricing below cost, with the deliberate intention of driving weaker competitors out of the market. This is not legal, but it is very difficult to prove intent. Consumers love low prices, so few people or politicians complain if a price war is raging.

E Exam insight

When answering a question on pricing, take care that the suggested pricing methods are realistic for the business and its market circumstances. A long list of possible pricing methods will not gain high marks.

Which?

Most businesses use a combination of pricing methods. In the long term, revenue must be greater than costs. The core of the business may be based on cost plus pricing but there may be opportunities to make additional profit using other methods. Pricing should be closely linked to the marketing strategy. Once this has been determined there are many different pricing tactics that can be used.

- *Loss leaders*: Prices are set deliberately low. This is to encourage customers to buy complementary goods that generate profit.
- *Psychological pricing*: Prices are set at a level that seems lower. A price of £19.99 seems lower than £20.
- *Promotional pricing*: A range of tactics which includes *special offer pricing* – 'buy one get one free' or offers made for a period of time or to clear stocks.

Application

Businesses use pricing strategies in many different ways.

Madonna's album *American Life* went straight to the top of the charts in its launch week in April 2003. The instant success was helped by aggressive price reductions. It was sold by some of the larger chains for half the normal retail price. Why did shops offer this reduction for an artist whose CDs would undoubtedly sell in any case? The shops used the Madonna CD as a loss leader, hoping that customers would leave the store with the Madonna CD and one or two others in their basket.

Other businesses price high as a demonstration of the confident, upmarket image they wish to portray, such as Mercedes, BMW, Chanel and Diesel jeans.

K Key Terms

Complementary goods – products bought in conjunction with each other such as shavers and razors

Economies of scale – cost savings made possible by increased production or sales

Elasticity of demand – a measure of how sensitive demand is to changes in other factors such as price or income

Monopoly – a market dominated by one supplier

S Student howlers

'If a business cuts its price it will lose money.'
'Price is the most important thing for the customer.'

T Test yourself

1. How does the availability of a product affect pricing? (3)
2. What is the relationship between price and revenue? (3)
3. Name and explain two pricing strategies for new products. (4)
4. Why might a firm offer a discount? (3)
5. What is meant by cost-plus pricing? (2)
6. What problems might occur if the price is too low? (5)

INTEGRATED MARKETING

The AQA specification for this unit states:

Candidates are expected to gain an understanding of marketing in an integrated context within the organisation. The study of marketing should focus on the processes of identifying, targeting and satisfying customers with an emphasis on marketing objectives, strategy and tactics.

When you are studying marketing, subjects such as market research or the Boston Matrix are taught as separate issues. If marketing in a business is going to be successful, however, these elements have to act together. A marketing strategy cannot work if it is not based on good market knowledge. It is also important to understand that marketing is not a separate business activity. It is part of the whole business operation. This is what integrated marketing is all about. Marketing objectives must be part of the overall business objectives.

Marketing strategy should be based not only on excellent market analysis and research but must also coordinate with the other parts of the business. There is little point in a marketing strategy to increase sales if there is no spare production capacity to make the additional products.

Marketing, like any other business activity, should contribute to profit. Remember the formula for profit:

Profit

=

Revenue (units sold × price)

−

Total costs (fixed costs + total variable costs).

Marketing can contribute by increasing revenue. It can generate more sales or it could help to sell the product at higher prices, perhaps by increasing brand awareness.

Increasing sales can also help to bring down costs. Average costs will fall as the fixed costs are spread over more output. Variable costs per unit may fall due to bulk buying.

Like any other business activity, marketing should be efficient. It should generate more revenue than it costs. This is where integration is also important. Good market analysis and research together with good product analysis (product life cycle and portfolio analysis) can lead to a workable marketing strategy.

Understanding elasticity of demand and using the marketing mix can help to develop the most effective marketing tactics.

T Test yourself (50 marks)

1. What is the difference between primary and secondary research? (2)
2. Explain the term 'product differentiation'. (1)
3. Describe two different ways of pricing a new product. (4)
4. What might a firm do if the sales of its product have levelled out? (2)
5. If a product is price inelastic, what will be the effect of cutting its price? (3)
6. What is market share? List two ways that it can be measured. (4)
7. What is the relationship between cash flow and product life cycle? (4)
8. What is the difference between market orientation and product orientation? (2)
9. A firm sells 100,000 units of a product that is estimated to have a price elasticity of (−)2. If the firm decreases the price of its product from £5.00 to £4.50 what will be the new sales volume? (6)
10. What is the difference between a random and a quota sample? (3)
11. What is a market segment? (2)
12. What does the term 'price taker' mean? (2)
13. List three pricing tactics for existing products. (3)
14. List two advantages for the firm of mass marketing. (2)
15. What is the difference between qualitative and quantitative research? (2)
16. How does the Boston Matrix help a business to analyse its product portfolio? (4)
17. With reference to income elasticity of demand, explain normal goods and inferior goods. (4)

Now try the following data response questions. Allow yourself 30 minutes for each one.

Data response: The Booze Cruise

Research by Switch (the debit card company) has shown that about 14% of British people go to France to buy alcohol and other goods. Majestic Wine, the bulk wine and beer retailers, has taken advantage of this. The British company has said that sales in its three French stores rose by 21.7% in the half year to September 2003. This compares with an increase of 12% in its UK sales. Majestic has 113 stores in the UK and sells over 800 wines from different countries. Paul Rossington, a broker from Williams de Broë, said that Majestic is gaining a bigger share of the 'booze-cruise' market because it offers wines differing from those at nearby French hypermarkets. Majestic Wine offers a product range similar to that of its UK stores, including many wines from Australia, Chile and elsewhere. This gives it a competitive advantage.

Below is a breakdown of the price of a typical bottle of wine and sales figures for a Majestic Wine Warehouse in the UK and in France.

	Wine in UK store	Wine in French store
Price to customer	£6.49	£4.99
Tax	£2.32	£1.00
Estimated profit margin per bottle	81p	77p
Store turnover	£1.3 million	£1.8 million
Volume of sales in bottles of wine per year	245,000	720,000

Source: adapted from *The Times*, 18 November 2003.

Questions

1. Why is the price of a bottle of wine lower in France than in the UK? (3)
2. As a percentage of the UK store turnover, how much higher is the French store turnover? (2)
3. Explain why the company takes a higher profit margin in the UK than in France? (5)
4. Analyse two possible benefits to Majestic of gaining increased market share. (6)
5. To what extent can any retailer differentiate itself from its competitors? (9)

Data response: Pearl of the Region

Five years ago hardly anyone had heard of Dubai. Now it is well known as a tourist centre attracting visitors year-round and from all over the world. The government's vision is to increase the number of tourists from 2.8 million visiting Dubai in 2000 to 10 million per annum by 2010. Tourism is the fastest growing sector within Dubai's economy. Dubai is highly accessible with more than 105 airlines providing direct links from Dubai to 140 cities worldwide.

The government has set up a Tourism Promotion Board (TPB) which plans and implements an integrated programme of international promotions in conjunction with 14 overseas offices. Innovative tourism campaigns, introduced over the past 5 years and spread throughout the year, have greatly increased Dubai's popularity as a year-round destination. In the very hot summer months hotels and shopping malls offer special activity and price promotions to attract visitors. In the second half of 2002, the TPB stepped up its international advertising in the print media. The campaign was directed at the travel trade and consumers, aiming to create clear-cut impressions of Dubai as a top class tourist destination. It spanned over 120 leading trade and consumer publications across Dubai's main target markets.

Questions

1. What is the Dubai government's tourism objective? (2)
2. Describe the marketing strategy used to achieve the objective. (3)
3. Explain why it is important to have the supporting infrastructure in place. (3)
4. It is very hot in Dubai during the summer, so it is difficult to attract visitors. Analyse ways in which marketing can help a business to iron out seasonal fluctuations in demand. (8)
5. Hotels often offer very low room rates, sometimes below cost. Discuss the value to a hotel business of this approach to pricing. (9)

REVENUE, COSTS AND PROFIT

What?

Business revenues

Revenue is the name given to the money that a firm receives from selling the product or service that it provides. The total revenue for a firm for any given period can be calculated by multiplying the selling price (revenue per unit) by the number of units sold in that period.

Costs

Accountants classify costs in several ways. For now, the important distinction to make is what happens to costs when the firm's output changes.

- *Variable costs*. A variable cost is one that varies in direct proportion to output. In other words, if a firm makes twice as many bags of crisps, they will need twice as many potatoes. Variable costs are often expressed per unit produced, i.e. variable cost per unit. They can also be given as the total variable costs, i.e. variable cost per unit × quantity produced.
- *Fixed costs*. A fixed cost is one that does not change in relation to output. An example might be managers' salaries – they remain the same whether 10,000 or 20,000 bags of crisps are produced per month.
- *Total costs*. This is the figure gained by adding the total variable costs at any level of output to the fixed costs being paid by the business.

Profit

Profit is the excess of revenue over costs. In terms of a formula, this can be expressed as:

$$\text{profit} = \text{total revenue} - \text{total costs}$$

This equation can be broken down as follows:

$$\text{profit} = (\text{quantity sold} \times \text{selling price}) - ([\text{quantity sold} \times \text{variable cost per unit}] + \text{fixed costs})$$

Why?

The quest for profit lies at the heart of the objectives of almost every business. Questioning in exams is likely to focus upon the ways to boost profit. The analytical approach to any question on profit is to consider how profit is calculated and work through each part of the profit equation.

Total revenue (selling price × quantity sold)

Increasing total revenue will boost profit unless costs rise faster. To increase revenue, one of two variables must increase:

- *Selling price*. Price can be increased, but, for most products, an increase in price will lead to a fall in quantity sold. Therefore, any decision on whether price would increase profit must be linked to the concept of price elasticity of demand (*see* Unit 1.8) – the responsiveness of demand to a change in price.
- *Number of units sold*. A firm trying to increase its profit may seek to boost the number of units sold, perhaps by promoting the product or changing the product in some way. Successfully increasing the quantity sold will increase the total variable costs. It may also go hand in hand with a change in some other part of the profit equation – perhaps the increase in sales was the result of an advertising campaign (increased fixed costs), or better quality materials (increased variable costs per unit). Another way of increasing the quantity sold is to reduce the selling price – but will this lead to an increase or decrease in total revenue? Only price elasticity has the answer to this question.

Total costs

Any action that successfully reduces total costs without hitting revenue will increase profit. However, you should always remember that no business will be deliberately ignoring easy cost-cutting measures – answers that suggest that cost cutting carries no further implications are simplistic and will not impress examiners.

Variable costs

Materials and components are the most obvious variable costs faced by firms. In order to reduce the variable cost per unit, you might suggest that the firm could use lower quality and therefore cheaper materials. However, a dip in the quality of the product might affect sales in the medium to long term. Therefore total revenue could fall in line with variable costs. Alternatively, a suggestion that buying materials in greater bulk would allow the firm to experience bulk-buying discounts should be qualified by an awareness that this may lead to increased stock-holding costs (usually fixed costs).

Fixed costs

A reduction in fixed costs is another route to greater profit. However, moving to a factory with cheaper rent may create very significant short-term relocation costs along with a probable halt to production while the move occurred. Cutting staff salaries would also reduce fixed costs but would do little to enhance staff morale and may therefore lead to less efficient production.

S Student howlers

'Fixed costs are costs that never change.'
'Firm A has fixed costs of £500 and variable costs of £5 per unit, so their total costs will be £505.'

How?

The answer is likely to lie in the question. Read stimulus material carefully in order to try to identify whether there are any potential cost savings that may be appropriate. Alternatively, increased profit may be achievable by boosting revenue in some way that avoids increasing costs significantly.

Application

Boosting profit in a favourable external environment	Boosting profit when the external environment is against a firm
In good trading periods, profit boosts are likely to stem from increases in revenue. These may be the result of increased sales volumes or the ability to increase selling price without significantly reducing sales.	If the external environment is unfavourable, a company will be very unlikely to be able to boost its revenues. Any increases in profit are likely to stem from cost reductions. However, it is important to consider the implications of any cost cutting, for example the effect on staff morale of laying off workers or the effect on the firm's image of using cheaper raw materials.

What next?

There are two ways that a firm can choose to use its profit:
- Retain the profit in the business and use it to buy extra assets that will help the firm in the future –

perhaps extra machinery or equipment that will allow them to grow.
- Pay out profit to the owners of the business. In some cases this will be necessary in order to keep the owners happy and avoid them withdrawing their investment.

The majority of businesses will actually choose to split their profit between these two uses, varying the proportion to each use depending upon their current circumstances and especially their need for extra finance.

K Key Terms

Fixed cost – a cost that does not change in relation to output

Profit – the surplus of revenue over total costs; if total costs exceed revenue the firm has made a loss

Variable cost – a cost that varies in direct proportion to output

E Exam insight

When proposing how to boost profit, keep thinking about timescale. Is the firm pursuing short- or long-term objectives? To increase short-term profit, higher prices and lower cost/quality materials may work well – but both approaches may damage long-term profitability.

T Test yourself

1. Identify two variable and two fixed costs of running a car wash. (4)
2. Firm X has variable costs per unit of £5. Revenue is £12,000 earned by selling 1000 units. If they made £2000 profit, what are their fixed costs? (4)
3. Firm Y makes a profit of £5000 by selling 1000 units for £10 each. If fixed costs are £3000, what are the variable costs per unit? (4)
4. SofaCo is a manufacturer of sofas.
   a) Outline one action it could take concerning its variable costs to try to increase profit. (2)
   b) Explain why that action might cause long-term problems for the business. (6)

BREAK-EVEN

What?

Break-even is the term used to describe a situation in which a firm is making neither a profit nor a loss. In other words, it is generating sufficient revenue to cover its costs, but no more. Break-even occurs at a level of output where total revenue and total costs are equal. A firm's break-even point is frequently shown on a break-even chart – a diagram that shows the firm's fixed costs, total costs and total revenue at all possible levels of output. The break-even point occurs where the total revenue and total cost lines intersect.

How?

In order to construct a break-even chart, it is best to draw up a table showing costs and revenues at three different levels of sales, usually where output is zero, at maximum output and at an easy figure in between. Take this example:
  • Selling price = £10;
  • Variable costs per unit = £5;
  • Fixed costs = £1000 per month;
  • Maximum output = 250 units per month.
The table used to construct the break-even chart would look like this:

Output	0 units	100 units	250 units
Variable costs	£0	£500	£1250
Fixed costs	£1000	£1000	£1000
Total costs	£1000	£1500	£2250
Total revenue	£0	£1000	£2500

With the table drawn up, the fixed and total cost and total revenue lines can be plotted on a graph, showing output on the horizontal axis and £s on the vertical.

Why?

Identify profit/loss at any level of output
The chart makes it possible to see profit or loss at any given level of output. Look along the horizontal axis to the output level that is being considered, then read upwards and measure the vertical gap between the total revenue and total cost lines. That gap represents the profit (if revenue is higher) or loss (if costs are higher than revenue). Figure 2.2A shows a loss of £500 if only 100 units are sold.

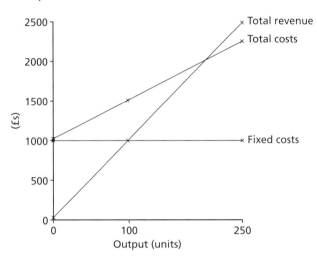

Fig. 2.2A: Break-even chart

Identify safety margin
Safety margin is the term given to the difference between the current level of sales and the break-even output. On the break-even chart, the safety margin is the horizontal distance from current sales to the break-even point, as shown:

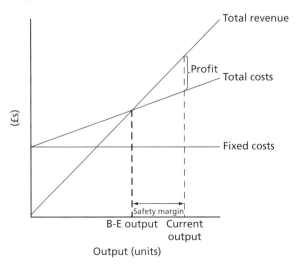

Fig. 2.2B: Break-even chart 2

How (without the graph)?

The break-even output of a firm can be calculated, without the need to draw a graph. The calculation required is shown below:

$$\frac{\text{Break-even}}{\text{point}} = \frac{\text{Fixed costs}}{\text{selling price} \quad \text{variable costs per unit}}$$

For example, the firm whose figures are shown above would have a break-even output of:

$$\frac{£1000}{£10 - £5} = 200 \text{ units}$$

Pros and cons of break-even analysis

'What if?' questions can be asked – the technique allows firms to see what would happen to costs and revenues if variables, such as selling price, or capacity, were changed by a simple adjustment to the break-even chart. The technique provides a graphical focus of attention for meetings.

But

Break-even is based on two key assumptions:

1. that the firm sells every unit it makes – in other words the firm is not manufacturing for stock.

2. that all the lines on the chart are assumed to be straight (linearity). This means that variable costs are the same for every unit manufactured, and every unit is sold for the same price. This is often far from the real situation, with some products sold at a discount and some firms able to bulk buy cheaper materials after reaching a certain level of output.

Application

Who does it work for?

Break-even is particularly useful for firms that:	Break-even is of limited use to firms that:
Make and sell one standard product	Find it hard to identify the actual variable and fixed costs involved in making their product
Only make products to order – meaning all output is sold	Are subject to severe seasonality
Only operate in one market	Operate in fast-moving markets

Application to business contexts

* *Manufacturing business*: Manufacturers will have a fairly clear idea of the variable costs and fixed costs involved in production. They will therefore be able to conduct break-even analysis to tell them how many units need to roll off the production line for sale in order to achieve break-even.

* *Service sector (e.g. a restaurant)*: Restaurants will be able to make a fair job of calculating the average number of customers needed per evening or per week in order to cover their costs. With an average cost per meal and an average revenue per customer established from previous experience, the manager will be able to calculate how many customers are needed to cover the costs.

Quality of information used

Any decision-making technique is only as good as the information used in its construction. Break-even charts will be of limited use if selling prices and cost levels are being roughly estimated e.g. in a business start-up.

Validity beyond the very near future?

Break-even is a technique used to try to assess the firm's future position. Many firms will be able to calculate how many units they must sell next week in order to break-even, but few will be in a stable-enough environment to work out an annual break-even output.

S Student howlers

'Calculating the break-even point will ensure that the firm covers its costs.'
'As Firm Y is 50 units short of break-even output, management should cut the selling price. This will mean that sales will go up by 50 units and they will break-even.'

T Test yourself

1. a) Calculate the number of units that would need to be sold to break-even if a firm sells its products for £5 per unit, has variable costs of £2 per unit and fixed costs of £6000. (2)
    b) If the firm is currently selling 2500 units, what is its safety margin? (2)
2. Briefly explain three key benefits of carrying out break-even analysis for a firm manufacturing toilet paper. (6)
3. Outline three problems that may be experienced by a computer manufacturer using break-even analysis to plan for the next year. (6)
4. Which key variables would a leisure centre need to identify in order to use break-even analysis? Use examples in your examples. (4)

CONTRIBUTION

What?

Contribution is the term used to describe the amount of money that is left over after deducting variable costs from revenue. The name comes from the fact that that money left after the deduction of variable costs is used as a contribution towards covering fixed costs. Once all fixed costs have been covered, any contribution is then pure profit.

How?

Contribution per unit

Every time a unit is sold, the transaction generates a contribution that is put towards covering the firm's fixed costs. The amount that is contributed from each unit is:

selling price – variable cost per unit = contribution per unit

If a firm makes shirts that cost £5 per unit in materials and labour, and can sell them for £12, every shirt makes a contribution of £7. If the firm's fixed overhead costs amount to £700 per week, the firm must sell 100 shirts to cover these costs. If it sells more than 100 shirts, every extra sale generates £7 of profit.

Total contribution

The total contribution generated by a firm is the value of all the individual contributions on each unit sold added together, so,

either

total contribution = contribution per unit × units sold

or

total contribution = total revenue – total variable costs

In the example used above, weekly sales of 300 shirts would generate total contribution of £7 × 300 = £2100.

Calculating profit using contribution

Profit can be calculated by deducting fixed costs from total contribution:

profit = total contribution – fixed costs

To continue with the example, £2100 total contribution *minus* £700 of fixed costs = £1400 profit.

What for?

Contribution is used in many important ways in business:
- for calculating a firm's break-even point (and therefore its safety margin);
- in making pricing decisions (contribution pricing and price discrimination are based upon calculating contribution);
- to calculate profit far more quickly than through the formula: total revenue – total costs.

Who?

Contribution for multiproduct firms

Contribution is very helpful for firms that make several different products. It may be hard to calculate the fixed costs for any of their particular products, but the variable costs associated with each product are likely to be clear. For example, a clothes shop may not know how to allocate fixed costs such as rent to menswear versus womenswear, but it will be easy to see the contribution made by each section – calculating the selling price minus the wholesale cost of all the garments sold. In this case, management can identify the total contribution generated by each section in order to identify its value to the firm as a whole. Any product that generates a positive contribution will be contributing something towards paying fixed costs.

Calculation

As previously stated, contribution can be a particularly useful concept for multiproduct firms. Take the firm below as an example:

Product	A	B	C	Totals
Sales	100	250	90	440
Variable costs	60	195	80	335
Contribution	40	55	10	105
Fixed costs				100
Profit				5

All figures £000s – this table is called a contribution statement.

Notice what would happen to the firm's profit if they stopped selling product C (assuming fixed costs are unchanged). Without product C's contribution the firm would make losses of £5000 instead of profits.

Application

A London clothing store had two floors of women's clothing and a basement selling menswear. The store manager divided the fixed costs of operating the store into three, to share them between the three floors. On this basis the basement was losing money. She therefore closed the menswear section and changed it to children's clothing. A year later a repeat exercise showed that the basement was still losing money. Fortunately, before she switched the children's clothes to a third floor of womenswear, a friend explained that as long as the basement's revenues were greater than its total variable costs, it was worth persisting with.

Themes for evaluation

There is a danger with the analysis of contribution that managers fail to see the big picture. They may tinker with the product range in order to ensure that each product generates a positive contribution. This may mean that they are missing the opportunity to expand by dropping a product that generates a positive contribution in order to free up resources needed to develop and produce an innovative new product.

E Exam insight

Keep an eye open for questions quoting average cost figures. It is much safer to work with price and variable cost figures, and therefore contribution per unit.

On questions showing contribution statements from multiproduct firms, be careful to avoid suggesting that the firm should automatically drop products that make a small contribution. Without the contribution they make to fixed costs, the firm may become a lossmaker.

S Student howler

'Since product C is making the smallest contribution to fixed costs, the firm should stop producing that product and concentrate on their other two products.'

T Test yourself

1. a) Calculate the contribution per unit if a firm sells its products for £8 and pays variable costs on each unit of £3. (1)
    b) What would the firm's profit be if they had fixed costs of £10,000 and sold 3000 units? (3)
2. Identify what would happen to total contribution if the following single changes took place:
    a) Suppliers charge more for materials;
    b) The firm sells more products;
    c) Selling price is increased due to increased demand. (3)
3. A firm has sales of 200 units a week at a selling price of £30 each. Its variable costs per unit are £18 and fixed costs are £2000.
    a) Calculate its current total contribution per week. (2)
    b) Use that information to calculate its profit per week. (1)
    c) Then a price increase of 10% pushes sales down to 190 units. Calculate the new total contribution and the new profit. What is the percentage increase in the firm's profit caused by the price increase? (6)
4. Briefly explain how multiproduct firms might use information on the contribution generated by each of its products. (4)

CASH FLOW MANAGEMENT

What?

Cash flow is the flow of money into and out of the business in a given period of time. *Cash flow is not the same as profit.* Profit is what is left for the business owners after all costs of operating have been deducted from revenue. Firms can be cash rich but unprofitable or profitable but have cash flow problems.

Why?

Cash flow is vital. It is essential that bills are paid when they come due. Suppliers will be reluctant to continue supplying raw materials if they are not paid. In extreme case *creditors* make take the firm to court, which could result in the company being put into *liquidation.*

Cash flow problems are the most common reason for business failure.

Who?

All businesses need to monitor their cash position. It is particularly important that *new firms* have sufficient funding if they are going to survive. It is estimated that 70% of new businesses fail in their first year because of cash flow problems. However larger *established firms* can also face cash flow problems. Marconi, MyTravel Group and Leicester City football club all faced cash flow problems recently.

When a firm wants to borrow money, the bank will almost certainly want to see a cash flow forecast. They do this to ensure that the business has enough cash to enable it to survive. They also want to be sure that the business will be able to repay the loan and to make the interest payments.

When?

Businesses need to manage cash flow by *continually* reviewing their present and future cash position. This allows the firm to:
* anticipate the timing and seriousness of any cash shortage;
* arrange financial cover for the shortfall period;
* review timings of cash received and paid out.

How?

The *cash flow forecast* helps the firm to review its *future* cash position. Each column shows money coming into and out of the business each month. It is like a mini bank statement. The firm can see the net cash flow by month (net cash flow = cash in – cash out). When this monthly net cash flow is added to the cash balance held by the business it shows if there is cash in hand or a cash shortage.

What then?

If the cash flow forecast shows that the firm is likely to have cash flow problems there are several things the firm can do:

1. Speed up cash inflows by:
   — giving less credit to customers; even a small reduction in the credit time will improve cash flow;
   — speeding up the production process, e.g. if a construction firm could build a new house in 3 months instead of 6, cash inflows from selling the finished product would arrive earlier;
   — factoring. In some cases the debt may be taken over by a factoring company. They immediately pay the money owed less a handling fee, then collect the money from the creditor when it becomes due. Cash flow is improved as the business receives its money sooner.

2. Delay cash outflows by:
   — negotiating longer credit, thus postponing cash outflows;
   — leasing rather than buying equipment, so delaying an expensive drain on cash;
   — renting rather than buying buildings, thus avoiding large cash outflows.

3. Cut or delay expenditure by:
   — cutting levels of stock;
   — cutting costs;
   — postponing expenditure on inessentials such as company cars.

But

The usefulness of cash flow forecasts depends on how well prepared the estimates are. A cash flow forecast can alert the business to possible future cash problems. It cannot take into account unforeseen circumstances that might affect the business. When a new business is starting up it can help to ensure that the venture does not fail for lack of adequate funding. This will depend on sales and costs forecasts actually being realistic.

K Key Terms

Creditors – individuals or other businesses that are owed money by the business

Debtors – individuals or companies that owe money to the business

Liabilities – what the business owes

Liquidation – being forced to hand your business over to a liquidator, who will sell off the firm's assets to repay its debts; this usually means the business closes down

Application

Research carried out in 2002 looked at new businesses that received support from local enterprise agencies. Their progress was compared with those that had not sought advice. The results showed that businesses that sought advice were more likely to survive and to do better than other surviving firms. The supported firms generally had better financial management and more careful risk taking and so tended to suffer fewer closures due to cash flow problems.

The foot and mouth disease which hit the UK during 2001 affected many businesses as well as farmers. Many small firms in the retail and tourist businesses such as holiday cottages, campsites and caravan parks, were also badly affected. In order to help these firms to overcome their cash flow problems the government extended the Small Firms Loan Guarantee Scheme. Under the scheme the government guarantees up to 85% of a loan up to £250,000. This gives the banks confidence to lend to businesses that otherwise may not have sufficient security. Even successful businesses can face cash flow problems due to a change in their trading environment. For many smaller firms this can be disastrous as banks will be unwilling to lend to a business with cash problems. In this case the government recognised the problem and took steps to help these businesses survive.

There is little doubt that cash flow management is important for businesses, especially new start-ups, which are more likely to face cash flow problems. Cash flow forecasting is also useful for existing businesses when they are looking at expansion or taking on additional business. However, cash flow forecasts are only a tool to assist managers. They do not ensure business survival. Managers need to be aware of any changes in the economic and market climate that they are operating in – and change their plans and strategies accordingly.

E Exam insight

When constructing a cash flow forecast, remember to show cash in and out *when* it is actually received or paid.

When suggesting how a firm can improve its cash flow position, look at what is realistic for the firm. A small firm is unlikely to be able to demand early payment from its customers.

S Student howlers

'Profit is more important than cash flow.'
'As long as an order is profitable the business should do it.'

T Test yourself

1. What is meant by cash flow? (2)
2. What is a cash flow forecast? (2)
3. Why is having sufficient cash important for the business? (4)
4. Which is more important: cash flow or profit? (4)
5. Give two reasons why a bank might want to see a cash flow forecast before giving the business a loan. (2)
6. Explain two things that a business could do to improve a poor cash flow situation. (6)

CONTROL OF WORKING CAPITAL

What?

Working capital is the finance available for the day-to-day running of the business. It is used for buying raw materials, paying the wages and other everyday bills.

Having enough cash to meet the company's requirements is vital for the business's survival. This is known as having enough liquidity.

Why?

If working capital is not controlled the business can experience several problems:

- *With suppliers*: If payment is delayed they may reduce the length of the credit period or refuse to supply future orders.
- *With banks*: Borrowing to cover cash shortages will result in additional interest charges. If the bank becomes concerned about the liquidity situation it may impose a higher interest rate. The firm will find it more difficult to get extra loans.
- *With missed opportunities*: The business may be unable to take advantage of bulk buying and the resulting lower average costs. It may have to turn down a profitable order because it does not have the necessary working capital.
- *With growth*: A firm that is short of working capital is unlikely to be able to grow, as no cash will be available for development.

How much?

The amount of working capital that businesses need varies from firm to firm. It depends on:

- *The length of the business process*: This depends on the length of the production process and the time taken to get the product to the market. Service industries tend to have shorter production time than manufacturing industries.
- *The credit given to purchasers*: This depends on market conditions. Generally business customers expect longer credit than private customers. Powerful, large firms may demand longer credit periods than small firms.
- *The credit obtained for purchases of materials etc.*: The credit given by suppliers will depend on:
  — the company's credit record;
  — how established the firm is;
  — market conditions.

Working capital requirements are specific to each business. It is often said that having *too much working capital* is wasting precious company resources. The cash that is not being used could be reinvested into long-term assets such as high-tech machinery. However a cash buffer is useful if the business faces any sort of downturn or unexpected event.

How?

A firm can manage its working capital by:

1. controlling cash;
2. obtaining maximum credit for purchases;
3. getting goods to the market in the shortest possible time;
4. collecting payments efficiently;
5. controlling costs;
6. careful stock management.

Why?

Liquidity problems can be caused by either internal or external problems, as shown in the following examples.

Internal problems

- *Production problems*: If production is delayed the product will take longer to reach the market.
- *Marketing problems*: If sales are slow cash will be slow coming in. Extra discounts may need to be given to shift stock.
- *Management problems*: Poor stock or production management can result in extra costs.

External problems

- *Changes to the economic climate*: For example, changes to inflation, economic growth or taxation.
- *Lower demand*: May be because of a recession, changes in taste or seasonal patterns.
- *Unexpected non-payment by customers*: Customers who themselves get into difficulty may delay payment. If the customer goes out of business this will become a bad debt.

How?

There are several measures that the firm can use to help resolve liquidity problems. The table below shows the advantages and disadvantages of these.

Measure	Result	Drawbacks
Discount prices	Increases sales Reduces stock Generates cash	May undermine pricing structure May leave low stocks for future activity
Reduce purchases	Cuts down expenditure	May leave business without means to continue
Negotiate more credit	Allows time to pay	May tarnish credit reputation
Delay payment of bills	Retains cash	Will tarnish credit reputation
Credit control – chase debtors	Gets payments in and sooner	May upset customers
Negotiate additional finance	Provides cash	Interest payments add to expenditure Has to be repaid
Factor debts	Generates cash	Reduces income from sales
Sell assets	Releases cash A proportion of the income is guaranteed	Assets are no longer available Costs can be high
Sale and leaseback	Releases cash Asset is still available for use	Increases costs – lease has to be paid Company no longer owns the asset

Application

In April 2003 The Birmingham Mint was placed in the hands of *administrators* with the loss of 51 jobs. The company, which was over 200 years old, was one of the makers of the new euro coins. In 2000 it won its largest orders ever – an order to supply Germany with euros worth £45m and another from Spain for 50m coins. But when these contracts were completed the orders dried up. The firm went into administration when they had insufficient cash to pay creditors or wages.

In April 2003 the shares of the nightclub and pub group PoNaNa fell to 6p, down from 172p when the business was launched. The reason for the dramatic fall was concern about the company's liquidity. PoNaNa had been trying unsuccessfully to sell 11 loss-making clubs. Poor trading over the Christmas period made the situation worse. The shares fell sharply after the group said that it was talking to its bankers to try to raise additional finance.

Getting the level of working capital right is about balancing company resources: too little and the firm could fail; too much and the business could miss opportunities.

Managing working capital is not just about cash flow management. It is about efficiency throughout the business. It is an integrated activity. Efficient production keeps costs down and gets the goods to the customer in the shortest possible time. Good stock management reduces waste and the amount of cash tied up in stock.

E Exam insight

Take care not to confuse creditors and debtors. *Creditors* are businesses etc. that the firm *owes money to*. *Debtors* are other firms or individuals who *owe money to* the company.

The circumstances of the business must be looked at carefully when analysing the reasons for liquidity problems and suggesting possible solutions. The solution should always be related to the problem as much as possible (e.g. if the firm is having problems with bad debts it should strengthen its credit controls).

S Student howlers

'This business could solve its cash problems by not paying its bills.'
'The more debtors the business has the better off it is.'

T Test yourself

1. What is working capital? (2)
2. What is working capital used for? Give two examples. (2)
3. Give two ways in which a firm can improve its liquidity position. (2)
4. List two factors that affect the amount of working capital required by a business. (2)
5. What is the 'right' level of working capital? (2)

SOURCES OF FINANCE

What?

All businesses need money invested in them. *Sources of finance* are the origins of that money.

When?

When a business starts out, it needs money for fixed assets, such as buildings and equipment. This is known as capital expenditure. It also needs money for its day-to-day spending on materials, labour, etc. This is known as working capital. Once a business is established it should generate enough income to pay its bills and to provide some profit. This profit can be returned to investors as dividends or reinvested into the business (retained profit).

If the business wants to *expand* it could need to find additional finance. If the firm runs into cash problems it may also need to find extra funding.

Where from?

Finance for business comes either from the business itself (internal) or from outside the business (external).

Internal finance

- *Retained profit*. Profit invested back into the firm is known as retained profit; this provides over 60% of the finance for the average business.
- *Sale of assets*. Selling assets that are no longer needed will release funding into the business.
- *Cash flow management*. Another way of generating cash is the careful management of working capital, such as cutting back on stock levels.

External finance

- For day-to-day working capital:
  — *trade credit*: when suppliers allow a firm time to pay its bills, often around 60 days.
  — *bank overdrafts*: the commonest form of borrowing for small businesses. The bank allows the business to go 'into the red' from time to time. The overdraft must be agreed with the bank and will be up to a specific amount.
  — *factoring*: factoring companies lend the business around 80% of an invoice's value. The remainder, less a fee, is paid to the company when the factor gets payment from the firm's customer.
- For growth and expansion
  — *loans*: medium-term finance (usually 2–5 years, and usually at a fixed rate of interest) provided by banks. Before lending, the bank will want to be sure that the firm will be able to meet the interest payments and repay the loan. Especially for a new business they will want some collateral (security) which may be a personal asset such as a house.
  — *owners' equity* (also known as share capital): money put into the business by the owners. If the business is a limited company it can raise finance by selling shares in the business.
  — *leasing*: the firm has use of assets without having to make the capital expenditure.
  — *debentures*: loans to big businesses from financial institutions or private individuals, for a fixed period of time and at a fixed rate of interest.
  — *venture capital*: venture capitalists invest in smaller riskier companies. They usually take a share in the company they are investing in.

Which?

The type of finance available will depend on several factors. These are:
- The type of business – sole traders will be limited to the owner's own funds and any loans that may be available. A *private limited company* can raise capital by selling shares to friends and family. A *plc* will be able to sell shares directly to the public.
- The stage of development of the business – new businesses will find it much harder to raise finance than established firms.
- How successful the firm is – a successful track record will encourage lenders and investors.
- The state of the economy – when the economy is growing business confidence is high. Lenders and investors are confident about the future. Interest rates also affect the amount of funding that is available. Higher interest rates make borrowing more expensive.

Why?

Firms generally seek finance for start up and growth. Growth is often seen as a natural development for successful businesses. Businesses may grow:
- to take advantage of economies of scale;
- to keep pace with competitors;
- to get sales above break-even level.

Being bigger will give the firm several advantages:
- It will find it easier to cope with changing economic circumstances.
- It will be able to deal with setbacks more easily.

But

Growth requires good planning and adequate financing. A firm that expands without adequate and appropriate financing is said to be *overtrading*. Adequate financing means that there must be sufficient funding. This is not just for the new machinery or buildings but also the working capital requirements to pay staff and buy raw materials.

Appropriate financing means that the funding should suit the project. The purchase of a fixed asset needs long-term financing. A short-term cash requirement requires a short-term financing solution.

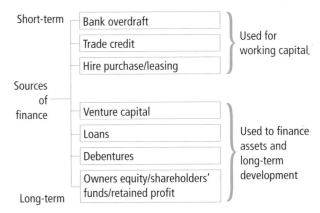

Fig. 2.6A: Short- and long-term finance

K Key Terms

Capital expenditure – spending by the business on fixed assets

Overtrading – when a firm expands without adequate or appropriate funding

Plc – public limited company; a business with limited liability whose shares can be advertised for sale, including on the stock exchange

Application

Robert Wiseman started out as a milkman and now his business is the UK's third largest milk producer. In 1985 Wiseman and his two brothers used their houses as security to raise enough funds to buy a dairy. This had five milk rounds and eight employees. Instead of supplying households the business concentrated on supplying shops. This strategy was very successful and enabled the business to grow significantly. However in 1994 they realised that they could not continue to finance expansion from cash flow. They decided to float the company on the stock market, selling 25% of the business to raise £14 million. With this funding they bought other Scottish businesses and built a dairy in Manchester and Droitwich. Now the business has annual revenues of around £390 million and employs more than 3000 people.

This successful business started with the usual difficulty faced by new businesses of how to secure funding. In this case the owners offered their homes as security so were able to obtain a bank loan, they reinvested profits and the stock exchange float enabled them to raise additional funding to continue to develop the business.

Businesses find it hard to strike the right balance when deciding on their finances. If the firm uses retained profits, shareholders may not get sufficient dividends. If the firm floats on the stock market then ownership and control of the business moves away from the original owners.

Raising finance does not guarantee success. The business world is littered with examples of firms that have successfully raised funding for expansion but have not succeeded. EuroDisney is constantly in the news, as it seems unable to generate enough revenue to repay its enormous debts of about £1.5 billion.

E Exam insight

When looking at business financing it is important to understand what the business needs the funding for. Above all else, is it a long-term project or a short-term cash flow problem? The financing solutions will be very different.

T Test yourself

1. What is meant by capital expenditure? (2)
2. List two internal sources of finance. (2)
3. Explain two types of business finance provided by banks. (4)
4. Outline how factoring works. (4)
5. Explain why a firm might find it difficult to get external finance. (4)
6. Outline two sources of finance suitable for long-term development. (4)

BUDGETING

What?

A budget is a target for costs or revenue that a firm or department must aim to reach over a given period of time.

Why are budgets needed?

Budgets are needed as a control tool once an organisation has grown to a size that prohibits the boss from making all spending decisions. Only the smallest organisations can operate without some kind of delegated spending power. In reality, most firms will need to have a system of budgets in place to allow those on the spot to decide where and when money needs to be spent, without the need to check with those in higher authority. A budget allows individuals or sections of the firm to be allocated a certain amount of money that they are permitted to spend. This frees up time for those who no longer need to sign off this expenditure.

How are they used?

- *As a control tool*: The allocation of sums that departments or individuals can spend allows spending to be constrained – ensuring that no area of the firm is running up costs that had not been planned for.
- *As a yardstick against which performance can be measured*: Successful departments will exceed budgeted figures for revenues and keep costs below budgeted figures. In either case, the success of the budget holder can be easily measured and therefore recognised.

What?

The use of budgets as a control tool relies on a process known as variance analysis. Budgeted figures are compared with actual results to identify any variance (difference) between the two figures. A difference that represents a positive result for a company's profitability is referred to as a *favourable* variance, whereas a result that suggests a decline in profitability is referred to as *adverse* variance (see the example in the table below).

Commentary: In January, sales targets were surpassed (a favourable variance of 20) and, possibly as a result of the increase in sales, direct costs were also higher than expected (an adverse variance of 20). With indirect costs higher than expected the month showed an adverse total cost variance which was big enough to outweigh the favourable revenue variance. This produced an adverse profit variance. February and March were better months, both showing favourable profit variances – in February as a direct result of a highly favourable total cost variance and in March due to a favourable revenue variance.

Meaning of variances

Variances such as these show very little in the way of clear facts. Instead they pose questions such as: What was happening to the average selling price of the products? Was the firm able to negotiate better terms with suppliers in February (causing the favourable direct cost variance)? A variance should be seen as a trigger for further investigation, rather than an answer in itself.

	January Budgeted	January Actual	January Variance	February Budgeted	February Actual	February Variance	March Budgeted	March Actual	March Variance
Sales revenue	500	520	20F*	520	510	10A	520	550	30F
Direct costs	200	220	20A*	210	200	10F	210	225	15A
Indirect costs	200	210	10A	200	190	10F	200	200	–
Total costs	400	430	30A	410	390	20F	410	425	15A
Profits	100	90	10A	110	120	10F	110	125	15F

* A – adverse; F – favourable.

How are budgets set?

- *Incremental budgeting*: Adding a certain percentage onto last year's budget to allow for inflation.
- *Zero budgeting*: Setting each budget to zero at the start of each year and asking each budget holder to justify every penny that is allocated to their budget. This is a time consuming and expensive process to go through each year but will ensure that budgets do not grow automatically.

Benefits of using a budgeting system

Budgets allow managers to practice what is known as management by exception. This is where they focus their attention on areas whose budgets show a large variance. This allows managers' time to be used more productively than if they were required to check every department's spending on a regular basis.

Delegating spending power to managers of separate departments may well have a motivational effect on the budget holders. Being trusted with the authority to decide how money should be spent may provide an increased feeling of responsibility.

What budgets won't do for you

Budgets are targets. There is no guarantee that targets will be met. Unrealistic targets may be out of reach even if staff are working well, although motivation is likely to fall as a result of being set unrealistic targets. Meanwhile, changing objectives may require an adjustment to corporate plans. Unless budgets are adjusted to account for strategic or tactical changes, targets will be irrelevant. Therefore variances need to be looked at within the bigger picture of what has been happening to the business. An adverse materials variance may have been caused by a large increase in output to meet a surge in demand.

How does culture affect the use of budgets?

The culture within an organisation will determine the way in which budgets are used. A culture that is dominated by autocratic attitudes is likely to find budgets used as a strict control system, with each budget holder being held accountable for minor variances. Budgets will be seen as enabling tools in firms with other cultures where budget overspends may be viewed as a chance taken to pursue an opportunity rather than an example of poor cost control.

How useful is variance analysis as a planning tool?

Although budgets are targets set for the future, the use of budgets as the basis of variance analysis must necessarily refer to the past. The variance cannot be calculated until the actual results for that period are in. A large adverse variance in the latest year's variance analysis may mean that a department has been working to an unrealistic target for the last 12 months, yet the problem has only been identified now.

K **Key Terms**

Budget – a target for costs or revenue that a firm or department must aim to reach over a given period of time

Business culture – the attitudes prevailing within a business

Variance analysis – a process of comparing planned with actual results

T **Test yourself**

1. Fill in the six gaps in the following table: (6)

	April			May			June		
	Budgeted	Actual	Variance	Budgeted	Actual	Variance	Budgeted	Actual	Variance
Sales revenue	500	500	0	520	530		520	510	10A
Direct costs	200	210	10A	210	220	10A	210		10A
Indirect costs	200	200	0	200	190		200	200	0
Total costs	400	410	10A	410	410	0	410		
Profits	100	90		110	120	10F	110	90	20A

A – adverse; F – favourable.

2. Explain the meaning of the term 'management by exception'. (3)
3. Identify two benefits of introducing a system of budgeting for a rapidly growing small firm. (2)
4. Outline two problems that may result from using budgets as a strict tool for controlling costs. (4)
5. Briefly explain why accurate budgeting may be much harder for a manufacturer of novelty items than a producer of washing machines. (5)

COST AND PROFIT CENTRES

What?

- *Cost centre*: An identifiable subsection of a company for which costs can be clearly identified.
- *Profit centre*: An identifiable subsection of a company for which revenues and costs – and therefore profit – can be identified.

Why?

A company as huge as Tesco has hundreds of thousands of staff working in thousands of different locations. If the business was run by one person (the Managing Director) it would be impossible to make all the necessary day-to-day decisions. Even if some authority was delegated to managers, trying to control the business would be a bureaucratic nightmare. Better, then, to divide the business up into smaller operating units, with the local boss having responsibility for the costs and/or profits generated. In effect, this could achieve the motivational benefits and flexibility of a small business, while operating under the umbrella of the hugely powerful parent.

A system of identifying cost or profit centres brings three main types of benefit:

1. *Accounting*: Splitting a large organisation into smaller sections eases the process of monitoring the financial performance of the organisation. With only small parts of the firm to be monitored, areas of concern can be identified and explored in more depth.

2. *Organisational*: The use of cost and profit centres allows delegation of authority to occur within the organisation with the manager of the cost or profit centre being held responsible for their area of control. In this way, firms can grow beyond the size that would be possible if senior management had to OK every item of expenditure.

3. *Motivational*: The manager of the cost or profit centre may be motivated by the responsibility for their particular area of responsibility.

How?

Identifying cost and profit centres

The way businesses split their organisations varies from firm to firm, but some ways of splitting the firm into cost centres are shown below:

- *Product*: Firms that make several different products may treat each product as a separate profit or cost centre.
- *Department*: Different functional areas (marketing, finance, production, etc.) can be used as the basis for a system of cost centres.
- *Location*: Firms operating in several geographical markets, either nationwide or globally, may treat different regions as separate cost or profit centres, while a firm with staff employed in various different locations can treat each location as a cost or profit centre.

Note that identifying profit centres requires dividing the business into particular areas that generate revenue as well as costs for a firm.

K Key Terms

Authority – decision-making power, backed by the resources (e.g. a budget) to achieve your goals

Delegation – passing decision-making power to lower levels within the organisation's structure

Application

Cost and profit centres are different by nature. Whereas a business may choose to identify each functional area (marketing, accounting, production, HRM, sales, etc.) as a cost centre, this basis for identifying profit centres would simply not work. Accounting departments, though necessary for the operation of the business, are never going to be profit centres since they generate no revenue for the business. The table below shows cost and profit centre applications to real companies.

	Profit centre	Cost centre
Marks and Spencer	Each individual shop	Head office HR department
Virgin Trains	Each route, e.g. London to Manchester	Head office Advertising department
Ford UK	Each factory, e.g. Southampton (makes Transit vans)	Research and Development department

Potential problems

1. The success of the department or branch can become more important than the success of the whole firm.
2. Not all costs and revenues can be easily linked to a particular section of the firm. Allocations may be perceived as unfair or unjust.
3. Performance of a particular cost or profit centre may be hugely affected by factors outside the manager's control.

Who?

As already noted, a profit centre can only be formed if the revenue generated by a section of the business can be identified. Not all businesses will be able to identify meaningful subsections that each generate revenue, so these will need to be happy with running a system of cost centres.

Profit centres could be identified by:	As:
Retail chains	Each shop
Any other service sector chains	Each branch
A multiproduct manufacturer	Each product line
A multinational company	Each country operated in

Cost centres would be more likely to be found in:
- manufacturers of single products;
- not-for-profit organisations (e.g. schools, government, local councils).

S Student howler

'The manager of a cost centre may be offered a financial bonus if they make a large profit.'

What next?

Cost and profit centres will almost always form the basis of a firm's budgeting system. Budgets will be agreed (or allocated) to a particular cost centre and the performance of that cost centre will be assessed by comparing actual with budgeted figures through the calculation of a variance. Sales budgets may be set for profit centres (though not for cost centres) and again, variances will form the basis for judging the success of that particular section of the business.

In attempting to offer some kind of judgement on the use of cost or profit centres, it is worth considering how each might be used. If operating a system of cost centres, a firm's management is likely to recognise achievements from managers of certain departments through praise and encouragement. If operating a system of profit centres, it is far more likely that staff may be offered a financial reward for achieving certain targets within the profit centre. This can lead to problems with the quality of the work produced or with an unhealthy focus on the need to generate sales at whatever cost. High Street banks such as Lloyds have received multimillion pound fines for mis-selling financial products to those who were better off without them. This can damage the bank's reputation in the medium to long term.

E Exam insight

Though many questions will expect you to be able to identify the advantages and disadvantages of using cost or profit centres, higher scores will be achieved by students who understand these concepts enough to know when they are applicable to different types of business.

Do not use the terms cost and profit centres interchangeably. Think carefully about whether the type of business in question has separate sections that can identifiably generate revenue and therefore be used as profit centres.

T Test yourself

1. Identify the three main benefits of operating a system of cost centres. (3)
2. Briefly explain how the figures from a profit centre could be used by the person responsible for running that profit centre. (4)
3. How would the figures from every cost centre be used by the Finance Director of a large organisation? (4)
4. a) Explain how the use of profit centres might help to motivate staff within each profit centre. (5)
   b) Outline any possible drawbacks of using profit centres. (5)
5. a) Suggest two possible cost centres within your school/college. (2)
   b) Suggest one profit centre and one cost centre for British Airways. (2)

INTEGRATED FINANCE

The AQA specification for this unit says:

Candidates are expected to gain an understanding of accounting and finance in an integrated context within the organisation and the wider environment. Emphasis is placed on the use of accounting and financial information as an aid to decision making and financial control.

Three fundamental issues should be considered when revising for AS level finance: the importance of cash flow, financial monitoring and control, and making a profit.

The importance of cash flow

Why?
Never lose sight of the fact that cash flow is the only thing that will let a firm pay its bills. With no cash and bills unpaid, businesses can be forced to cease trading when their creditors take them to court to recover the unpaid debts. It is therefore vital to ensure that there is enough cash within the business to allow short-term debts to be paid when they are due.

How?
Careful financial planning should decrease the chances of cash flow problems. Cash flow forecasting is a highly effective way of focusing on the necessity of a healthy cash flow in the weeks and months to come, although it is important to remember that a cash flow forecast is never 100% reliable. Since the forecast can never be wholly relied upon, problems do occur, and the various methods available to businesses to ease cash flow problems should not be overlooked.

Who?
Cash flow is more often a problem for small firms than for larger organisations. The immediacy of cash flow problems for a small firm is great – if the wages are not paid, no-one turns up for work next week. However, even the very largest firms can fall victim to cash flow problems. Those that over-borrow in order to finance growth will find heavy interest payments a substantial drain on cash flow.

What it's not
Cash flow is not the same as profit. Profit is not cash, and sales do not mean immediate cash inflows. The most significant cause of differences between cash flow and profit is credit sales. A sale is made, recorded as such and a profit recorded on that sale. However, if the credit terms offered to the customer are too generous, the business may not be able to bridge the gap between cash outflows (spent making the product) and the inflows that will only arrive once the customer is due to pay up.

Financial monitoring and control

Why?
Tight financial controls are needed in business to keep fixed overhead costs down and to ensure that variable costs stay in line with revenues. Achieving this level of financial efficiency is the role of senior financial staff within the organisation and/or lower levels of management who have been set budgets to monitor their own department's finances.

How?
A budgeting system is the vehicle through which firms are able to delegate spending power to managers. Centrally determined budgets will allow clear control over planned expenditures and variance analysis should ensure that potential problems can be identified early enough to be dealt with. Most budgeting systems are hung onto an internal framework of cost and/or profit centres. These will allow the organisation to monitor the financial performance of each subsection, allowing the identification both of successful areas and those which are struggling.

Monitoring the finances of the business is the only sensible way to ensure that decision makers can continue to make informed decisions that will allow the business to make a satisfactory profit.

Making a profit

What?
Any business featured in an exam question will be concerned with the amount of profit it generates. It is therefore critical to develop a thorough understanding of the concept. Profit should be viewed as a relatively simple concept – the excess of revenues over costs. As discussed in Unit 2.1, generating or increasing profit will come from boosting revenues and/or cutting costs.

How?

Reading student answers to finance questions can often lead an examiner to question why any business fails. There is a tendency to assume that any firm can cut its costs at any time without any significant reduction in its performance. Think again. Reducing material costs may hit product quality, cutting wages or shedding staff will demotivate the workforce, while the often suggested move to a cheaper location never quite seems to consider the massive cost, disruption and general upheaval involved in shifting an entire business (especially a manufacturer). If profit were easy, how could any business struggle?

| Evaluation

Finance is only a support function within a business. Those whose roles involve planning, monitoring and evaluating financial performance do not make anything or generate any profit. If businesses exist to make a profit, then the role of the finance people is simply to measure success. It is the marketing people who come up with the ideas and the operations staff who create the products and services being sold. Managing these people, getting the most out of them and any equipment they may be using, as well as effectively communicating your company's message to customers are what will make a firm successful. Of course finance departments have a key role to play in advising these other areas of the firm, but a business is more than just a set of numbers.

E Exam insight

Finance questions may need you to make calculations. These calculations are not mathematical challenges – they will test your ability to apply business studies knowledge. Try to ensure a full mastery of any financial calculations you may be required to make (break-even analysis, profit calculations, cash flow forecasts and budget variances). The big marks, however, tend to come from being able to show a written understanding of the importance of financial matters to the running of a business.

T Test yourself (50 marks)

1. Analyse the potential benefits to a firm from effective financial monitoring. (5)
2. Explain why financial forecasts can never be 100% reliable. (5)
3. Outline two possible solutions to a cash flow crisis caused by a short-term dip in sales for a crisp manufacturer. (4)
4. Explain why cash flow may be more important than profit to a firm that is expanding. (6)
5. Fill in the blanks on the following cash flow forecast: (10)

Month	January	February	March	April
Cash in	100	110	120	120
Cash out	90	110	130	
Net cash flow		0		20
Opening balance	10			
Closing balance				

6. Identify two benefits of cash flow forecasting. (2)
7. Explain what is meant by the term 'factoring'. (3)
8. Briefly explain how improved working capital control can aid cash flow. (4)
9. State three internal sources of finance. (3)
10. Identify one long-term source of finance only available to limited companies. (1)
11. State two methods that banks may use to provide finance to a business. (2)
12. Explain what is meant by the term 'zero budgeting'. (3)
13. State two limitations of break-even analysis. (2)

Now have a go at these data response questions. You should allow yourself 30 minutes for each.

Data response: Celebration Cakes

Robtel Ltd, manufacturers of high-quality baked goods have seen significant recent success following a deal with several major supermarket chains to supply celebration cakes featuring popular children's characters. Success has come rapidly for the firm which has been struggling to meet the orders from the supermarkets along with those of their regular customers. Kate Dougall, the firm's finance director, has drawn up the following figures relating to a proposal to rent new factory space dedicated to meeting the orders from the supermarkets, leaving the firm's existing production facilities to cope with existing customers and smaller scale new business.

Average selling price (price paid by supermarket)	£2.60
Variable cost per cake	£0.80
Rent on extra factory space (per month)	£44,000
Other overheads (per month)	£28,000

Given the power of the supermarket chains, Robtel is unwilling to purchase extra premises or machinery and are therefore renting all the equipment they need. This means that the only extra finance that needs to be found is an estimated £80,000 to fund the extra working capital requirements. This will be necessary because of the generous credit terms offered to the supermarkets, and the inability of Robtel to negotiate longer credit terms with their own suppliers. Robtel's Managing Director, Liz Green, has expressed concern over the strained cash flow position that will be created by accepting this new business from the supermarkets. Cash flow forecasts suggest that the firm will have to endure several months of negative net cash flows in the near future.

Questions

1. State what is meant by the term 'overheads'. (2)
2. Outline two internal sources of finance that could be used to generate the extra working capital required. (4)
3. Calculate the expected break-even output of the new factory for Celebration Cakes. (4)
4. Analyse *one* reason why this break-even analysis may prove unreliable. (6)
5. Discuss the possible solutions to Robtel's cash flow problems relating to the supermarket orders. (9)

Data response: Nurwoo Noodles

Nurwoo Ltd is in the rapidly expanding noodle market. The firm's no-frills approach to Chinese fast food has allowed for rapid expansion in its 5 year history, with eight restaurants now operating in South East London and Kent. The founders of the business, Mr Nurthen and Mr Woo, oversee the operations of the firm but the manager of each restaurant is responsible for hitting budgets agreed with the founders on a 6-monthly basis. With each restaurant treated as a profit centre, the founders are growing concerned over the performance of the Bromley branch, managed by Tom Way. Recruited straight from university, Tom oversaw the successful opening of the restaurant in January 2003, but performance has dipped in the second half of the year and Tom has been called to a meeting with Mr Nurthen and Mr Woo to explain the budget statement shown below for July–December 2003 at the Bromley restaurant:

	Budgeted (£)	Actual (£)
Eat-in sales	16,000	11,200
Take-away sales	20,000	19,500
Total revenue	36,000	30,700
Ingredients	12,000	10,500
Wages	13,800	13,600
Overheads	6000	6900
Total costs	31,800	31,000

Questions

1. Explain the meaning of the term 'total revenue'. (2)
2. Outline one benefit that Nurwoo may experience as a result of using profit centres. (5)
3. Calculate the profit variance for Bromley for the period July–December 2003. (4)
4. Analyse one reason for keeping the Bromley restaurant open. (5)
5. To what extent would tighter budgetary control have prevented problems at the Bromley branch? (9)

PRODUCTIVITY AND PERFORMANCE

What?

Productivity measures the efficiency with which a firm turns inputs into output. The commonest type of productivity measured is labour productivity, i.e. output per worker.

Productivity – not output

Productivity is not the same as total output. Productivity measures output per employee. One firm may have a higher output than another, yet a lower rate of productivity. If this is the case, the smaller, more efficient firm is likely to prove more successful in the long term.

Why?

The more units of output each employee produces, the lower the labour cost per unit (unless they are paid purely on piece rate). Higher productivity creates lower input costs per unit which means a lower total cost and a more competitive business. It is therefore able to charge lower prices, or generate more profit per unit, than its less productive rivals. Productivity is therefore a hugely important variable for many firms. Managers will focus a great deal of time and energy on finding methods of raising productivity.

Different measures of productivity

There are different measures of productivity, as shown in the following table:

Context	Measure of productivity
Manufacturer	Units of output per worker per week
Supermarket checkout	Average number of items 'zapped' per minute
Call centre	Calls answered per hour
Fruit picking	Kilograms per day
Insurance company	Number of claims processed per week

How?

Increasing productivity

1. *Training*: Better trained staff will be capable of working faster and more accurately. Better quality means that fewer materials will be needed to produce the same output, and a higher rate of productivity due to less time wasted correcting mistakes.

2. *Motivation*: A more motivated workforce is likely to work harder and in a more focused manner, showing commitment to the job. Staff are also more likely to come up with ideas for improving productivity levels.

3. *Management*: Organisation of the workplace and the production process can be a crucial factor in achieving higher levels of efficiency. Management may also encourage staff to share their ideas for improving productivity.

4. *Technology*: More advanced machinery and equipment can speed up processes – allowing higher levels of output reduced levels of labour and time input.

E Exam insight

Students use 'productivity' as if it is a posh way of saying 'production'. It is not. Productivity and production are quite different. Productivity is efficiency; production is the total quantity produced.

What next?

With higher productivity more units of output can be produced at a lower cost per unit. This provides the opportunity to increase sales by cutting price.

Higher productivity also allows output levels to rise without taking on any extra staff. If a firm had been struggling to meet demand, this is great news. So rising productivity is especially valuable to firms with products in the growth stages of their life cycle, or at times when economic growth is boosting demand.

On the other hand, firms may decide that there is unlikely to be any significant extra demand for their product and take the opportunity to reduce

**Productivity is up -
can we increase sales?**

Yes → Maintain current sales, Cut price

No → Cut staff, Find alternative use for staff

Fig. 3.1A: Productivity diagram

their workforce. The same number of units can now be produced by fewer staff. This course of action has significant implications in terms of employee job security and levels of trust between management and staff. A more positive alternative would be to find some other way to use the staff no longer needed for their original purpose, i.e. to redeploy them to a new task. This alternative is clearly preferable to redundancy, as far as staff are concerned.

Application

Faster inquiries

In 2003 the new Directory Inquiry service 118 118 set up a bonus system based upon the speed with which operators answered calls. This gave staff a financial incentive to increase their productivity. In response, some staff gave out wrong numbers or just put the phone down on customers, in order to keep within the deadline for their bonuses. When this was uncovered by journalists, 118 118 suffered embarrassing publicity and made 30 staff redundant. This shows that boosting productivity must be handled with care.

Slower food

Market research by McDonalds in the 1990s demonstrated the limitations of a total focus on increased productivity, with customers complaining that staff were rushing their orders and not paying enough attention to satisfying customers. McDonalds moved the focus of their staff away from speed (customers served per hour) towards customer satisfaction (happy customers per hour?).

Themes for evaluation

Managers can make the mistake of seeing high productivity as an end in itself. Yet it is important to consider the effects of achieving a higher level of productivity. Increasing productivity can bring fears of redundancy unless the firm is in a position to increase output. This can damage the relationship between staff and managers, especially if managers are seen a slave drivers, continually pushing for higher levels of productivity.

Other negative side effects may evolve as a result of attempts to boost productivity. Any increase in productivity that leads to quality problems may well be a major problem. Employees rushing to finish more work in a given time may be forced to cut corners in their jobs, leading to poorer quality standards. Simply encouraging employees to work faster is likely to cause deep problems relating to the firm's reputation amongst its customers. Firms that pride themselves on customer service may suffer as a result of frantic attempts to increase productivity, with staff rushing through their dealings with customers in an attempt to serve more customers per hour. In both cases attempts to increase productivity may damage the firm's overall performance.

S Student howlers

'Although firm A has 50% more workers than firm B, they have a higher productivity because their output is 25% higher than firm B.'
'Increasing productivity will mean that the firm sells more units and will make a higher profit.'

T Test yourself

1. Calculate the output per worker of a firm with a workforce of 500 that manufactures 20,000 units per month. (2)
2. Identify the four main routes to increasing productivity. (4)
3. Outline two potential benefits of achieving a higher level of productivity on supermarket checkouts. (6)
4. Explain how a drive to increase productivity may result in employee dissatisfaction. (8)

UNIT 3.2
MOTIVATION IN THEORY

The question of what motivates people to work has been studied formally for most of the last 100 years. There are four key motivation theorists with whose work you must be familiar: F.W. Taylor, Elton Mayo, Abraham Maslow and Frederick Herzberg.

▌F.W. Taylor

What did he say?

Taylor was admittedly more than just a motivation theorist, concentrating on how work should be organised. Working at the start of the twentieth century, Taylor's work was rooted in his belief that the only factor that motivates people to work is money.

How to organise the workplace

- *High division of labour*: Taylor felt that any production process should be split into as many separate tasks as possible. This allowed for the identification of small simple jobs that could be repeated over and over to allow unskilled workers to become specialists in that job very quickly and thus achieve high rates of output with virtually no training or experience. In 2002 McDonalds in America planned to achieve zero training, i.e. hire new staff and put them to work immediately.
- *Payment by results*: Taylor favoured piece rate, in other words paying per unit produced. He believed that this would encourage people to work hard without the need for tight supervision. All a supervisor would need to do is to count the quantity of work produced.
- *Time and motion study*: Taylor advocated taking a scientific approach to organising work. He studied the way work was done and identified the 'one best way' to do the job. Each part of the job could be timed to identify how much each worker should be expected to achieve in a day. This could then be used to set challenging piece rate targets.
- *Best tools for the job*: A key part of Taylor's scientific approach was to ensure that his workers were given tools that were designed carefully to make their job as straightforward as possible – thus speeding up production.

▌Elton Mayo

What did he say?

Mayo was originally a keen advocate of Taylor's ideas and his most famous set of experiments were designed to examine Taylor's theories. The results of the 'Hawthorne experiments' led Mayo to take motivation theory a step forward. The acknowledgement that factors other than money could impact on the motivation of staff altered the way that many firms treated their staff.

How to organise the workplace

- *Teamworking*: Mayo identified the importance of 'group norms'. A team could work together for the good of all, or be obstructive and negative. Taylor thought of workers as individuals; Mayo saw the importance of managing their team spirit.
- *Social facilities*: Since workers work better if they feel part of a team, any opportunity should be taken to encourage this feeling of togetherness. Social facilities or sports clubs at the workplace are examples of ways in which firms have tried to develop this feeling of belonging.
- *Hawthorne effect*: This describes the beneficial impact on staff workrate and morale of managers taking an active personal interest in their staff. You have probably already seen this in action at school – you worked harder for teachers who actually seemed to care about what and how you were doing. Likewise in the workplace – if the boss is interested in what you're doing, this provides a boost to morale and performance.

E ▌ Exam insight

The first step to success is to know the work of these theorists exactly – vague references to motivation theorists add little to an answer. The best approach is to choose one relevant theorist and use the theory to analyse the business situation in detail. Avoid briefly saying: 'Taylor would say this, Mayo would say that and …'

Abraham Maslow

What did he say?

Maslow's hierarchy, shown below, identifies five types of need that human beings will try to satisfy. Knowledge of these needs should encourage a manager to apply them to the workplace (see the table at the foot of the page).

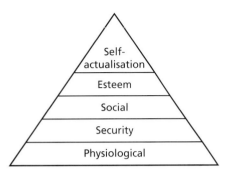

Fig. 3.2A: Maslow's hierarchy of needs

Frederick Herzberg

What did he say?

Herzberg's two-factor theory suggests that there are two groups of factors that affect job satisfaction: 'motivators' such as responsibility can lead to positive job satisfaction; 'hygiene factors' such as working conditions can cause job dissatisfaction, but have no potential for causing lasting job satisfaction. The identification of factors that determine workers' levels of job satisfaction and dissatisfaction allows managers to get the highest possible level of performance from staff. Herzberg's two different sets of factors determining motivation are shown in the table below.

Hygiene factors (remove dissatisfaction)	Motivators (provide positive job satisfaction)
Company policy and administration	Achievement
Supervisor's competence	Recognition for achievement
Salary	Work itself
Relations with supervisor	Responsibility
Working conditions	Psychological growth and advancement

How to motivate workers

Herzberg's advice in bitesize chunks is as follows:

1. Address both hygiene factors and motivators – poor hygiene means unhappy staff, weak motivators leads to an 'acceptable' (but no more) level of performance.

2. Jobs should be designed to allow workers to learn and grow.

3. A job should involve the opportunity to produce a complete unit of work (finish a whole project or produce a whole product from start to finish).

4. The process of designing jobs to include as many motivators as possible was what Herzberg referred to as 'job enrichment'.

Criticisms of the theorists

Theorist	Criticisms
Taylor	There's far more to it than money. Repetitive jobs and piece rate can lead to quality problems, boredom, resentment and high labour turnover
Mayo	Mayo's views were radical, even revolutionary, but managers turned his theory into bland ideas such as social clubs and football teams at work
Maslow	Does everyone have the same five-stage hierarchy, or are some people satisfied to work for money and a good time with their mates, i.e. uninterested in stretching themselves?
Herzberg	Theory based on research conducted amongst accountants and engineers – is the theory applicable to other types of job?

Can any theory explain human behaviour at work?

There are likely to be so many different variables that influence workplace performance that any attempt at a single explanation of motivation may be doomed to failure. This argument would suggest that every single individual must be treated differently according to their own personal situation.

How many people actually know about this?

Few of those responsible for managing people at work have actually spent any time studying motivation theory. More advanced theories – such as Herzberg's two-factor theory – may therefore be completely ignored in many workplaces. In a few lucky instances managers may have a natural feeling for what is likely to motivate their staff, yet many tend to assume that money is enough. In these cases, staff may not give their best and therefore a key resource is being underused. It could be argued that motivation theories are the most important piece of business knowledge available to managers.

How to apply Maslow to the workplace

Hierarchy	In a work context	Role of manager
Self-actualisation	Develop new skills	Implement a training programme and create challenging assignments for staff
Esteem	Recognition, status, power	Praise staff who achieve, offer promotions and/or bonuses
Social	Opportunities for teamwork	Create a team environment with effective communication systems and social facilities to allow staff to mix after work
Security or safety	Job security	Clear job description, simple lines of accountability – just one boss
Physical or physiological	Adequate pay and breaks should ensure a worker's physiological needs are met	Appropriate pay, breaks and comfortable physical working conditions

K Key Terms

Division of labour – splitting a process into small simple repetitive jobs

Job enrichment – designing a job to include as many of Herzberg's motivators as possible

Time and motion study – watching the way a process is completed and identifying standard times for each section of the process to be completed in order to identify the best way and expected time for that process.

S Student howlers

'Herzberg's ideas were revolutionary because he said that money doesn't matter.'
'Herzberg believed that the motivators were more important than hygiene factors.'
'Managers taking an interest in staff is likely to boost staff morals.'

T Test yourself

1. Identify three modern business practices that flowed from the work of F.W. Taylor.　(3)
2. Outline two pieces of advice that Mayo might give to new managers, explaining how each would help to bring the best out of their staff.　(4)
3. Briefly explain how each of Maslow's sets of needs might be achieved in the workplace.　(10)
4. For each of the following, identify whether Herzberg classed it as a motivator or a hygiene factor:
   a) Salary;
   b) Recognition for achievement;
   c) Relationship with supervisor.　(3)

MOTIVATION IN PRACTICE

▌ What?

Culture

Culture is the accepted set of attitudes, behaviour and beliefs within an organisation. Each organisation, department or classroom will have its own culture. Culture will be affected by the make up of the group, the attitudes of any official or unofficial leaders within the group and the traditional approach to doing things within that business.

Job enrichment

Herzberg's prescription for motivating staff is to provide them with what he termed job enrichment. An enriched job has several key features:

1. A complete unit of work – each employee should be able to see their work as contributing to the production of a complete and identifiable finished product.
2. Direct feedback – a worker should know how they are doing without someone else needing to tell them. There should be no need for a quality control inspector.
3. Direct communication – if a worker needs to talk to anyone in another department, they should be permitted to do so, without needing to go through traditional channels of communication.

▌ How?

Some examples of how to enrich a job are illustrated in the following table.

▌ What else?

Other means of job enrichment include job enlargement, empowerment, teamworking and financial reward systems.

Job enlargement

This is the process of building a wider range of tasks into a job, possibly including a variety of tasks with different levels of responsibility. This can allow employees to grow within their working lives, enabling them to feel a sense of self-actualisation. However, job enlargement is frequently used as a euphemism for increasing the workload of staff without making their jobs any more interesting.

Empowerment

Empowerment means passing genuine decision-making power to a worker – not just how to do a job but to decide exactly what job needs doing. Such an initiative usually requires deep-rooted cultural change since managers need to trust in the instincts and skills of their staff. A genuine theory Y manager should be able to operate a system of empowerment effectively. Managers who are unwilling to trust their staff completely will fail to see the benefits of empowerment, since staff will always feel they are being checked up on or over-supervised.

Teamworking

This describes introducing a system where groups of employees are split into identifiable teams. These teams work together to improve performance within their area of the firm and are held responsible for the level of performance they produce. Though this approach undoubtedly helps to meet employees' social

	Job enrichment in a manufacturing plant	Job enrichment in a clothes shop
A complete unit of work	Each member of staff takes a product through the manufacturing process from beginning to end	A shop assistant offers advice to a customer, perhaps helps in trying on the clothes and then goes to the till to take payment for the item
Direct feedback	Workers should check the quality of their own work, to provide feedback on whether they have done it effectively	The customer's reactions to the shop assistant will provide feedback on how well he has done his job
Direct communication	A worker finding a faulty component can go directly to the storage area to get a replacement without needing to check with a supervisor	The assistant can phone the warehouse to check whether or not that particular size can be ordered for the customer, without needing to consult with the manager

needs, other benefits are expected, such as better problem-solving performance since the team can pool their ideas. However, teamworking can fall victim to reduced levels of productivity, as noticed by Mayo in his Hawthorne experiments, if workers within a group lower their work-rate to conform to 'group norms'.

Financial reward systems

All the theorists agree that money is an important factor to consider in the performance of staff. A number of payment methods have been developed that try to use the power of financial reward to stimulate staff to work harder:

Financial reward system	What is it?	Advantages	Disadvantages
Piece work	Paying workers a fee for every unit of output completed. It is used most commonly on a production line	Encourages a fast rate of production by rewarding those workers that achieve the highest output	Can lead to poor quality of output as work is rushed Makes workers less willing to accept changes to working practices, since they are likely to be slower at a new process
Performance-related pay	PRP links pay (often bonus payments or annual rises) to an assessment of the employee's job performance	Rewards good job performance, judged according to pre-set criteria	Those who fail to 'make the grade' may be extremely de-motivated May take up significant amount of management time
Profit sharing	Workers are paid a bonus related to the amount of profit generated by the company or the site at which they work	Should encourage workers to work in a way that maximises profit, e.g. increasing productivity or reducing defect rates	May encourage a short-term approach to solving problems in order to protect this month's profit bonus
Share ownership	Involves issuing shares in the company to the workforce as part of their remuneration package	Ties the objectives of the workforce to shareholder objectives, since anything that causes the share price to rise should make both groups better off	Workers may feel that the total value of the shares they receive is insignificant
Fringe benefits	Non-financial rewards that can be given to staff, such as a company car or private health care	Can help meet employees' security needs, while some fringe benefits may go untaxed	Workers may prefer an increased pay packet that allows them to spend their money as they choose

Themes for evaluation

Is it real or just an illusion?

Take empowerment as an example. Many firms will happily use the term to describe how they treat their staff, but there is a genuine difference between empowering a worker and simply piling more jobs on their shoulders. Many of the motivational techniques suggested above have failed when put into practice simply because firms paid lip service to the ideas without ever fully committing to the cultural change required to make ideas such as empowerment provide the expected benefits.

E Exam insight

Will you be able to spot a case study where the management are saying the right things but failing to act in a way that reflects what they are saying? Too often in exam questions, students take an uncritical approach to considering motivational tools. If empowerment is mentioned in a case study, the standard arguments in favour of empowerment come back at the examiner, despite the possibility that the firm is not managing to motivate its staff because of over-supervision. Be willing to be critical.

S Student howlers

'If the loss-making company in the case study introduces a profit-sharing payment system instead of this year's pay rise, the workers will be more motivated and everything will be good for the firm.'
'Piece rate pay will help to improve the image of Safeway's because customers will not need to wait as long at checkouts.'

T Test yourself

1. Identify three features of an 'enriched' job. (3)
2. Briefly explain two reasons why an advertising agency might benefit from moving towards a more team-based system. (4)
3. Explain the business significance of organisational culture. (5)
4. Explain two reasons why empowerment may not be an effective motivational tool for summer farm workers. (4)
5. Identify (explaining your reasons) the financial reward system that might work best for:
   a) sales staff in a fashion clothing shop;
   b) the manager of a branch of a chain of fashion clothing retailers. (4)

LEADERSHIP AND MANAGEMENT STYLES

What?

The easiest way to classify the different approaches to management is to think of a spectrum, ranging from a purely autocratic approach to an approach that allows subordinates to carry on with their jobs with virtually no interference from management. Various labels can be attached to different management styles and these labels are shown below the spectrum below:

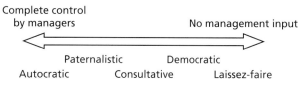

Fig. 3.4A: Leadership styles

How do they differ?

There are pros and cons at each end of the spectrum. At the left of the spectrum, managers may find it hard to fully motivate their staff. Staff will feel that they are not being paid to think at all, with managers taking all decisions. Therefore, autocratic managers may need to use threats or bribes in order to get staff to work harder. However, these managers will have a far clearer picture of what is going on within their area of responsibility, since all decisions have been made by them. Decisions can be made quickly and this feature may be critical in the event of a crisis situation.

Managers to the right of the spectrum will be more likely to be able to claim that their staff really enjoy their jobs and feel that their work is meaningful. However, decisions may take longer if consultation is

Leadership style	Pros	Cons
Autocratic	• Decisions can be made quickly and decisively • Practical, if most staff are part-time and/or temporary, e.g. at a seaside fast-food restaurant	• May damage motivation among staff who want to contribute ideas • Hard to spot potential new leaders, if only the existing leader has authority
Paternalistic	• Being 'part of the family' will meet the safety, physiological and social needs of staff • Training provision is likely to be good, giving staff a strong base for career success	• The higher order needs (Maslow) may be unfulfilled, if the leader treats staff like his/her children • The 'family' may not cope well with a trading downturn; trust would be broken by redundancies
Consultative	• Consultation based on open information and two-way communication is motivating • It should also improve the quality of decision making	• Consultation must be genuinely based on a wish to learn from staff views, not pick and choose • Consultation can be a slow process, especially if the firm operates on many sites
Democratic	• Effective delegation of authority is one of the most important human motivators • Passing authority down the hierarchy ensures that decisions are made by those who understand the day-to-day issues	• Democratic leadership requires trust and the willingness to accept mistakes as part of a learning process • Democracy must be genuine, i.e. not merely 'delegating' unwanted, dull or unpleasant tasks
Laissez-faire	• Allowing staff freedom to set their own goals and strategies can be hugely motivating • This approach is effective (and may be necessary) in creative professions such as advertising	• The lack of coordination implied by laissez-faire may cause a lot of staff effort to be duplicated or misdirected • It may only be effective in small teams, so firms hit problems if they grow too fast or too much

used, and staff may feel unsettled by the openness of a laissez-faire style. They may want to ask 'the boss' what to do next, but the leader is leaving it entirely up to them. These styles of management tend to be more effective with skilled rather than unskilled and experienced rather than brand-new staff. Roles where creativity is crucial may also benefit from a leadership style nearer the right-hand end of the spectrum.

K Key Terms

Autocratic – a management style characterised by issuing orders and demanding unquestioning obedience

Democratic – managers make decisions that are supported by the majority of staff, preferably through a consensus of opinion

Laissez-faire – managers do not interfere with the way in which staff work, leaving staff to make decisions themselves

Paternalistic – a management style that mirrors the way in which a father treats his children; the manager will make decisions based upon what he/she feels are in the best interests of staff

What?

Douglas McGregor classified managers according to the assumptions they hold about their staff using a 'theory X and theory Y' system.

- A theory X manager assumes that:
  — employees dislike work and will avoid it if they can;
  — employees want to be told what to do, have little desire for improvement and try to avoid responsibility wherever possible;
  — employees must be controlled and threatened or bribed to work.
- A theory Y manager assumes that:
  — work is as natural as play or rest for humans;
  — staff welcome responsibility if rewarded fairly;
  — most employees are capable of offering their own ideas when approaching problems.

Why are these assumptions important?

The assumptions that each type of manager has will determine the way in which they treat their staff. Theory X managers will believe that their staff need to be given clear instructions and closely supervised. A manager with theory Y assumptions will treat staff in a very different way, being more trusting and therefore less bossy. Opportunities to involve staff in decision making will be created, and there will be an emphasis on consultation and, especially, delegation.

S Student howlers

'A theory X worker is lazy and will need to be threatened to work.'
'Autocratic leaders use delegation; democratic ones use consultation.'

Attempts to identify a 'best' style of management may founder on the different and changing circumstances of different firms. There can be no one best management style – the best a firm can hope to find is the right style for their existing set of circumstances: an autocrat in a crisis, a democratic or even laissez-faire leader to encourage innovation in the good times. However, with most managers tending to favour a particular style, individual managers may need to change their approach as circumstances change. This risks insincerity – for example a theory Y leader attempting to be autocratic at a time of difficulty for the business. Unless managers are able to adjust their own style, a previously successful management team may need to be replaced when circumstances change. The right approach in boom times might not work well when cutbacks are needed.

E Exam insight

There is a big difference between leadership labels and leadership in practice. Many bosses call themselves democratic, but they actually only allow subordinates to get involved in minor or trivial decisions. Many staff resent sham democracy, and would prefer to have a boss who is honestly bossy!

Look for evidence of a prevailing leadership style at a company. This means the style that most managers seem to display. If you can identify a common style, this will allow you to perhaps offer some insight as to how this type of leadership style may affect a company – for example, a company where most of the managers seem to take a paternalistic attitude to staff may have low staff turnover but have a poor record for creativity and innovation.

T Test yourself

1. Distinguish between a theory X and a theory Y manager. (3)
2. Explain one advantage and one disadvantage of a laissez-faire management style in a school. (6)
3. Analyse the factors that might influence the most appropriate leadership style in any given company. (7)
4. What might be the implications of a sales manager adopting an autocratic leadership style (4)

ORGANISATIONAL STRUCTURE

What?

The structure of an organisation shows the formal relationships between the staff within a business.
- NB: Check that you understand the key terms listed at the end of this unit before embarking on your revision of structures.

Why?

The people within an organisation need to identify who to go to for advice, who is their boss and who they are in charge of. A formal structure makes these issues clear and helps the people within an organisation to understand what authority they have and who they are accountable to.

How?

Designing a structure
Organisations have traditionally been hierarchically structured, i.e. the structure resembles a pyramid with the highest levels of authority at the top of the pyramid and power flowing downwards to the lower, wider, levels within the structure.

Functional or divisional hierarchies
These hierarchical structures are split into separate sections within the business. A functional structure separates each business function and lays out a hierarchy for the people within that function – so, for example, there will be a marketing director in charge of the whole marketing department. Divisional structures split the organisation into different sections according to the different products made by the company or the different geographical locations, so a major multinational may have separate divisions for Europe, The Americas and Asia – each with its own boss.

Functional hierarchy   Divisional structure

Fig. 3.5A: Functional hierarchy/divisional structure

Hierarchical structures can vary significantly in their shape, with some companies preferring a flat structure with few layers of hierarchy and wide spans of control. Other firms prefer a structure with narrow spans of control – this will lead to the appearance of a tall, thin structure.

Advantages of a flat structure	Advantages of a tall structure
Encourages delegation	Allows far greater control
Reduces distance from senior management to shop-floor staff	Less likelihood of mistakes, as supervision is tighter
Encourages bottom-up communication	Better promotional prospects

Who?

Different businesses will find differing structures more appropriate:
- A tall structure would be particularly effective when most staff are unskilled or inexperienced, perhaps part-time or temporary, or where the smallest mistake can have huge consequences, such as in the design and production of aircraft components.
- A flat structure would be useful when highly skilled staff should be encouraged to take their own decisions or when market trends are rapidly changing.

Centralised or decentralised power
These differing shapes of structure can also be described by referring to where the decision-making power tends to lie. A tall structure tends to keep authority in one place – at the higher levels of the structure – and is therefore referred to as centralised. A decentralised structure is one where power is spread throughout the organisation, with even lower levels of staff empowered to make decisions that concern their own jobs. Such a phenomenon is more likely to be found in a flatter structure.

How else?

Matrix
A matrix structure is one where lines of authority run both vertically and horizontally. Superimposed on top

of a traditional functional structure are project teams set up to work on a particular project that is current to the firm's needs. These project teams will include people from whichever departments are necessary – perhaps someone from marketing, someone from finance, an engineer and a couple of scientists might be working on developing a new product line.

Fig. 3.5B: Matrix management

What next?

Leadership styles
Flatter structures with wider spans of control tend to be accompanied by a more democratic leadership style. The increased amount of delegation required by such structures requires a leadership style that places decision-making power in the hands of subordinates. Meanwhile, taller structures would tend to indicate a more autocratic leadership style with the emphasis on control.

Themes for evaluation

The right structure for the organisation
Firms have control over their organisational structures. With this in mind, it is important for a company to ensure that the structure it has in place suits the staff within the firm and the operations of the business. Different structures have different strengths and the directors of any organisation should decide which are the key features that suit their particular position and which structure best meets their needs.

Changing the structure
Changing an organisation's structure can be a theme within exam case studies and can be viewed (at least superficially) as a tough job. Structural change, as with any major change within an organisation can cause uncertainty, even fear. During the economic downturn in 1990 to 1992 'delayering' was widespread. This meant eliminating a whole management layer from a hierarchy, usually by making experienced managers redundant. Whatever long-term benefits might stem from a flatter hierarchy, in the short term the key was to manage the change effectively and sympathetically. For more information on managing change, refer to Unit 3.8.

K Key Terms

Accountability – identifying who an employee is answerable to, and for what

Authority – the power to make decisions over what to do and how to do it

Chain of command – the vertical lines of authority within a structure

Functions – the major types of activity necessary for a firm to function, e.g. marketing, finance, personnel (Human Resources), operations

Span of control – the number of subordinates for whom a manager is directly responsible

E Exam insight

Successful exam answers require precise knowledge of the terminology involved in organisational structures. Only then will an examiner be convinced that the student understands the issues raised by the firm's organisational hierarchy.

It is crucial to be aware of the implications that certain structural types and shapes carry for the way in which the business is run. Consider how the working experience might differ if you move from a firm with a matrix structure to one with a tall hierarchical structure.

S Student howlers

'A flat structure has wide chains of command and tall spans of control.'
'A narrow span of control will help all internal communication.'

T Test yourself

1. Explain what is meant by the following terms:
   a) wide span of control;
   b) long chain of command;
   c) centralised structure. (6)
2. Outline two benefits to an advertising agency of ensuring that its structure is flat. (4)
3. Briefly outline two possible problems of a matrix structure. (6)
4. Explain two benefits of ensuring that an organisation has a clear organisational structure that all staff understand. (4)

MANAGEMENT BY OBJECTIVES

What?

Management by objectives (MBO) is a system for delegating control within an organisation by devising mutually agreed objectives for each member of staff that flow from the corporate objectives.

How?

In order to move any group of people in a desired direction, the job of the leader is easier if people are all individually moving in the same direction as the group needs to travel. Note the diagram below, with each large circle indicating an organisation and the small arrows within showing each member of staff and their own personal objectives from their job.

No sense of direction   Clear sense of direction

Fig. 3.6A: Objectives provide direction

Why?

As countless examples can illustrate, any group of individuals will achieve an overall result far more effectively if they are all working in the same direction. Imagine a 'tug of war' team that had each individual pulling in a slightly different direction and you can see what MBO can avoid.

Once objectives have been agreed, managers can allow their subordinates to pursue those objectives in whatever way they see fit. Decision-making power can be delegated and thus employees can gain motivational benefits from a sense of achievement and control over their own job.

Application

- *Small business*: The concept of formal management by objectives is hardly relevant to small organisations. Staff should be fairly clear about the direction the firm is heading in. They will therefore understand relatively easily what they can do to help the firm achieve its overall objectives. In this case the value of formalising the MBO process may be questionable.
- *Large business*: Larger organisations are often victims of diseconomies of scale (see Unit 4.1), one example of which is the lack of motivation that comes from feeling an insignificant part of a large faceless organisation. MBO can help to overcome this problem since staff are set objectives that hopefully allow them to see how they are personally contributing to the firm's overall success. In a large firm, the process needs to be formalised, and therefore a fairly substantial investment of time, training and money will be required for MBO to operate effectively.

E Exam insight

Management by objectives is an area often overlooked by students. The result is that answers to examination questions rely solely upon an explanation of what is meant by an objective. In fact the key point of MBO – getting everyone pulling in the same direction – is frequently absent from students answers to MBO questions.

What can go wrong?

- *Costs*: A system of management by objectives costs time (for meetings between managers and staff to take place) and money (for training for those involved in running the scheme). It can be quite hard to quantify the actual financial benefits of the system and so the obvious costs may be seen to outweigh the less quantifiable benefits.
- *Paperwork*: With the need for formally agreed objectives, there will often come a heavy burden of paperwork to be completed. Perhaps forms will need to be filled in to record the agreed objectives, while employees may need to provide written evidence of the objectives achieved. After a while,

the benefits of the system can be lost as employees and managers start to lose heart with the system – seeing it as too much work for minimal gain.

What else?

- *Diseconomies of scale*: MBO can help to retain control and coordination within a large organisation. At the same time the system allows staff to avoid feelings of isolation as they feel they are contributing to the firm's success by achieving their own objectives.
- *Motivation*: Responsibility for setting an agreed objective, along with the sense of achievement that comes from meeting the target, are both motivators according to Herzberg. MBO should allow managers to enrich the jobs of their subordinates.
- *Delegation*: The clear definition of a target that is desirable for the firm allows delegation of decision-making power throughout the organisation. This means that the benefits that flow from delegation should result from the successful operation of a system of management by objectives.

Themes for evaluation

Establishing a system of management by objectives can be a time-consuming process that may or may not be worth it. At its worst MBO may encourage short-term thinking in order to hit targets. At its best it will help to make a democratic leadership style work.
MBO will prove most effective where the business already has a strong, positive culture and high ethical standards.

T Test yourself

1. Explain the meaning of MBO. (4)
2. Outline three benefits of MBO. (6)
3. Outline two reasons why a small firm may not introduce a system of MBO. (6)
4. State two possible objectives that may be pursued by:
   a) the Purchasing Director of a medium-sized computer manufacturer. (2)
   b) a football team's goalkeeper. (2)

HUMAN RESOURCE MANAGEMENT

What?

Human resource management (HRM) is the management function responsible for recruiting, developing and using the people that work for an organisation in order to assist the firm in achieving its stated objectives.

In order to fulfil its purpose HRM undertakes four major tasks within the company: workforce planning, recruitment and selection, training and appraisal.

Workforce planning

What?

Workforce planning allows a firm to identify the staffing needs it is likely to have in the future. This involves not only the number of staff but also the skills that they will need.

How?

These staffing needs are identified by carefully studying the firm's corporate strategy for achieving its stated objectives. Having identified what staff the firm will need and what particular skills they will require, the firm will undertake any recruitment or training that is necessary.

In some cases firms will need to get rid of existing staff. If the workforce planning is carried out well in advance, the pain of redundancy can be minimised as much of the reduction in numbers can come from 'natural wastage' – not replacing staff who retire or leave the firm.

Recruitment and selection

How?

Staff may be recruited internally (existing employees) or externally.

Benefits of internal recruitment	Benefits of external recruitment
Firm already knows member of staff – lessens danger of a disastrous appointment being made	There will be a far wider pool of applicants to choose from
The member of staff already understands the firm's culture; induction training will not be necessary	New staff may bring in fresh ideas from outside the company

One or more of the following methods of selection may be employed:
- Application forms – used to draw up a short-list;
- Interview – ranges from informal 5 minutes to interviews that can last several days for more senior members of staff;
- Psychometric tests – allow a firm to assess the attitudes held by applicants: this can help to ensure that the recruit will fit into the firm's culture;
- Aptitude tests – test the actual skills of the employee – usually mental reasoning skills rather than hands-on practical skills;
- Role plays – can allow firms to assess the way that recruits might react in a range of different work scenarios.

Who?

Job	Recruitment method
Temporary fruit picker	Application form (perhaps); possibly a very brief, informal chat with the boss
Retail store manager	Application forms and CVs will be requested, then short-listed candidates will probably be required to take part in a whole day of interviews, including various types of testing and possibly some role play activities
Finance Director	Adverts appearing in the *Financial Times* may attract a number of applicants who will be short-listed on the basis of CV and reputation. The short-listed applicants are likely to undergo a rigorous series of interviews, quite possibly over several days. This process may well be handled by a specialist (and expensive) recruitment consultant

Training

Why?

Training may be used to fulfil the following needs:
1. The need to introduce new staff to the firm's systems and procedures. This is known as induction training.
2. The desire to increase the range of skills available within the firm to allow for flexibility or future changes.

3. To increase the knowledge and commitment to the firm of the workforce.

4. To enhance the quality of work produced by staff.

Note that a paternalistic employer would be inclined to train staff for life as well as for the job, i.e. offer training for personal development such as a foreign language and courses in public speaking or assertiveness. An autocratic employer is more likely to focus upon skills related directly to the job in hand.

E Exam insight

Human resource management is a term that is frequently misunderstood in exams. Remember the four functions of HRM listed at the start of this unit. Do not assume that anything that relates to managing people will be classified as HRM – this is not the case. Questions about HRM expect you to be able to define the term and indicate a clear understanding of the components of HRM.

Appraisal

What?

Appraisal is a system whereby each employee's performance is assessed formally and regularly.

Why?

Such systems tend to be implemented for a variety of motives. Most firms will suggest that their appraisal system exists to identify staff training needs and career plans. Some firms use an appraisal system as a basis for offering staff financial rewards. Others will claim that their appraisal system is an opportunity to recognise achievements of staff. The true motives behind an appraisal system will offer an indication of the attitudes of management towards their staff.

How?

Appraisal is likely to be carried out as a rolling programme, with every employee appraised once in a period of time that could range from a year, to as little as 3 months. It is most commonly the role of an employee's line manager to conduct their appraisal; however, appraisal could be carried out by peers, or even subordinates.

Application

Churchill Insurance Ltd prides itself on the ability of its appraisal programme to identify good performance as a means of highlighting staff capable of rising to higher levels within the organisation. Appraisal is felt to be an extremely valuable process for both the firm and employee being appraised. The firm's recent massive growth in staffing levels has, however, necessitated a slowing down of the appraisal process, since it was taking up too much management time – staff are no longer appraised once every 12 weeks.

Effective HRM brings a number of benefits to firms. However, there is no question that certain aspects of HRM will actually increase costs in the short term. Training costs money in the short term, yet in the medium to long term it can enhance productivity and therefore reduce costs. It may also improve staff motivation and reduce labour turnover, further reducing costs. The attitude of senior managers towards their staff is likely to be the key factor in deciding how seriously those benefits are set against the obvious costs. Look for indicators within a case study as to management attitudes towards staff before judging their approach to managing their human resources.

K Key Terms

Induction training – training that introduces new staff to the firm's systems and procedures when they join the company

Natural wastage – reductions in staff numbers due to natural causes such as retirement, choosing a different career, or staff moving to a new region or country

Workforce planning – identifying the number and type of staff needed to achieve the firm's objectives

S Student howler

'Better HRM will make employees more motivated because managers that decide to use Maslow's theory will meet staff needs better.'

T Test yourself

1. Explain what is meant by the terms:
   a) external recruitment; (3)
   b) workforce planning. (3)
2. Outline two benefits to an employer of running an appraisal scheme for all staff. (4)
3. Explain how a major car manufacturer might use workforce planning to prepare for a strategic reduction in total capacity. (5)
4. Analyse the potential benefits to staff of being trained to take on new, more demanding roles at work. (5)

CHANGE MANAGEMENT

What?

Managing change involves planning, implementing, controlling and reviewing any major organisational changes that may occur within a business.

Why?

The problem with change

Any organisational change is likely to come up against resistance for a number of reasons:

- Resistance from individuals, resulting from:
  — a desire to protect the existing routine;
  — staff wanting to maintain the membership of existing formal or informal groups;
  — the desire of staff to protect payment levels and jobs;
  — avoiding the worry caused by the unknown;
  — preserving psychological feelings of security (as identified in Maslow's hierarchy).
- Resistance from the organisation:
  — mainly revolves around preservation of the existing culture;
  — may be linked to the prevailing leadership style.

How?

Those tasked with managing organisational change must overcome all of these potential barriers. This can be done by following through four phases of a change management programme: planning, implementation, control and review.

Planning

This must be based on three key questions:

1. *Where are we now?* What is it about our current position that necessitates a change?
2. *Where do we want to be after the change?* What will the firm look like after the change?
3. *How should we get there?* What alternative methods do we have available to move us from where we are to where we want to be?

This is unlikely to be successful unless the staff involved in the change are the ones answering these questions. In fact, many top-down managers think that their wisdom allows them to ask and answer key questions about 'their' organisation. This is forgiveable (though arrogant) if the leader has risen to a leadership role from the 'shopfloor' of the organisation. In such cases, the individual will have learned about most aspects of the business, and be in a position to take a paternalistic view of the best way forward. A top-down approach has little credibility, though, when it comes from a newly appointed leader who may not yet have any meaningful grasp of the strengths and weaknesses of the business, let alone how to change them.

Implementation

It is the staff within the firm that must implement the change, and therefore overcoming their likely resistance is critical to successful change management. If they have been fully involved in identifying what changes are necessary and how they can be achieved, staff are far more likely to support the change. This sense of ownership – where staff feel that their own ideas are being implemented – is the critical feature of the implementation process.

Control

Controlling a change process is likely to involve setting and monitoring the achievement of a number of targets that will mark the route from where the firm stands before the change to where it will be after the change. It is important that these targets are closely watched – diversion from them may mean that the change fails to meet its objectives.

Review (What next?)

Once change has been successfully achieved and the organisation has reached the point it had planned to reach at the start of the change programme, further questions should be asked. Sitting back is rarely a valid option, so, having arrived, management needs to consider whether its new situation remains the right place for the firm. Furthermore, managers need to identify the next step in the development of the business and begin to plan how to get there.

Judging how well change has been managed is often fertile ground for evaluation marks. Consider the ease with which the organisation has moved from an original situation to that presented at the end of a case study. Successful change may not be the fastest change, nor may it be the most simple – it is likely to be a change that has attempted to involve all staff affected at all times. Change that is not managed is likely to lead to a series of difficulties that management may fail to see as being linked to change.

K Key Term

Culture – the accepted norms of behaviour within an organisation – 'the way we do things round here'

E Exam insight

Case study exams almost always relate to the management of change. This makes this a critical unit in your revision programme. The key is to understand the process of change within an organisation. If you are able to explain how change occurs, and offer observations judging the skill with which the change was managed by the firm, you should be able to offer some well-developed insight relating to the case study. Look for the implications of the changes implemented: what were the results of the change programme – both good and bad, planned and unplanned?

S Student howler

'I would advise the firm to make a number of major changes to the organisation. These will be easy to accomplish.'

T Test yourself

1. Outline the four major phases of a change management programme. (8)
2. a) What reaction would you expect from staff at a factory when management announces that 50% of assembly workers will be replaced by robots? (3)
   b) How would you, as a manager, attempt to manage such a change? (7)
3. Why may the firm's existing culture affect the success of the change programme being undertaken? (7)

INTEGRATED PEOPLE

The AQA specification for this unit says:

Candidates are expected to appreciate the contribution of selected management theories to an understanding of motivation and leadership. They are required to understand the significance of various management and organisational structures for a business and its employees. Also they should recognise the opportunities and constraints, in relation to people in organisations, created by the business/legal environment.

The key issue is maximising the return from investing time, effort and resources into the people you employ. The investment can be measured in terms of the results from effective recruitment, training, motivation and organisation of staff.

Why?

People management is so critical to a business' success because people are capable of operating at many different levels of performance, and just as a manager would be distraught at a piece of machinery operating at only half its capabilities, so managers should be unhappy if the people they manage are only operating at half of their potential level of performance.

How much can they give?

This depends on how much you let them do, how much they can do and how you treat them. Theory X managers assume workers have little to offer and therefore ask for little. The result is that they tend to get as little as they expected. However, firms that carefully design jobs that allow their staff to achieve, be creative and take some genuine control over their working lives, are likely to gain much more than just average levels of output from their staff.

How do you get the most out of them?

- *Get the right people in at the right time with the right skills:* That's successful HRM and is the process of planning, recruiting and training staff. It is then important to actually organise staff in the right way – hence the need to carefully consider the organisation's structure.

- *Get them fired up and wanting the firm to succeed:* Theorists can tell us what it is that motivates people in theory, but putting that into practice is a tricky job for managers. With the need to keep staffing costs within budget, motivational techniques must pay for themselves. How? By providing more efficient workers, able to work to higher levels of quality, faster and probably more creatively.

- *Leadership and management style will have a crucial influence:* Your own experience will tell you that some managers (or teachers) can get more from you than others. Some managers expect staff to simply follow instructions, whereas other management styles place a far greater decision-making burden upon subordinates. Different circumstances require different leadership styles. Of course a democratic leader will be more likely to stimulate a level of interest and enthusiasm in her staff than an autocrat, but sometimes the autocrat will produce measurably better results.

Themes for evaluation

Straightforward knowledge and application of the theoretical aspects of people management should allow you to explain how better performance can be achieved through appropriate people management. Better answers should show an appreciation that different circumstances require different approaches. The best answers will demonstrate an awareness that managing people is a very tricky business. There are no magic solutions. Good people management is difficult and quite rare.

E Exam Insight

Beware overuse of motivation theory. Every question you are asked is a specific question that needs a directly related answer – don't assume that all 'people' questions will always relate to motivation theory. Exam questions on HRM tend to be answered purely in terms of motivation – ignoring recruitment, training and workforce planning.

T Test yourself (50 marks)

1. Outline two reasons for using a centralised organisational structure. (4)
2. Briefly explain the relationship between spans of control and the height of an organisational structure. (4)
3. Explain the term matrix management. (3)
4. State two benefits to an employer of introducing a system of management by objectives. (2)
5. Explain the term delegation. (3)
6. Briefly explain F.W. Taylor's approach to paying staff. (3)
7. Explain what is meant by the Hawthorne effect. (3)
8. What steps can a company take to meet employees' social needs? (4)
9. State three of Herzberg's hygiene factors. (3)
10. Explain what will occur, according to Herzberg, if an employee's hygiene needs are met? (3)
11. Using a motivation theory, explain why team working may help to motivate staff. (4)
12. List four financial incentives that may be offered to employees to encourage them to work harder. (4)
13. Outline two assumptions held by theory X managers. (2)
14. Distinguish between an authoritarian and a paternalistic leadership style. (3)
15. Explain the term workforce planning. (3)

Now try the following data response questions.

Data response: Mainwaring and Werge

Mainwaring and Werge Childcare Ltd provided Britain's first nationwide babysitting service. From small beginnings, the company grew gradually to cover all of the UK's major cities. From a central call centre, customers can request babysitters with as little as 1 hour's notice and be sure that well-trained, police-checked staff will look after their children.

Careful HR management allows the firm to recruit, train and check local staff before declaring the service available in each new location. The firm has a recruiting officer in each UK county responsible for visiting and organising training for new babysitters. However, much of the firm's operations are still controlled from Head Office by its founders Cath Mainwaring and Sam Werge. They feel that this level of control is crucial to ensure that all police checks are thoroughly handled and that customer service levels are maintained at the highest standards.

The firm now plans to diversify into dog-walking services. Mainwaring and Werge are setting up a separate division under a new divisional manager to avoid over-extending the founders' span of control.

Questions (allow 30 minutes)

1. Explain the term span of control. (3)
2. Outline the benefits that Mainwaring and Werge experienced as a result of careful workforce planning. (6)
3. Analyse the reasons why the firm may have decided to use internal rather than external training. (7)
4. To what extent would Mainwaring and Werge benefit from a more decentralised structure? (9)

Data response: Ramsbottom Engineering

Lydia Edwards runs a small company producing specialised industrial equipment. In the 8 years she has been in charge, Lydia has introduced sweeping changes to the way in which the firm is run, having taken over from Tom, the son of the company's founder. When the Ramsbottoms were running the firm, a paternalistic leadership style was in evidence, with staff being given very little freedom while management looked after what they perceived to be the staff's interests. Lydia's arrival prompted a major shake-up, as she took all four supervisory staff away on a training weekend designed to encourage them to take a more democratic approach to management.

Within a few months of Lydia taking charge, the workforce had taken on much more responsibility for production planning and Lydia's introduction of quality circles a year later proved a great success. With a surprisingly small number of staff leaving the firm, Lydia had managed to hold on to what she perceived to be their key asset – a vastly experienced and highly skilled staff. Further moves included the adoption of single status for all staff, a move welcomed by shopfloor staff and supervisors alike.

Unfortunately, tough trading conditions led to a significant downturn in industrial investment. Work for the firm started to dry up. Lydia reached the point where she called her supervisors together to discuss the most likely candidates for what seemed to be the unavoidable round of redundancies. One supervisor suggested that they share the details of their problems with the shopfloor staff to see whether they were able to come up with any solutions. Desperate to avoid making compulsory redundancies Lydia agreed, despite worrying about how the harsh reality of the firm's prospects might affect the morale of the workforce.

Questions (allow 30 minutes)

1. Explain what is meant by the term 'single status'. (3)
2. Analyse one benefit that Ramsbottom Engineering may have gained as a result of the switch to a more democratic style of management. (6)
3. Explain why Lydia was fearful of sharing the harsh truth with her staff. (6)
4. To what extent is Lydia's approach transferable to all companies? (10)

ECONOMIES AND DISECONOMIES OF SCALE

What?

- Economies of scale are *average* cost savings that businesses make as the level of production increases. A firm may be able to produce 1000 units for £6 each, so total cost is £6000. If it increases production to 3000 units with a total cost of £15,000 then the average unit cost will be £5. This reduction in average unit cost is due to economies of scale.
- Diseconomies of scale occur when higher output leads to an *increase* in average unit costs.

How?

As a firm grows it should be able to become more efficient. It is this increase in efficiency that reduces average unit cost.

There are several ways in which the business can become more efficient:

- *Managerial economies*: In larger firms the business can benefit from *specialisation*. The managers can concentrate on their areas of knowledge rather than being 'Jacks of all trades'. This should mean that fewer mistakes are made.
- *Technical economies*: As the firm increases output it can initially make use of its available capacity. Instead of a machine operating for 8 hours a day it could be operated over two shifts. The cost of the machine will therefore be spread over a larger number of units. As the firm gets bigger it will be able to invest in larger, more efficient machines. It may also become more automated and so save labour costs.
- *Financial economies*: Small firms often find it difficult to borrow money. Banks are reluctant to lend and if they do the rates of interest are often high. Larger firms are considered to be less risky so banks are willing to lend at lower rates of interest.
- *Marketing economies*: Marketing is expensive. The firm will gain cost advantages by spreading the cost over a larger number of sold items. It will also get benefits from easier recognition, as its name becomes known.
- *Purchasing economies*: Suppliers are generally more willing to give a lower price for a larger order.

Larger firms have more bargaining power and can often negotiate both lower unit prices and more relaxed credit terms.

Who?

Any firm, large or small, can benefit from economies of scale. Taking advantage of economies of scale is often given as a reason for company growth. In competitive markets the ability to make cost savings can make all the difference to business performance. The theory of economies of scale tends to focus on levels of output and production. However, the theory is just as applicable to retail and service businesses as it is to manufacturing. Superstores are a retail example; centralised call centres for banks or insurance companies are a service example.

But

Businesses can grow internally by just getting bigger or they can grow externally by taking over or merging with another business. Not all growth is good. Sometimes when businesses grow they become more inefficient and unit costs begin to increase. This is due to *diseconomies of scale*. This can be caused by:

- *Management problems*: The main problem is with coordination. In a small firm the owner may decide what the firm's aims are and tell the staff how to operate. As the firm gets bigger there is a larger number of staff and maybe processes. This may all become too much for one person and they may need to delegate some of the tasks. Unless this is well coordinated some managers may be trying to achieve different aims than others.
- *Employee problems*: In a large firm, workers may have less contact with their managers. They may therefore feel isolated and lack the feedback and recognition that most theorists feel is essential for staff motivation. Poorly motivated staff do not work as hard and absenteeism increases.
- *Communication problems*: As the firm grows, the distance the message has to travel increases. Unless the business has good communication systems there could be problems with getting the same message across the whole organisation. More levels of management mean that there are more

opportunities for misunderstandings. This links into poor motivation. Workers may often feel that they do not know what is going on and that management does not listen to them.

What?

As businesses grow there are bound to be both economies and diseconomies of scale. The business needs to find the *optimum level of production*. This is the point where it takes full advantage of available economies and avoids the inevitable diseconomies. Economists show this in a diagram, as follows:

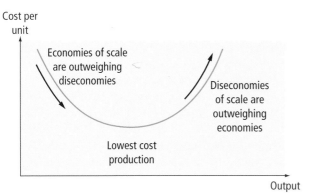

Fig. 4.1A: Production costs and production scale

Unit costs are plotted against output. As output increases unit costs fall as economies of scale are greater than diseconomies. When diseconomies of scale outweigh the economies the costs begin to rise again. The lowest point is the point where costs are at their lowest. This is the optimum level of production.

How?

Achieving the optimum level of output is not easy. It is often difficult for firms to recognise that diseconomies of scale are occurring. It is easier if growth is planned and reviewed. Rapid growth is less controllable. Good management will address the problems of diseconomies of scale and focus the solution on the problem areas.

If problems are occurring with motivation, the firm could look at different ways of working such as setting up *cell production* or it could introduce *job enrichment programmes*. If communication is a problem the firm could look at introducing quality circles or works councils.

K Key Terms

Average cost – total cost divided by the number of units

Cell production – breaking down part of a business process into smaller working units

Job enrichment programmes – programmes designed to make work routines more interesting; can be done by changing the process or adding responsibility

Specialisation – concentrating on what a person or organisation does best

Application

Six London councils have got together to take advantage of economies of scale. Using on-line ordering they are able to cut costs on basic items such as stationery and cleaning products. The six councils – Tower Hamlets, Lewisham, Barnet, Redbridge, Newham and the Greater London Authority – combine their orders and so get bulk-buying discounts. Suppliers make savings on bulk orders so are able to pass these on to the purchasers. It might only mean a small saving per item but when added up they make massive savings. On one contract for paper it is estimated that they will save £30,000 per annum. This is a good example of economies of scale at work.

Many people think that discussion of economies and diseconomies of scale is just academic. In the real business world, businesses are just getting on with the job. In reality, businesses need to be aware of costs if they are to be competitive and successful. They may not be able to break down each contributing factor but achieving optimum cost and production levels is an important aim. Firms also need to be aware of the dangers of becoming too big. Growth needs to be carefully managed and an understanding of the relationship between growth and costs is a vital element in that management.

E Exam insight

Do not always assume that growth is a good thing for a business. Look at the circumstances of the business. Is management able to manage the growth? Does the firm have the necessary financial and people resources?

As a business grows it is likely to experience both economies and diseconomies of scale. The important thing is to ensure that the economies outweigh the diseconomies.

S Student howlers

'Large firms have all the advantages.'
'Diseconomies of scale mean that the firm should not grow.'

T Test yourself

1. What is meant by economies of scale? (2)
2. List three ways in which economies of scale occur. (3)
3. Why do diseconomies of scale occur? (3)
4. What is meant by optimum level of production? (3)
5. If economies of scale are so important, how do young, small firms survive? (4)

CAPACITY UTILISATION

What?

Capacity utilisation is a measure of the extent to which a firm is using its maximum possible output. Expressed as a percentage, capacity utilisation can be calculated by expressing current output as a percentage of maximum possible output:

$$\frac{\text{current output}}{\text{maximum output}} \times 100$$

Why is it important?

The single most important concept related to capacity utilisation is that of fixed cost per unit. The closer a firm gets to its maximum capacity utilisation (100%), the lower the amount of fixed costs carried by each unit of output. Fixed costs in total stay the same from 0 to maximum output, so the more units of output they are spread across, the lower the fixed costs carried by each unit and the greater the profit per unit.

Fig. 4.2A. Spreading fixed costs

How does it look?

Capacity utilisation in a factory	Capacity utilisation in a restaurant
A factory measures output in terms of the number of units produced per week or month. Maximum capacity utilisation occurs when all equipment is being used flat out, with two or even three 8-hour shifts and the factory working continuously. Any periods when the factory is quiet would indicate a capacity utilisation less than 100%	If a restaurant is completely full all the time it is open (as at Jamie Oliver's restaurant '15'), the restaurant is working at 100% capacity utilisation. Restaurants with empty tables and waiters standing around doing very little would be operating at less than 100% capacity utilisation

What?

The ideal capacity utilisation should be 100% since this will allow the firm to minimise fixed costs per unit and therefore maximise profit. Though this logic is sound, few firms can safely operate at 100% capacity utilisation for any length of time. This is because there would be no time available to carry out routine maintenance tasks. In reality, most firms like to operate at just below 100% of capacity.

How?

There are two ways to increase capacity utilisation: increase current output and reduce maximum capacity.

Increase current output

Increasing current output will spread fixed costs over more units and therefore achieve the objective behind increasing capacity utilisation. However, there is little point in increasing output unless you can sell the extra items you are producing. It is vital to consider how you will sell those extra items. If extra sales are the result of a price cut, have you actually reduced your price by more than your fixed costs per unit have fallen?

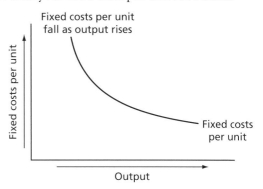

Fig. 4.2B: Falling fixed costs per unit

Reduce maximum capacity

Reducing maximum capacity will also have the desired effect of reducing fixed costs per unit by reducing your total fixed costs. Laying off staff, closing down an under-used factory, or moving to smaller premises will allow a firm to reduce its total fixed costs. Therefore, with an unchanged output, fixed costs per unit will be lower as there are fewer fixed costs to be covered.

Why may utilisation be low?

Business	Cause
At a leisure centre	Demand is high after work in the evenings, but low during the working day
At a third division football club	The ground was built when larger crowds were common, perhaps when the club was doing better
Producing Cadbury's Creme Eggs	Production is flat out from the Autumn through to Easter, but halted between Easter and the late summer

Which is the best choice?

The solution to a problem of low capacity utilisation should be appropriate to the causes of the problem.

If the causes of the capacity utilisation problem are short term (such as a seasonal dip in sales), a short-term solution should be found. This will usually involve marketing activities such as price discounting.

Cutting capacity will be a longer-term answer to a longer-term problem. If a market has declined and the firm feels unable to reinvigorate sales in that market, it may decide to reduce capacity. It may lay off staff or even close down a production line or a whole factory. These actions are hard to reverse so the firm is unlikely to rush into such decisions.

What next?

Flexibility is crucial in coping with low levels of capacity use. If the company is able to identify a core of key staff and assets that will allow it to function at a low level of output while keeping fixed costs low, they know they have a 'fall back' position when demand is low and output needs to be low. Extra production, when required, can be added through the use of temporary staff, rented machinery and premises, or even through the use of subcontracting. In this way, a firm would be able to operate at a high level of capacity utilisation even when demand is low, while retaining the flexibility to increase output when the need arises.

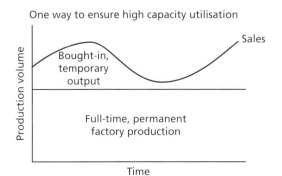

Fig. 4.2C: The value of flexibility

How big a problem is it?

A firm with low capacity utilisation may not have a particularly big problem. In some cases firms will expect a low level of capacity utilisation during certain periods of the year. They may have already taken steps to cope with this, by using quiet periods to train staff or update machinery and equipment. Although fixed costs per unit will be high during these periods, the firm may benefit from higher quality standards in the medium term.

Is the capacity utilisation the cause or effect of the problem?

Low levels of capacity utilisation cause higher costs per unit and therefore may tempt firms to charge higher prices. This may be the reason why demand for the product is low, so low capacity utilisation is the cause of the problem. Alternatively, the weak demand could be the effect of external factors such as the arrival of a new competitor. This would mean that the low level of capacity utilisation is simply an indicator of a problem elsewhere.

T Test yourself

1. What is the current level of capacity utilisation for a firm with a maximum output of 25,000 units per month that is currently making 20,000 units? (2)
2. If the firm's fixed costs per month are £100,000, what are fixed costs per unit at:
   a) their current output? (3)
   b) 100% capacity utilisation? (3)
3. Briefly explain how you could see that capacity utilisation was low at:
   a) a manufacturing plant; (3)
   b) a hotel. (3)
4. Outline two actions that could be taken to increase capacity utilisation at a leisure centre. (6)

TYPES OF PRODUCTION

What?

Types of production means the methods used to produce goods or services: job, batch or flow.

Why?

Businesses are concerned with turning inputs into outputs. If the business is to be profitable this process should add value. This means that the end product is sold for more than it has cost to produce it. In order to maximise this added value, firms need to find the most efficient method of production.

How?

There are many different production methods but the three main classifications are job, batch and flow.

Job production
This is about producing items specific to the customer's requirements. It is clearly seen in service industries such as accountants or solicitors where each client is different. It is a very flexible approach to meeting customer requirements, requiring a highly trained, skilled workforce. It is also expensive and provides no scope for economies of scale.

Batch production
Batch production produces several items at one time. If there are several steps in the production process, each stage is completed before the batch moves on to the next stage. A baker may use this system. Batches of breads or cakes are made, then moved to a different part of the factory for finishing or packaging.

Flow production
This is the process that we associate with mass production. The most common form is an assembly line. This process takes raw materials in at the start of the process, adds components as required and produces the end product at the finish. Each individual item flows through each stage (often moving along a conveyor belt) until it emerges as a finished product. Car production is a typical process. The body and engine are assembled then other parts are added as the car moves along the production line. Individual workers will have responsibility for a particular part of the process, often leading to repetitive, low-skilled jobs.

In many flow production systems computer-aided technology has speeded up the process. In some areas robotic machines have replaced assembly workers.

Which?

The process that is most suitable in any one case will depend on the nature of the business and the types of product it is producing. A small business making individual products for single customers will obviously use job production. In a market where identical products are acceptable but the market is not large, batch production may be more suitable.

Mass marketing requires mass production so a flow system is usually used. Firms may use several different production methods within one factory.

But

Henry Ford was the father of the assembly line. His invention of this method of production was the start of mass marketing. Subsequently, many firms adopted the flow production method. Following the success of different methods of working such as those adopted by Volvo and Toyota, many firms have modified the use of flow production (see Unit 4.4 on lean production and Unit 4.5 on Kaizen). It is seen by many to be an outdated way of working.

Criticisms are:
- It is demotivating: the work is repetitive and workers have little responsibility for their output.
- A stoppage in one part of the line can hold up all the factory production.
- It is hard to spot quality problems until the product is complete.
- It is inflexible: changes in output are difficult to manage, and it relies on high and constant demand for a product.

In reality firms may use a mixture of all types of production. Some factories may have a main assembly line with smaller batch production units feeding component parts into it. Developments in computer-aided production have opened up many new ideas about production systems. They allow the production process to be modified much more easily and enable firms to be much more flexible with output. This has led to the concept of *mass customisation.*

Who?

Most operations management theory tends to be based on manufacturing businesses. However, it is relevant to most businesses. The type of production that is most suitable will usually be related to the type of market. Products sold to *niche markets* will usually be made using either job or batch processes. Mass marketed products are made using flow production. In service industries the process used will depend on the product and customer requirements. Package holidays, which are a form of batch production, helped to bring down the cost of international travel. However, some customers want a tailor-made package. This is job production.

K | Key Terms

Kaizen – a management philosophy that looks for continual improvement in the business process

Lean production – an attitude to production that concentrates on reducing costs and minimising waste

Mass customisation – mass-produced products that can be individually tailored to customer specifications

Niche markets – small parts of a larger market; markets where individuals demand a tailor-made product

Application

Honda's UK factory at Swindon could produce 250,000 vehicles annually if it used its full capacity. With this sort of output most car manufacturers opt for some form of flow production.

Another large output industry is bread manufacture. The total market for bread and bakery products in the UK is around £2.8 billion annually. Bread manufacturing used to be batch production by small local bakers, but they now have less than 10% of the market. Today, most bread is mass produced by a few large companies. Warburtons is one of the three largest bakeries in the UK and produces 100,000 loaves each day. This is an example of an industry that has been totally changed. The introduction of flow production has shifted production away from the traditional batch method of production.

LUSH (the bathroom and cosmetics firm) now has over 100 shops worldwide and operates mail order businesses in the UK, Canada, Australia, Italy and Japan. This is a big leap forward from one shop in Poole that opened in 1994. The company's web site (www.lush.co.uk) says:

> We hand-make our cosmetics in Europe, Canada, Australia, South America, Singapore and Japan, in our own production facilities, so that every product available in our shops or sent to you by mail is as fresh as it can possibly be because fresh products work better and use fewer preservatives.

This business is a good example of a marketing link to production. They are appealing to a niche market and offering something different from mass-produced cosmetic products.

Although we discuss types of production as different and separate processes, in reality businesses often use a combination of methods. The latest trend in car manufacturing is to make mass-produced, one-off models. With the aid of advanced technology, car manufacturers are able to produce a car to customer specifications on the production line – this is known as mass customisation. They can take advantage of the speed, efficiency and cost saving that can be gained from flow production but produce individual items. On the other hand, many businesses such as restaurants now use a combination of batch and job production. Many of the ingredients for restaurant chains such as *Pizza Express* are prepared in batches, delivered to the outlets and then tailored to individual customer requirements.

E | Exam insight

Do not automatically assume that moving to flow production will be beneficial for a business. If demand is erratic (e.g. seasonal), a flow system is unlikely to be economic.

Remember that no single production method is 'the best'. The key is to assess the one that best fits the situation of the firm.

S | Student howlers

'Batch production is only suitable when small quantities are being produced.'
'Manufacturers can save a lot of costs by moving from batch to flow production.'

T | Test yourself

1. What type of production is likely to be used by:
   a) a supplier of shopfittings to the Next chain of clothes shops; (1)
   b) a producer of tailor-made wedding dresses; (1)
   c) a producer of small, standard calculators. (1)
2. State two advantages for each of:
   a) job production; (2)
   b) batch production; (2)
   c) flow production. (2)
3. What types of product might be produced by job production? (3)
4. Explain what is meant by mass customisation. (3)

LEAN PRODUCTION

What?

Lean production is a company-wide approach that concentrates on making the production process as efficient as possible. It aims to produce the maximum output using the fewest resources. It involves both management and the workforce.

Why?

If a business can streamline the production process to minimise wastage of materials, time, human or capital resources or finance, there should be considerable savings. This will create a cost advantage for the company that can give them a *competitive advantage* in the market place.

How?

The main focus is on achieving high levels of *labour productivity*, high utilisation of fixed assets such as machinery, and low levels of stock. There are of course many ways in which businesses can make the production process more cost efficient and eliminate waste. The three main approaches are total quality management, time-based management and just-in-time.

Total quality management

Total quality management (TQM) is a philosophy rather than a technique. The idea is that quality is the responsibility of each worker in the organisation. In most production systems quality control is usually done at the end of the process when quality controllers check the finished goods. By this time it is too late to correct most faults so the product has to be scrapped or sold off as a reject. With TQM, workers have the authority to stop the process if they are aware of a fault. This means that faults can be corrected earlier in the process. The aim is to eliminate the waste caused by rejected goods.

Time-based management

This approach focuses on how time is used. The aim is to reduce the time spent on any particular task and to eliminate dead or wasted time. It focuses on both people and machinery. Training plays a large part in

this. Operatives are trained to be multiskilled. This avoids time being wasted while another person takes over the job. In terms of machinery, management will focus on why machines are lying idle. This may be due to technical problems. Old machinery that is constantly breaking down may need to be replaced.

The process will also be looked at. It may be beneficial for the factory to produce shorter runs of different products. This may require investment in more flexible machinery.

Just-in-time

Just-in-time (JIT) focuses on *stock management*. Lower stocks mean lower costs. The ultimate aim of the JIT approach is to make products to a specific customer order. Once the customer places the order the process begins and stocks of components are bought in. As soon as the production is completed it is delivered to the customer. This cuts down on holdings of raw materials, work in progress and stocks of finished goods. For this system to work there needs to be an excellent and reliable relationship with the materials or component supplier. The operation also needs to be of a size that makes it worthwhile for the supplier to deliver stocks on a more regular basis. The best-known user of this approach is the computer manufacturer Dell, which has grown to become the world's No. 1.

K Key Terms

Competitive advantage – having an advantage over competitors in the market place; this may be because of the product or price

Labour productivity – a measure of how productive the workforce is

Stock management – the process of controlling all the elements of stock handling; this involves ordering, processing and storing of stock

Who?

Toyota was the first company to develop lean production. Toyota aimed to make the production process continuous so they designed machines that had many different applications. They also concentrated on reducing the waste caused by poor quality on their production lines. The improvements that followed gave the Japanese car industry a competitive advantage over other car makers. On the basis of this, many western manufacturers started adopting the Japanese approach to production management.

Lean production is not just applicable to mass production. Any production process – in fact any business process – can benefit from TQM, time-based management and JIT. Many savings can be made in office-based functions by looking at how long people spend on a job or how much time is spent passing paper from one department to another.

Of course some ideas will be best suited to larger and more complex operations. Some ideas of JIT cannot be applied to smaller concerns. Nevertheless, all businesses can benefit from becoming 'leaner and meaner'.

But

The introduction of lean management requires good management and good worker relations. Buffer stocks exist to protect the business from mistakes. Adopting JIT exposes inefficiency, because delivery failures will mean workers cannot work. Moving to lean production would rarely be a successful approach if the firm is currently being run inefficiently. Managers need to ensure that the ideas being introduced are appropriate for the business and that the workforce understands how and why the ideas are being introduced.

Problems with lean management can also occur if there is a change in demand. If the production set-up is too lean, it may struggle to react to increased demand. This may mean the loss of business opportunities.

Criticism has also been made of the JIT stock management system. Very low buffer stocks can leave the business very vulnerable if a supplier has delivery problems.

Application

The Chloride Motive Power factory in Bolton makes batteries and power cells for electric vehicles. The company has recently introduced lean production. David Ling (a spokesman for the business) said: 'The lean initiative is difficult and the work involved is enormous but, after much effort from the team and all employees at CMP, the end results speak for themselves.' Raw material stocks have been reduced by 65% and total stock holding including finished goods by 31%. Factory maintenance costs were reduced by 45% and – equally as important – CMP recorded an 80% reduction in accidents. Strict targets were set and were exceeded.
(www.engineeringtalk.com: Company news received, 3 November 2003, from Chloride Motive Power)

The suitability of lean production must be questioned. For lean production to work it requires good management and workforce cooperation. The processes need to be well considered and not just bolted on. Many businesses use a partial approach where they adopt some aspects of lean production, perhaps to tackle a particular problem. Lean production needs to be a long term business strategy, not a quick fix.

E Exam insight

Remember that lean production does not apply only to mass production; elements of lean production can be used in any business process.

Lean production is not a quick fix solution to production problems. When looking at how a business can use lean production, take care to ensure that the suggestions are relevant and practical for the business. A large mass producer might be able to redesign its production line but does a smaller business have the financial resources to do that?

S Student howlers

'Lean production is just for large firms like car manufacturers.'
'Lean production means just making as much as you can sell.'

T Test yourself

1. What is meant by lean production? (2)
2. What three approaches do businesses use to achieve lean production? (3)
3. Why is quality control important? (3)
4. What sort of problems can the introduction of JIT cause? (4)
5. Analyse two ways in which Chloride Motive Power can benefit from the results of its lean production programme. (8)

KAIZEN

What?

Kaizen – or *continuous improvement* – looks for ways of improving business productivity or quality on an ongoing basis. Kaizen is about making small changes in the production process, often stemming from suggestions by staff. These small changes can add up to a significant impact on the whole business.

How?

If Kaizen is to work, the entire business must understand the philosophy and have a commitment to it. Each individual will be encouraged to do his or her job but at the same time to think about how it could be done better. Managers have to be receptive to ideas coming from the shopfloor. Management and employees are encouraged to:

- ignore conventional fixed ideas;
- think of how to do it rather than why it cannot be done;
- not make excuses;
- question current practices.

There are four main principles that underlie the philosophy:

1. *Individual responsibility*: Kaizen recognises that each individual is an expert at their particular job and that staff are the company's most important resource. It recognises that the person doing the work will have a better idea of what the problems are and how to solve them than a manager sitting in an office. It encourages the individual to make suggestions.

2. *Teamworking*: Another strong feature of Kaizen is group working. Workers are often organised into teams known as cells. This 'cell' is the basic work unit and has responsibility for the output and quality of the work coming from their section. Workers in the cell will meet regularly to discuss issues – a sort of mini *quality circle*.

3. *Empowerment*: If Kaizen is to work, employees need to have the power to make changes. If each small change had to be discussed and approved by management, progress would be limited and slow.

4. *Targets*: An important part of Kaizen is that each work unit (cell) is given targets for production and quality. Targets can also be used to monitor the effect of any changes that have been suggested.

Why?

Kaizen is another way in which businesses can improve the efficiency of their operations. The advantages affect:

- the business – by increasing output, unit costs can be reduced. This gives a competitive advantage. If quality is improved there is less wastage and fewer problems with dissatisfied customers.
- customers – reduced costs mean prices may be lower. Improved quality gives more customer satisfaction.
- Employees – empowerment will improve employee motivation.

But

If Kaizen is to work it requires commitment from both management and employees. Kaizen is a way of working and to be successful it must be accepted by all. Workers coming into a factory that already has a Kaizen system will find it easy to accept; it is much harder to introduce into a workplace with old established ideas. If there is a history of poor industrial relations there is likely to be an unwillingness to change. *Autocratic managers* may also resist the changes. They may see it as a threat to their power and position.

Introducing Kaizen is not cost free. It will require some elements of retraining. Time out for quality circle or cell meetings has a cost impact. Changes to working patterns or adjustments to machinery will take time and there may be some need for additional *capital investment*.

Critics of Kaizen say that, after the initial spurt of ideas when it is introduced, the ideas begin to dry up or become insignificant. There is also the worry that employees may be looking for problems in order to keep up the flow of ideas. Subsequent changes may do more harm than good.

Another criticism is that making continual small

changes may blind management from the need for a radical change. Efficiency may benefit more from the installation of a new machine than tinkering with an old one.

K Key Terms

Autocratic managers – managers who are unwilling to share authority, e.g. unwilling to delegate or to share information

Capital investment – investment in fixed assets such as machinery

Quality circle – a group of employees who meet on a regular basis to discuss quality issues and to make suggestions for improvements

Who?

Typically Kaizen is thought of as a process that is useful for manufacturing businesses. However, the philosophy can just as well be applied in a retail outlet or an office situation. Any business process that can be improved can benefit from Kaizen. Tesco and Barclaycard both claim to have benefited from introducing Kaizen.

Application

'Are you a Kaizen kind of person?' (this is the heading on the Nestlé recruitment page). The page goes on to explain what Kaizen is and how the people that they wish to recruit will become part of this. 'It [Kaizen] demands a special attitude, a constant vigilance for better ways of doing things – and the confidence to make the necessary changes.' This is a good illustration of how important people are in the Kaizen process. Nestlé has 508 factories and employs over 250,000 people worldwide.

The GSM Group supplies metal and plastic components worldwide, and has around 200 workers at three sites in the UK. GSM has introduced Kaizen throughout its factories. The system is focused on eliminating time wastage. One of the initiatives is a Kaizen form on all the notice boards. Suggestions are reviewed and a response given within a week. If a suggestion is accepted, costs are worked out and a time scale for the implementation is agreed. One successful suggestion was to cut down on the wrapping of some goods. This saved the cost of the wrapping material and the time taken to wrap the product and unwrap it when it arrives at the customer. This is a good example of how a medium-sized firm is using Kaizen principles.

Kaizen, like most business processes and ideas, will work in some situations but not in others. Traditional autocratic firms will find it very hard to introduce. It is also possible that it is helpful when times are good, but not when cutbacks are required that may imply job losses. If a sharp recession hits, Kaizen will not provide a solution. More drastic cutbacks or changes may be essential.

E Exam insight

A Kaizen system should involve the whole workforce and not be ideas passed down from management.

Take care when answering a question on Kaizen that you do not just outline the theory. That will only earn you content or knowledge marks. Try to apply the theory to the particular business. For example: 'The management in this business is autocratic and may find it difficult to let employees have responsibility. This will make the introduction of Kaizen difficult.'

S Student howlers

'In a Kaizen system every employee has to come up with new ideas.'
'Kaizen only works in Japanese firms.'

T Test yourself

1. What is meant by Kaizen? (2)
2. What is necessary for successful implementation of Kaizen? (3)
3. Why might the introduction of Kaizen fail? (3)
4. Why may staff feel more secure with small, step-by-step improvements than with major changes to working practices? (4)
5. Re-read the Application section about Nestlé and GSM Group. Explain two benefits each firm could gain from its Kaizen approach. (3)

BENCHMARKING

What?

Benchmarking is a management tool that helps companies to improve their performance. It involves comparing aspects of business performance with those of other companies. The purpose is to identify the best achievements within the industry. The business will then change some or all of its practices in order to try to be as good as the best company.

When?

Having realised that they were not performing as well as their Japanese competitors some American and British companies started to look at what these competitors were doing. They began to incorporate some of the Japanese ways of doing things in order to try to catch them up.

Why?

Benchmarking arose from a recognition that profitability and growth come from improving performance. This is not just year-on-year improvement; it needs to be improvement compared to the best performers.

Some advantages of benchmarking are:

- It saves companies from having to solve problems from scratch. It makes companies aware of their relative performance. If their performance lags behind they can take action to catch up.
- Benchmarking can spark ideas about other ways of doing things. A process that might help to improve performance in one area might also be applied to another activity.
- Benchmarking can improve international competitiveness. As companies become aware of the need to compete with the best in the world this will improve their international performance.

How?

Benchmarking is not about spying on competitors to discover their secrets. Most benchmarking exercises are done with complete cooperation between the partners.

Benchmarking is not the same as competitive market research. Information about a competitor's performance and products is still a vital marketing activity.

A typical benchmarking system will involve:

1. Identifying an area that is underperforming – Benchmarking begins when the company recognises that it could do better. It may have worries about falling sales or lower profitability. It needs to identify specific areas for benchmarking.
2. Measuring the process – If the process cannot be measured, businesses cannot compare performance.
3. Identifying the best company – The business may already be aware of the best performer. Information may be available from government-sponsored schemes and industry databases. Some companies use management consultants to find the best performer.
4. Agreeing with the best-practice business on exchange of information – Clearly this may be difficult. A business may not want to share the secrets of its success. Yet a business may be brilliant at stock control but may produce at quite a high cost per unit. It may be happy to swop information so that both companies can do better (perhaps enabling both to cope better against overseas rivals).
5. Comparing processes and identifying areas for change – By comparing how the best company operates, the business can identify activities that could be changed to improve performance.
6. Changing processes – Specific changes can now be made, perhaps to the whole process or to a small part of it. It may involve tackling a process in a completely different way or adjusting part of the existing activity.
7. Remeasuring – Once the process has been completed, the whole cycle will start again to determine if the changes have had the desired effect.

Which?

Benchmarking can be used to look at almost any aspect of the business. It is an appropriate way of:

- improving waste management;
- improving personnel practices;
- simplifying office systems;
- controlling manufacturing costs.

As long as the process or activity is measurable it can be benchmarked.

Who?

Early benchmarking exercises used Japanese companies for comparison. Now companies are looking at the best performing company wherever it is in the world.

Benchmarking initially tended to be industry specific. A carmaker would benchmark against another carmaker. Today this is less likely to be true. Companies benchmark against a best performer even if the other company is in a totally different industry. This has often produced some new ways of thinking about processes:

- Xerox used L.L. Bean, a mail-order clothing company, when it was looking to improve the way it dealt with customer orders in its warehouse.
- IBM looked at casinos in Las Vegas when it was trying to solve problems of theft by employees.

But

Benchmarking has some disadvantages:

- If companies are just copying others then they will not develop new ideas.
- The company may focus on processes, losing sight of its primary objectives (e.g. worrying more about minimising stock than satisfying its customers).
- The costs may not be recovered in savings or increased efficiency.
- Successful companies may become complacent.

K Key Terms

Efficiency – making the best use of the resources available to the business; this can be measured in several ways such as output per worker or cost per unit produced

Inter-firm comparison – looking at statistical information that is available about other firms in an industry

International competitiveness – the ability of firms to compete with overseas firms, both overseas and at home

Processes – the activities that enable the company to produce and deliver its goods and services to the consumer

Application

Wessex Water has a monitoring programme at all its water and wastewater treatment sites. This has enabled it to introduce benchmarking to optimise performance at its plants. This form of internal benchmarking is used to identify areas where operating costs are unnecessarily high and where the use of power, water or raw materials can be reduced. The comparative data identified two sites with a 40% higher than average energy consumption for 'activated sludge treatment'. Although the project required additional expenditure for monitoring it has already saved £50,000 at one

activated sludge works, where the waste was being 'over-treated' by excessive aeration. The company is optimistic that they can save 5% of the process budget by benchmarking energy costs.
(Adapted from *Wessex Water Cuts Energy Costs* by Melanie Brown. First published in *Water & Waste Treatment*, July 2002)

Benchmarking has proved to be a useful exercise for many businesses. One of its major contributions has been to encourage businesses to recognise that they could do better. Having recognised that there may be a problem, it is easier to find solutions. Some businesses have found that they can usefully copy methods or processes used by other businesses. Other businesses have discovered that it does not work to try to 'bolt on' someone else's processes to their existing way of working.

The concept of benchmarking is fairly simple but the practice is rather more complicated. It may not be a case of using the 'best' but often what is available. Comparing processes may also be a problem in that it is not always comparing like with like. Nevertheless companies have found that even if benchmarking does not provide a quick-fix solution it does encourage thinking about the problem. This often leads to the discovery of alternative solutions.

E Exam insight

Students often think that benchmarking is just about finding out how a business compares with other firms. But it is more than that: it is about finding out who is the best and then incorporating some or all of the ideas that make the best company succeed.

S Student howlers

'Benchmarking is about finding out where you are in the business league table.'
'Only manufacturers use benchmarking.'

T Test yourself

1. Explain the purpose of benchmarking. (5)
2. Identify two activities that might be suitable for benchmarking at:
   a) a manufacturer of buses and coaches;
   b) a Sainsbury's supermarket;
   c) a driving school. (6)
3. State three requirements for successful benchmarking. (3)
4. Explain three reasons why benchmarking does not always work. (6)

QUALITY MANAGEMENT

What?

Quality management is the maintenance of consistent levels of quality. Quality management prevents defects, controls costs and generates customer satisfaction.

What is quality? Deming, the American quality guru, said: 'Quality is defined by the customer'. In other words, people do not always want the highest quality – sometimes cheap and cheerful is right. A golf beginner should buy lots of cheap, low-quality golf balls because they will get lost very quickly.

Another definition is 'fit for use'. For some products quality is defined by law. The law lays down minimum quality standards. This particularly applies to products where health or safety is involved. Food must be fresh and has to be handled in certain ways. It is illegal to sell electrical equipment without a plug fitted.

Who?

Quality is important for all firms. In a competitive market it will be more significant. In industrial markets firms will often define minimum standards for their suppliers. This helps them to maintain their own quality standards. Large businesses such as supermarkets and chain stores are able to insist on quality standards. They have the buying power to force their suppliers to conform. They may insist that their suppliers have obtained *ISO 9000* which is an internationally recognised quality accreditation.

Some large industries have watchdogs that ensure that minimum standards are met. OFWAT (the water industry regulator) has the task of ensuring that water quality is maintained.

Why?

Quality is an important competitive issue. Its importance will depend on how competitive the market is. A good quality product will:
* be easier to establish in the market;
* generate repeat purchases and therefore a longer life cycle;
* allow brand building and cross-marketing;
* allow a price premium.

Quality problems will have cost implications for the firm, as shown in the table:

Marketing costs	Business costs
Loss of sales	Scrapping of unsuitable goods
Loss of reputation	Reworking of unsatisfactory goods – costs of labour and materials
May have to price discount	Lower prices for 'seconds'
May impact on other products in range	Handling complaints/ warranty claims
Retailers may be unwilling to stock goods	Loss of consumer goodwill and repeat purchases

How?

The ideal is to detect quality problems before they reach the customer. Most quality control processes are concentrated in the factory. These aim to prevent faults leaving the factory. This can be done by:
* inspection of finished goods before sale – this may be all goods or only a sample;
* self-inspection of work by operatives – this is being used more as businesses recognise that quality needs to be 'everyone's business';
* statistical analysis within the production process – this can be used to ensure that specifications stay within certain limits.

A good quality management system will have four stages of quality control: prevention, detection, correction and improvement.
* *Prevention*: To try to avoid problems occurring, for example at the design stage.
* *Detection*: To ensure that quality problems are spotted before they reach the customer. The use of computer-aided statistical analysis has given firms better tools to detect faults. Increasingly businesses are making detection the responsibility of every employee.
* *Correction*: This is not only about correcting faults – it is also about discovering why there is a problem. Once the problem is identified steps can be taken to ensure that the problem does not recur.
* *Improvement*: Customer expectations of quality are always changing. It is important that businesses seek to improve quality.

Quality initiatives

As the importance of quality has been recognised there has been a growth in initiatives to control and improve quality. Techniques for quality control such as inspection and statistical control continue. They have been supplemented by other initiatives such as:

- *Total quality management* – see Unit 4.4.
- *Continuous improvement* – see Unit 4.5.
- *Quality circles* – groups of employees that meet together regularly to identify problems and recommend adjustments to the working processes (often used as part of total quality management or Kaizen).
- *Training* – this can make an enormous contribution to quality. It might be specifically job orientated such as training a machinist, or a sales assistant in customer care. It is important where the company is trying to introduce a 'quality culture'.
- *Benchmarking* – see Unit 4.6.
- *Quality assurance* – schemes such as ISO 9000 provide customers with confidence that a supplier has a documented quality system operating throughout the company and involving suppliers and subcontractors.

K Key Terms

Benchmarking – comparing a firm's performance with the best practice in the industry

Continuous improvement – a management philosophy that encourages everyone in the business to look for ways of making improvements to the company efficiency

ISO 9000 – an internationally recognised quality assurance certificate; firms have to show that they have quality maintenance processes, which are documented and inspected (formerly known as BS5750)

Total quality management – a management philosophy that insists that quality is the responsibility of everyone in the organisation

But

Quality initiatives may be expensive. It is possible to get 100% quality at a cost. It is necessary to balance the cost of quality control and improvement with the costs of poor quality. The company needs to be aware of how much the customer is prepared to pay.

Application

Having a quality image is one of the main ingredients for a good brand name. Many household names such as Marks and Spencer and Tesco have used their reputation to launch other products such as financial services. Quality builds reputations, but a quality problem can have an enormous impact on a business.

When bottles of Perrier water were found to be contaminated, the costs were enormous. Over 600 million bottles had to be recalled and production fell drastically as customer demand fell. It took over 3 years for the company to regain its position. When the Mercedes A Class car proved unstable just before it was launched, the cost of rectifying the problem was estimated at over £500 million.

Often quality initiatives require a long-term view. There may be a conflict between short-term costs and longer-term results. Shareholders may want returns today but the benefits may take some time to show.

Increased quality brings its own rewards in the market place. Companies have also found that the initiatives, especially where they are people-based, have also brought other advantages. Changes in working practices have improved motivation and efficiency and have reduced waste and costs.

E Exam insight

When answering questions about quality management, think beyond the production department. Quality issues are often closely interwoven with other parts of the business. Links with motivation theory and the role of the employee in quality control are important issues.

When suggesting quality initiatives or solutions to quality problems, remember to consider not only how the initiatives work but also the problems that they may cause.

S Student howlers

'The firm should ensure that it has 100% quality.'
'Quality is less important in niche markets.'

T Test yourself

1. What is meant by quality management? (2)
2. Give two reasons why quality management is important. (2)
3. Explain two ways to control quality in a factory. (4)
4. What management initiatives contribute to quality management? (4)
5. Outline two advantages and two disadvantages of improving quality by continuous improvement instead of by dramatic changes to working practices. (8)

STOCK CONTROL

What?

Stock control includes all the management systems involved in the handling of stock. This includes ordering, processing and storing stock.
Manufacturing businesses hold three types of stock:

1. *Raw materials*: These are the products and components required to make the finished product (e.g. aluminium for making the aircraft wings).

2. *Work in progress*: This is part-finished products (e.g. the aircraft wings).

3. *Finished goods*: These are the finished products that are waiting for shipment to the customer (e.g. the completed aircraft, awaiting collection).

Other businesses will have different types of stock. Retail outlets will have stocks of the products that they sell plus disposables. Hairdressers will have stocks of shampoo.

Who?

Most business study textbooks deal with stock control as if it is an issue only for manufacturing businesses. However, all businesses need to control stock. Even a small business may tie up a large proportion of its *working capital* in stock holding.

Why?

There are several reasons why stock control is important:

1. *To keep the manufacturing process running smoothly*: To do this, raw materials or components need to be available as required.

2. *To minimise costs*: Having too much stock could mean extra expense for storing, handling, and insurance; having too little could mean having to buy in emergency stock to be able to satisfy customer demand. See Figure 4.8A.

3. *To avoid wastage*: Wastage is expensive. It can be due to:
   — stock deteriorating whilst being stored or handled;
   — loss of stock due to theft;
   — material wastage caused by an inefficient production process;
   — problems with manufacturing which cause the item to be reworked or scrapped;

4. *To avoid losing customers*: In retail outlets customers expect a full range of goods on the shelves. The opportunity cost of excessively low stocks may be the loss of customers who cannot find the size 8 pink dress they really want.

5. *To avoid liquidity problems*: Holding stock uses *working capital*. It ties up money in the business. If the firm is unable to move its stock it may face cash flow problems.

How?

There are several elements to good stock management, for example:

- *Purchasing*: Having too little stock could slow production. Firms use a stock control chart to control the timing of purchases. *Buffer stock* is held in case there are problems with delivery or exceptional usage of stock.

- *Stock handling*. Most firms rotate the stock to try to use the oldest stock first. This is known as 'first-in-first-out'. This is particularly important where stock deteriorates or if it is likely to become obsolete such as with foodstuffs or high tech components.

IT developments allow businesses to manage their stock purchasing and handling much more efficiently. Computers enable much more data to be processed. Bar coding of items coming into and going out of stock make the recording of stock movements much easier. Orders for the next delivery can therefore reflect very accurately what is needed to refill the shelves. These records can be processed and sent to the supplier overnight for next day delivery.

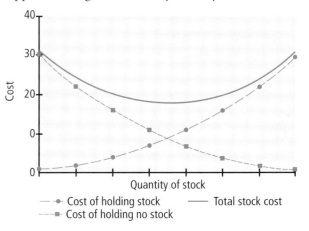

Fig. 4.8A: Minimising stockholding costs

What?

Just-in-time (JIT) is a system of stock management that tries to minimise the level of stock held. The ideal of JIT is zero buffer stocks. The ultimate system is to receive customer orders, get the material and component stock delivered, and then to despatch the finished goods to the customer. This way no stock is actually held apart from some work in progress. In reality this system is almost impossible to operate so firms use elements of this idea. Many companies have successfully applied JIT to stock ordering and delivery. With this system stock is ordered so that it goes straight to the factory floor.

JIT has both advantages and disadvantages as can be seen in the table below.

Advantages of JIT	Disadvantages of JIT
Less space is used for storage – this can be used for production instead	Production can be stopped if there is a problem with supply of materials
Costs of stock holding are reduced	More orders may mean higher costs for delivery and processing of orders
Liquidity is improved as less cash is tied up in stock	Heavy dependence on supplier(s)
Stock wastage is reduced	Heavy dependence on staff to get production right first time

How?

If JIT stock control is to work, one essential feature is to have a *good working relationship with suppliers*. JIT invariably means that deliveries of materials will be smaller and more frequent. Obviously not all firms operate on a scale that will allow this to happen. Suppliers will only cooperate if the size of the delivery is economically feasible.

Another important feature is that *estimates of stock requirements must be accurate*. If too little is ordered, production will stop as there is no buffer stock – too much and the company has the problems of handling and storage that the system is trying to avoid. IT systems allow much better estimates of stock requirements. In practice many firms hold buffer stock to avoid this problem.

K Key Terms

Buffer stock – additional stock held in case of problems with stock delivery or in case orders increase

Liquidity – the day-to-day cash position of the business; a firm is in a good liquidity position if it has sufficient funds to pay its debts as they become due for payment

Opportunity cost – the cost of missing out on the next best alternative when making a decision

Working capital – money used for the day-to-day running of the business

Who?

Stock management is essential for all firms. However, JIT is not the answer for them all. It is more likely to be successful in organisations large enough to force their suppliers to cooperate.

Application

Dell Computer Corporation is the world's No. 1 computer systems manufacturer with an estimated 14% of the global market. One factor in this success is the careful management of stock. Computers are made to the customer's specification. At the assembly plant they do not keep stocks of finished machines, only component parts. After an order is received the computer is constructed. It is then shipped to a distribution centre. Minimising its investment in working capital in this way has helped Dell to finance and maintain its incredible growth. It has also helped the company to avoid the problems of holding stocks of computers when a change in technology makes yesterday's models obsolete and slashes their value.

S Student howlers

'Firms need around a week's buffer stock.'
'JIT is the best system of stock control.'

T Test yourself

1. What is the aim of stock management? (3)
2. What are the three elements of stock for a manufacturer? (3)
3. What is meant by JIT stock control? (2)
4. Outline two advantages and two disadvantages of JIT stock control for a fashion clothes business such as Next. (8)
5. For a retailer, what are the opportunity costs of:
   a) holding too much stock;
   b) holding too little stock. (4)

INTEGRATED OPERATIONS MANAGEMENT

The AQA specification for this unit says

Candidates are expected to gain an understanding of operations management in an integrated context within the organisation and the wider environment. The study of operations management should focus on the way organisations use inputs and manage business processes efficiently to satisfy customers. These efficiencies should be related to financial controls and marketing benefits.

As you study the topics within operations management you should keep being struck by the importance of efficiency and how it interlinks with business profitability. Capacity utilisation is important to minimise costs, thus enabling competitive pricing or enhanced profitability. Understanding economies and diseconomies of scale makes the business aware of costs and what it can do to minimise them. Cost savings obviously help profitability.

Remember: profit = revenue – costs.

Improved profitability means that the business can grow and it has resources to invest in research and development or in better machinery or even staff training. Having lower costs also helps in the market place. If costs are lower, the business has more pricing options. It could also use some of the costs saved in production for other marketing initiatives such as advertising and branding.

Good quality contributes not only to the marketing effort but also improves profitability through savings on reworking and reduction in wastage. Initiatives such as Kaizen and lean production not only improve production efficiency but also contribute to motivating and empowering the workforce. Effective stock control improves cash flow and makes savings to variable costs and fixed overheads.

As you answer questions linked to operations management, try to see these topics in this wider context. If you are analysing a process improvement, try to consider what other effects it will have on the business:

- How are people affected?
- Does this contribute to the marketing effort? (perhaps by producing a better quality product or by producing it cheaper so enabling the business to be more competitive)
- How does it affect the finances of the business? (perhaps by reducing costs or cash flow needs or increasing profitability)

Doing this will enable you to see the whole picture, which is the starting point for effective evaluation.

T Test yourself (50 marks)

1. What is meant by benchmarking? (3)
2. What is a quality circle and what does it contribute? (4)
3. How could a firm increase its capacity utilisation? (3)
4. Explain how economies of scale reduce unit costs. (2)
5. Why might diseconomies of scale occur? (2)
6. What is the difference between batch and job production? (3)
7. What problems might occur if the firm is using just-in-time stock control? (4)
8. What influences the minimum level of stock a business needs to maintain? (3)
9. How does quality management contribute tothe marketing effort? (3)
10. Why do average costs generally fall when output is increased? (3)
11. What sort of business processes can be benchmarked? (3)
12. Which sort of production process is most suitable for mass-produced goods and why? (4)
13. What is Kaizen and what is required for it to succeed? (4)
14. What is the principle behind total quality management? (2)
15. How does good stock control help to improve cash flow? (3)
16. What are the advantages and disadvantages of automating parts of the production process? (4)

Now try the following data response questions. Allow yourself 30 minutes for each one.

Data response: On-line stock management

Internet-based stock management systems are now available to help local authorities manage their gritting programmes. The *De-Icing Business*, which supplies salt products to local authorities, has a web-based stock management system that allows local authorities and contractors to manage their stock of salt on-line.

De-Icing Business customers are able to access daily stock data and see exactly how much stock has been used at each depot. On-line reporting allows customers to accurately monitor salt stocks and gritter performance to ensure that every penny of the winter salting budget works as hard as possible. The Wintranet uploads data from each salt storage location. The gritters drive over a weighbridge every time they leave and return to the depot. This enables the calculation of how much salt has been spread en-route. By comparing daily stock usage figures against agreed stock profiles the system can provide early warning of potential low stock and automatically generate an order to restock when necessary.

Another feature is the use of global positioning satellites to track the precise position of gritters, providing proof of the exact times and route on which salting occurred. As well as enabling accurate monitoring of gritter performance, these data are crucial for managers and local authorities in case of legal action from road users involved in accidents. These highly advanced features can improve control over the gritting operation to ensure that adequate service levels are delivered.

(Source: Adapted from *The De-Icing Business* website)

Questions

1. Why is it important for local authorities to maintain adequate stocks of salt? (2)
2. What advantages does an automated stock management system give? (4)
3. Consider the advantages and disadvantages of a computerised production process. (6)
4. In this case the system helps the business to deliver a quality service. Why is quality control important for businesses? (5)
5. Some businesses use a just-in-time system of stock management. Explain how this works and evaluate the pros and cons for a medium-sized business producing sandwiches for sale in supermarkets. (8)

Data response: Challenge 50

The Maruti car factory in India had set its workers and management a challenge. Challenge 50 aims for a 50% improvement in productivity and quality and a 30% reduction in costs over 3 years.

The first year of the challenge has shown remarkable results, as shown in the table below.

As a result of cost savings Maruti has been able to reduce the price of its small car, the Maruti 800, to below the price in 2000. Consequently, sales have increased by over 30%. Maruti also experienced a 45% increase in sales of the Alto, another car in its portfolio. The company decided to make this car cheaper as well. This was not a forced price reduction and the forecast profit for this model was expected to stay the same. The company was hoping to take advantage of growing sales. Both of these moves signal a change from the business being production led to being market led.

So how have Maruti managers achieved this:

- They have benchmarked against the 'best in class' Suzuki's Kosai plant in Japan. Among other things this has led to a redesign of the working area to reduce the number of steps taken to perform a task. As the chairman of Suzuki says: 'We pay people to work, not walk.'
- They have made changes in philosophy and application of the Kaizen system that has been operating for several years.
- They have extended the Kaizen ideas to their suppliers. The car factory is an assembly plant and 80% of the car is produced by suppliers. By visiting suppliers' factories, the managers have managed to reduce the number of suppliers and cut costs by 4% each year.

	2001–02	2002–03
Man hours per vehicle index (base 1999–2000 = 100)	76	59
Ratio of stock to sales index (base 1999–2000 = 100)	59	41
Average defects per vehicle	60%	33%
Direct pass rate	20%	40%
Inspection workers per shift	8	2
	1995	**2002**
Cars per day (output)	730	1700
Employees	4800	4600
Kaizen suggestions	60,000	72,000
Number of suppliers	300	245

(Extracted from *Business Standard*; India)

Questions

1. What is meant by the sentence: 'Both of these moves signal a change from the business being production led to being market led'? (2)
2. Explain briefly how the number of cars produced per day can increase when the number of employees is falling. (3)
3. Why did the company choose to reduce the price of the Alto following an increase in demand? (4)
4. Explain why the company has benchmarked against the Suzuki plant in Japan and the benefits of this process. (7)
5. The business is operating a Kaizen system. Evaluate some of the advantages and disadvantages of this. (9)

MARKETS AND COMPETITION

What?

A *market* is a place where buyers and sellers meet. Most markets consist of many buyers and many sellers.

How?

Markets work because of the interaction between buyers and sellers. If no-one wants to buy the product it will not sell. If there are many buyers and few sellers then the seller will be able to sell and be able to set a high price. This balance of supply and demand is what determines the *market price*. In a perfect market, i.e. a market where there are many buyers and sellers (and all have full information), the balance of supply and demand will set the price. A good example of a perfect market is the foreign exchange market, where the £'s exchange rate is determined by demand and supply for £s compared with other currencies.

The diagram below shows quantities of supply and demand at various price levels. When the price is high there will be lower demand. A lower price will encourage more buyers. When the price is high there will be a high level of supply. Suppliers will be happy to put their products onto the market as they will be getting good margins. As the price falls some suppliers will leave the market so supply will fall. The point at which the two curves cross is known as the

market equilibrium point. At this point supply and demand are equal. The price at this point is the market price.

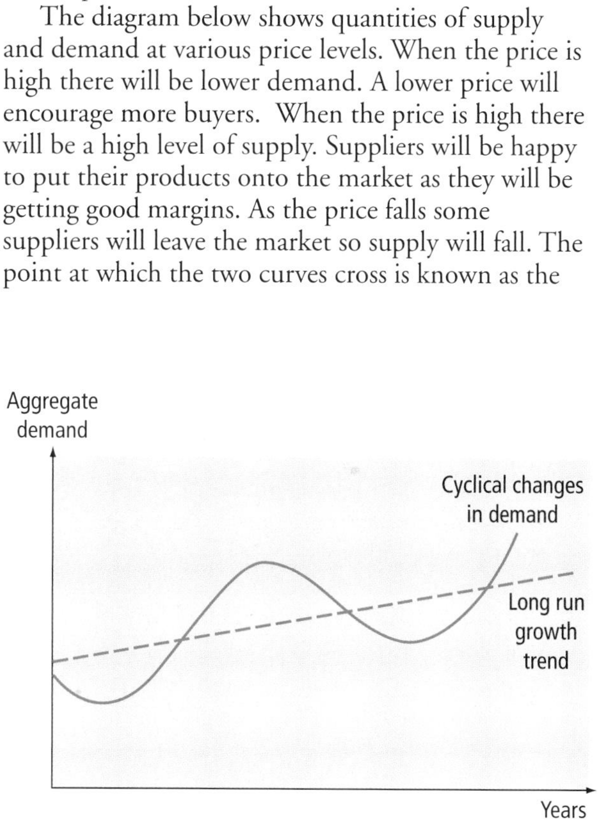

The degree of competition in any market can be categorised as follows.
- If there is only one seller in a market selling a product that has no substitutes it is known as a *monopoly*. It will be difficult for other firms to enter the market. As a consequence the monopoly business will be able to set the price.
- *Perfect competition* defines a situation where buyers have perfect knowledge of the market and are therefore able to choose the best product from those on offer. A perfectly competitive market has many sellers selling an identical product. There is *free entry* into the market and the balance of supply and demand determines the price.

(Most markets lie between these two extremes.)
- *Monopolistic competition* – in this market there is free entry into the market, many sellers, the price is determined by the market, but influenced by the producers. The major difference to perfect competition is that the product is differentiated.
- *Oligopoly* – here the product is also differentiated but the market is dominated by a few large suppliers. The sellers tend to set the price in the market.

Who?

There are very few pure monopoly firms. Water companies have a monopoly of water supplies in regions of the UK. Some train operators have a monopoly over certain routes.

Oligopoly is quite a common situation. The washing powder market is dominated by two large firms: Procter & Gamble who make Ariel and Daz and Unilever who make Persil. Between them they have over 75% of the market. If you look in a supermarket you will see that these products are often sold at very similar prices.

Why?

Governments will try to encourage competition and discourage monopoly. The Competition Commission

Fig. 5.1A: Supply and demand

exists to ensure that firms do not become dominant in the market. If a take-over bid or merger is likely to make one company dominant or lessen the number of firms competing in the market, the Commission can prevent the merger from taking place.

Competition is considered to be healthy for consumers and the economy.

- For *consumers* the advantages are:
  — there is more choice: if customers are dissatisfied they can find another supplier;
  — the price will be lower;
  — product features and quality are likely to improve when firms compete against each other.
- For the *economy* the advantages are:
  — businesses become more efficient;
  — prices are kept down, thus avoiding *inflation*;
  — businesses are more efficient so can compete more effectively internationally, thereby contributing to a healthy *balance of payments*.

K Key Terms

Balance of payments – the balance between exports and imports; if exports are higher than imports the balance of payments will be positive

Free entry – new businesses are able to enter into a market without restrictions; they are able to compete with existing sellers in that market

Inflation – a general rise in prices across the economy

Price skimming – a policy of charging high prices for innovative goods in a market; the company takes advantage of the lack of competition to charge high prices which it then reduces as competitors enter the market

Is it fair?

In an oligopoly, firms may decide not to compete on price. This is when businesses artificially alter the market. Illegal unfair trading activities include:

- *Price fixing*: Businesses may watch other firms and fix their price accordingly, but managers are not allowed to get together to determine prices.
- *Market sharing*: Businesses who agree to divide markets by region or some other criteria are acting illegally. There is, however, no problem if a firm decides not to operate in a certain area for business reasons.
- *Cartels*: These are agreements between businesses that restrict free competition. Supply is limited in order to maintain higher prices. Cartels, too, are illegal.

The line between fair and unfair practices is often very thin. If companies knowingly act together to harm the customer's pocket, then they are breaking the fair trade laws.

Application

The Office of Fair Trading (OFT) imposed fines of £23 million against GUS who run the Argos chain and Littlewoods. Both companies are appealing the decision. The fines are a result of a price fixing allegation with Hasbro UK, a toy manufacturer. The firms are accused of agreeing with the toy maker to keep prices at the level recommended by Hasbro. This meant that prices in the stores would be higher than on the open market. As many shops use Argos as a price guide the OFT felt that this was pulling up prices in the market.

Although the company denies that it has been involved in price fixing the OFT feels it has acted unlawfully.

Most markets are imperfect. Consumers do not necessarily have all the knowledge of all the products and services that are available. Although competition is seen as a healthy thing, many firms are happy to stay with the status quo. If the firm is making an adequate profit it may deliberately choose to keep things as they are rather than trying to capture more market share. This may mean that competition is too weak to serve the consumer's best interests.

E Exam insight

The competitive situation of a business is essential background to its marketing strategy and plans.

S Student howlers

'Perfect competition is the best market situation.'
'The Government is in control of the competitive situation.'

T Test yourself

1. What is meant by competition? (3)
2. What are the four different kinds of competitive situation? (4)
3. How does an oligopoly differ from monopolistic competition? (3)
4. Why does the government try to prevent one company from having too much power in the market? (4)
5. What disadvantages may there be for customers, when firms like Procter & Gamble and Unilever have a combined market share of more than 75%? (6)

DEMAND AND THE BUSINESS CYCLE

What?

Demand is the amount of a product or service that the market wishes to purchase; the *business cycle* describes the pattern of changes in demand nationally.

Demand for all goods and services throughout the economy is known as *aggregate demand*. Aggregate demand does not stay the same in an economy: it may rise or fall. When it is rising the economy is said to be growing. If aggregate demand shrinks the economy is said to be going into a decline or *recession*. A long period of growth is referred to as a *boom*, a long period of recession is a *depression* or *slump*.

Both growth and recession do not occur evenly across the economy. Often in a recession one sector (e.g. manufacturing) is affected initially. As businesses close or cut back on production, jobs are lost. This will have a knock-on effect on suppliers to the business so more jobs will be lost. In the area where jobs have been lost local businesses will also begin to feel the effect of unemployed workers having less disposable income.

Similarly, in a growth period, the opening of new factories will result in growing local prosperity.

E Exam insight

Technically, a recession is two consecutive quarters of negative growth. However, in case studies you may see indications that the economy is approaching a downturn. Look for lower demand, increasing unemployment, falling inflation. All of these indicate that the economy may be slowing.

How?

Recession is a slowing down in economic activity. It will not affect all businesses in the same way and the impact will be very different for each business. The effect of a recession on businesses will normally follow the following pattern:

1. The business will experience lower demand.
2. It may then increase marketing effort, perhaps by reducing prices to stimulate sales.
3. This may reduce profitability, especially if rivals do the same.
4. If the reduction in demand persists, the firm will reduce production and lay off workers.
5. This may take the firm below *break-even* so it will start to make losses.
6. If the firm is not able to support these losses it will go out of business.

As demand falls, firms may try to maintain current output but will put any *investment plans on hold*. This will affect the suppliers of any equipment etc. that they may have ordered.

If a firm is struggling or goes out of business its suppliers may not get paid. *Delaying payment to creditors* is often used as a tactic if there are cash flow problems. This will make the suppliers more vulnerable and could cause them to go out of business.

A slump – a prolonged period of recession – will exacerbate all of the problems experienced during a recession. Some business may be able to ride out a short period of recession but will go under if it is extended.

Who?

The cyclical movement in demand affects all businesses. Some businesses are affected more than others. Sellers of luxury goods may find that demand for their products falls when income is lower and aggregate demand is lower. Manufacturers of staple products such as foodstuffs may find little alteration to total demand. However, within this some products may be replaced by others. There may be a move away from branded products to cheaper own brands.

Small businesses tend to be more vulnerable to recession. If they experience delayed payment of bills or have *bad debts* this will affect their cash flow and may cause them to fail. Larger, established firms are more likely to be able to survive, as they are less likely to be reliant on one product or market. *Firms that are already having problems* will probably not survive.

Some businesses may do better during a recession. Firms supplying cheaper ('inferior') goods may find that sales increase as customers shift to their products.

But

Business life is not just about recession. The UK has experienced average growth of 2.9% over the last 10 years. Following a recession there will be a *period of recovery*. This may be very slow to take hold. Firms that have cut back on production will initially be very reluctant to increase output or capacity. It will take time for firms to become confident enough to take on more staff and make new investment. Once firms do become more confident the economy will move into a boom period. The effects of this are:

- There will be an increase in output and investment.
- This may lead to a shortage of workers.
- It may also lead to a shortage of materials.
- This may mean that there is a shortage of goods for sale.

All of these factors may cause a rise in prices. Firms will have to pay more to attract workers with the required skills. Material costs may rise, as other suppliers need to be found. Shortage of supply in the market will pull prices up. This could lead to inflation.

One of the major problems with a cyclical pattern of economic activity is the effect on business confidence and therefore future development. Even in a boom period firms may be reluctant to invest in case another recession is coming along.

However, when businesses find themselves facing problems they look at how to improve performance. Is the stock holding too high? Could labour productivity be improved? Is there wastage that could be eliminated? During boom times firms may get complacent so a recession may help to improve overall performance.

K Key Terms

Average costs – total costs (fixed cost + variable costs) divided by the number of units produced

Bad debts – debts that are unpaid and are unlikely to be paid in the future

Break-even – the point of output at which total revenue equals total costs. No profit or loss is made

Cash flow – the flow of cash into and out of the business

Fixed costs – costs that stay the same regardless of the level of output

What then?

If the recovery and subsequent boom leads to inflation the government will try to reduce the level of inflation. They may do this by raising taxes or increasing the rate of interest. Both of these strategies will help to reduce demand. If demand is reduced it may lead to recession and so the cycle of boom–bust continues.

Application

The 10-year period from 1992 to 2002 was one of the most economically stable periods that Britain has seen. Growth averaged at 2.9%. Unemployment fell from 10 to 3% – its lowest for 30 years. Inflation averaged 2.5% and never got above 3.5%.

This period of stability was beneficial for British firms: a low rate of inflation allowed them to compete both at home and overseas against international competition; the lower unemployment meant that there was less labour wastage, and the steady growth and price stability allowed firms to plan for the future.

Heidelberger Druckmaschinen, a German company, is the world's largest maker of printing machinery. Over the last 2 years it has been making losses and reducing the workforce. The latest cut of 1000 jobs follows a decision to sell the unit that makes presses for magazines and newspapers. The reason behind this is the slump that has been affecting advertising and in particular newspaper and magazine advertising over the last few years.

Historically the UK economy has seen continuous cycles of growth and recession. This has made it very difficult for businesses to plan. However during the last 10 years the cycle has been much less dramatic. No extended recession and no exaggerated growth. This stability has helped many firms. Unfortunately it is impossible to predict whether or not this is a new pattern of economic activity.

E Exam insight

Take care when talking about the effects of growth or recession to relate your answer to the business in question. What sorts of products do they sell/make? Do they have cash flow problems? How easy is it to alter the level of production?

S Student howlers

'All businesses suffer in a recession.'
'During a boom period this business will be able to grow much faster.'

T Test yourself

1. What is meant by recession? (2)
2. What problems might a firm face during a boom period? (5)
3. Why might a firm fail during a recession? (8)
4. Which firms are more likely to succeed during a recession? (5)

INTEREST RATES

What?

Interest rates are set by an independent committee of the Bank of England. The Bank's Monetary Policy Committee (MPC) sets the current rate of interest. This is known as the *base rate*. The rate is used to calculate the cost of borrowing or the return on money lent. The interest rate is the annual cost of money. When a firm takes out a loan it will pay interest on the loan. If it borrows £100,000 at an interest rate of 5% per annum, it will have to pay the lender £5000 each year as interest.

How?

The MPC meets monthly to set the interest rate. One of the main tasks of the MPC is to ensure price stability. Set up in 1997, it was given responsibility for achieving the government's inflation target. From 2004 that target is for an inflation rate of around 2%.

In order to do this the committee takes into account the level of growth in the economy, the rate of exchange and the level of unemployment. If growth is high the committee will look at the reasons behind the growth. If consumer demand is excessive and likely to lead to higher prices, they may decide to increase the rate of interest to dampen down demand. If they wish to stimulate the economy they will reduce interest rates.

What effects?

Increases in interest rates have an impact on businesses.

1. If interest rates are increased it will *make the cost of borrowing more expensive*. Firms will have to pay the lender a greater amount. As a cost to the business this will immediately affect profit.

2. It could also make it *harder for the firm to raise finance for expansion*. Less money will be available from investors. Investors want to get the best return possible. If they can get a high rate of interest on bank deposits, why should they look for a risky option?

3. The firm *may postpone investment plans*. New projects will need to show a higher return than previously.

4. Higher interest rates will also affect the market. *Customers will have less disposable income.* Customers will be deterred from taking out additional loans. The loans and mortgages that they already have will be more expensive. This will affect demand, particularly for luxury products.

Who?

All businesses are affected in some way by changes in interest rates. When interest rates are high small firms may find it harder to find lenders. Lenders will be concerned to know if the firm is capable of repaying the interest as well as the loan. Businesses that are in difficulty – especially those having cash flow problems – will be very vulnerable to rate rises.

Application

Amicus-AEEU is the UK's largest manufacturing union. It has 730,000 members throughout the private and public sectors. It has expressed concern about the increase in interest rates in November 2003. The base rate was increased by 0.25% to 3.75%. They estimate that this increase will accelerate the rate of loss of manufacturing jobs. It is estimated that around 10,000 manufacturing jobs are lost each month. The Joint General Secretary Roger Lyons said: 'Any increase will spell disaster for British manufacturing and squash any signs of recovery.'

When Gordon Brown established the MPC in 1997 the idea was to separate the government from decisions about interest rates. Previously the government had made the decisions. However, many would argue that, as the MPC has responsibility for achieving government targets and supporting government economic policy, it is not independent. Setting the rate of interest is rather like walking a tightrope. Every time the MPC meets and makes a decision about interest rates there is a chorus of approval or disapproval from interested parties. The Confederation of British Industry is always supportive of any lowering of the rate. House builders and mortgage lenders also welcome no change or a rate lowering. People concerned about the rising level of debt in the country feel that higher rates are the only solution.

There are also regional problems. A countrywide interest rate will affect different regions in different ways. A rise in interest rates to dampen a buoyant housing market in London and the South East may cause problems for firms in less affluent areas.

K Key Terms

Base rate – the interest rate set by the Bank of England's Monetary Policy Committee

Disposable income – income available to spend

Inflation – a general rise in price throughout an economy

Mortgages – loans secured against property such as houses

E Exam insight

Take care not to confuse interest rates with the rate of inflation or exchange rates. Interest rates are the cost of money. Inflation is a general rise in the level of prices and exchange rates are the value of the country's currency compared with those of other countries.

S Student howler

'A high interest rate means that the business will need to increase prices.'

T Test yourself

1. What is the rate of interest currently? (1)
2. What impact does a raised interest rate have on consumers? (6)
3. Why does a rising interest rate make it harder for businesses to raise finance? (6)
4. Why may an increased interest rate hit jobs in manufacturing industry? (7)

INTERNATIONAL TRADE, EXCHANGE RATES AND COMPETITIVENESS

What?

International trade is the buying and selling of goods and services between businesses in different countries: *imports* are goods brought into a country, *exports* are goods sold to other countries. The export and import of goods such as bananas or cars is known as *visible* trade; export and import of services such as insurance, banking or tourism is known as *invisible* trade.

In order to conduct international trade, businesses need the currency of the country they are trading with. *Exchange rates* are the rates at which different currencies can be bought or sold. If an American firm wishes to buy goods from a business in the UK it will need to buy UK pounds. The rate at which the firm can exchange dollars for pounds is the rate of exchange.

Which?

The goods and services that are imported and exported are constantly changing. The UK exported over £270,000 million worth of goods and services in 2002. Imports in the same period were about £300,000 million. This meant that there was a *deficit* in the balance of payments. The country imported £30,000 million more than it exported. Services such as insurance, banking and tourism made up about 30% of total exports. Manufactured products such as cars were 36% of total exports. Other important exports are North Sea oil, chemicals and foodstuffs. Hidden within these figures are the contributions of a huge number of British firms who have found markets for their products abroad. One company in Bedfordshire exports sand to Saudi Arabia.

Where?

Large global corporations such as Coca-Cola sell their goods all over the world. Other companies may sell to only one other country. There are many factors that affect where goods are sold. Fresh produce will need to be air freighted if it is to arrive fresh in the market. Other bulky goods such as cars will generally be shipped, as the costs of other forms of transport are too high.

Some countries also limit the amount of goods that can be imported or impose an import duty that raises the price of the product above locally produced equivalents. These *trade barriers* try to protect home industries from international competition. Trading groups such as the European Union have abolished trade barriers between member countries.

How?

Selling in other markets is a risky business. If it is to succeed the company will need to be *competitive*. As in any other market it needs to be able to supply goods that are either able to be sold at a better price than rival goods or are superior in some way. One of the factors in the competitiveness is the exchange rate. This is constantly fluctuating and makes it very difficult for exporting and importing firms to set prices and to plan.

£ strengthens against other currencies	£ weakens against other currencies
Value of £ rises	Value of £ falls
Exporters will receive fewer pounds for goods sold abroad	Exporters will receive more pounds for goods sold abroad
Exports become more expensive abroad	Exports are cheaper abroad
Imports are cheaper	Imports are more expensive
UK firms' competitiveness worsens	UK firms' competitiveness improves

In the short term the value of currencies is often affected by *speculation*. This makes currency movements more frequent and dramatic and contributes to the uncertainty felt by exporters and importers. Another point to remember is that the pound could rise against one currency and depreciate against another.

But

Exporting is not easy. Apart from the many uncertainties there are also additional costs involved, such as:
* *Transportation of the goods*: There will be additional costs of getting the product to the foreign market.

- *Administrative costs*: Paperwork involved with shipping and invoicing will be greater. There may be additional legal requirements such as customs clearance.
- *Exchange costs*: There is a cost involved in changing from one currency to another. One of the aims of the single EU currency (the euro) is to reduce exchange rate costs and fluctuations.
- *Representation costs*: There may be a need to establish a representative office or to employ local agents to sell the goods.
- *Product adjustment costs*: Products may need to be labelled or packaged differently for different markets.

Any business involved in international trade needs to be fully prepared. As in the home market it needs to have an excellent understanding of the market(s) so that it can ensure that it is able to trade profitably.

Most governments encourage businesses to seek export markets. Exporting brings in revenue that can be used to buy imports. Many firms seek to export to expand their businesses, particularly if they have no growth potential in their home country. However, moving into overseas markets is not always successful and can be extremely risky. To compete abroad often means that businesses have to be very competitive and that requires good management and excellent market knowledge.

There is much discussion about the fall in UK manufacturing exports. However, it has to be remembered that the UK also exports high value services. These have become more expensive whilst mass produced manufactured goods have fallen in price.

K Key Terms

Currency speculation – dealing in currency in order to make a gain out of exchange rate movements

Internationally competitive – able to compete effectively against overseas firms

Trade barriers – a measure taken by a country to restrict imports

Trade deficit – when a country's imports are greater than its exports

E Exam insight

A common student error is to confuse interest rates and exchange rates. The interest rate is the rate charged for borrowed money or paid on savings. Exchange rates are the value of one currency compared to another.

When considering if a firm should enter into the export business, look carefully at the circumstances of the business. Exporting is unlikely to be a solution for a business that is struggling in the home market.

Application

B&Q, the DIY retailer, has invested over £70 million in China. It has built 14 stores so far. The largest to date in Beijing was opened in October 2003. The stores have been very successful. B&Q, which is owned by Kingfisher, plans to invest a further £50 million next year and has a target of 58 stores in China by 2007. They have taken advantage in the massive growth of home ownership in the country. This is a good example of a business that understands its market and has positioned itself to take full advantage.

The British government is keen to encourage international trade. UK Trade & Investment is a government organisation that offers support to UK companies that want to export goods or services. Among the success stories is Panesar Foods of West Bromwich which produces a range of speciality foods including organic products, egg and dairy-free soya products and bottled sauces including Mexican pepper sauce, Cajun pepper sauce, Caribbean pepper sauce and Jalapeno chillies. They have just started exporting two types of chilli sauce to Mexico! They also export to the USA and Sweden. Panesar Foods is hopeful that its export business will help it to increase its turnover by 40% to £3.5 million by the end of the year. This shows how successful exporting can help a business to grow.

S Student howlers

'High exchange rates make international trade easier.'
'Small firms cannot export because of the language barriers.'

T Test yourself

1. What is meant by international trade? (2)
2. What are barriers to trade and why do countries use them? (5)
3. Identify three possible reasons why a country's export levels might increase. (3)
4. Outline the possible effects on Cadbury's of a 10% increase in the value of the £ against all other currencies. (6)
5. What additional costs might firms encounter when trading abroad? (4)

INFLATION AND UNEMPLOYMENT

What?

Inflation is the rate of rise in the average price level within an economy. It is measured in the UK by the consumer Price Index (CPI). The base year, currently 1995, is given an index of 100. In 1996 the index was 102.4. This shows that prices rose by 2.4% from 1995 to 1996. CPI is measured by collecting a considerable amount of data on prices of goods and services bought by typical households. The index figure is therefore an average across a wide range of products and services. It should be remembered that if inflation is rising, not all prices are increasing. Some may be going down.

Why?

Most governments and economists watch the rate of inflation very carefully. This is because it is often an indicator of what is happening in the economy. But why is it important?

The main problems with inflation are:

1. It reduces spending power so may reduce overall demand. If the price of goods has risen by 4% in a year, each £1 will buy fewer goods. This does not matter so much for people who are working, as their wages will probably increase by a similar amount. It will affect anyone on a fixed income and it will reduce the value of savings.

2. It reduces international competitiveness. If British manufacturing costs are rising they will become uncompetitive compared to goods being produced in a country whose inflation is lower.

3. Price rises are a cost to industry. The cost of labour will rise as workers demand increased pay.

These factors are not important, though, when inflation is relatively low. Prices rising at 2% or 3% a year will not cause any difficulties for firms or for consumers.

Deflation, which is when prices are falling, occurs when there is intense competition in a weak economy. It can be a serious problem. If firms are unable to make cost reductions to keep pace with the fall in prices their profitability will fall and they may eventually go out of business.

Both inflation and deflation can occur in sections of an economy. The seriousness of the impact is often shielded by the average figure.

How?

Inflation occurs in two ways:

1. *Demand–pull* inflation is caused when there is excess demand in the economy. If the economy is buoyant there may develop a shortage of materials or labour. This situation is referred to as 'overheating'. Employers will have to pay higher wages to find and retain good staff. This may feed a wage–price spiral that forces prices up. As it becomes widespread it will start to push the inflation figure higher.

2. Inflation can also be caused by a rise in the price of materials. This is known as *cost–push* inflation. If the rate of exchange falls, rising import prices can push prices up generally. Workers will then look for wage increases to keep pace with expectations about future inflation.

Governments will try to control inflation. The government may try to reduce demand by increasing taxation or cutting government spending. Alternatively, it may try to control the supply of money by raising interest rates.

E Exam insight

The annual percentage change in the rate of inflation is:

$$\frac{\text{index for year 2} - \text{index for year 1}}{\text{index for year 1}} \times 100$$

CPI for 1999 was 111 and was 114.2 in 2000. Therefore:

- the change in the index was 114.2 – 111 = 3.2.
- the annual percentage increase was (3.2/111) × 100 = 2.88%.

But

Inflation is not bad news for everyone. Households with high mortgages will be pleased to see the real value of the debt reduced by the increase in prices. It is not always bad news for businesses either. If firms have loans the real value of their repayments will fall. They may also be able to take advantage of rising prices to improve profit margins.

What?

Unemployment is when people are willing and able to work, but are unable to find jobs. There are several different types of unemployment: structural, cyclical and frictional.

Structural unemployment
In most economies, even when the economy is buoyant, there is a core of unemployed people. The reason for this is that changing patterns of employment in the economy mean that the skills demanded differ from those available among the unemployed. In recent years there has been a shift from manufacturing. The manufacturing sector has declined and automation has reduced the need for many jobs. Some of these people will not have skills that can be used in other sectors. They may be unwilling or unable to be retrained. This is known as *occupational immobility*.

Cyclical unemployment
This occurs when the economy goes into recession and so businesses cut back on the number of employees. As the economy recovers so unemployment should fall.

Frictional unemployment
Frictional unemployment is the effect of people changing jobs. The gap in employment between leaving one job and moving to another contributes to the unemployment statistics.

Why?

Unemployment is undesirable because it can severely affect the self-confidence of those who have lost their jobs. It can also affect the level of crime and social unrest, especially if the unemployment is concentrated in small local areas.

The national economy suffers as unemployment is a waste of a nation's resources. It is also expensive, as unemployed people may claim benefits to support themselves and their families. Some unemployment may be good for industry as it may bring down labour costs if there is a ready availability of labour. However, this depends on the available workers having skills that match those required.

Application

China is hitting the headlines. Growth has been estimated at 7–9% a year for the last 10 years. It is now one of the top six world economies. With growth figures at this level, analysts would normally expect inflation to occur. However, two factors are limiting price rises: one is that labour costs are not growing as

China has a huge labour market so there is no wage inflation; the other is that although output is growing, demand for the products is not growing at the same rate. This is because the Chinese do not have high disposable income. In terms of gross domestic product (GDP) per head, the country ranks about 100th in the world.

This shows that growth in itself is not the cause of inflation. There need to be other factors such as an increase in input costs and/or demand exceeding supply.

A worrying trend is causing the loss of thousands of jobs in the UK. Aviva, the UK's biggest insurer, announced in November 2003 that it was planning to relocate around 2300 call centre and office jobs to India. Other banking and insurance groups have made similar plans. Lloyds TSB will move 1500 jobs to India. Analysts think that this could result in a loss of 100,000 jobs in the UK.

Successfully starting and running a business is hard enough at any time, as there are so many internal factors to consider. Unpredictable external factors such as the economy can only make things harder. So firms crave predictability: a steady inflation rate of 2–3% is fine, as is a stable level of unemployment. Few firms would like to see unemployment so low as to make it difficult to find suitable people to fill vacancies.

Another area of discussion is the extent to which governments should get involved in the management of these aspects of the economy. The seesawing nature of the British economy as it moves from overheating to recession and back again has been blamed on the intervention of successive governments. Certainly it is difficult to get the balance right.

K Key Terms

Interest rates – the rate that is paid for borrowed money or given for money lent

Occupational immobility – the inability of workers to move from one type of job to another

T Test yourself

1. What is inflation? (2)
2. How is it measured? (2)
3. What effects might high inflation have upon a manufacturer of jeans? (6)
4. Why is unemployment bad for the economy? (5)

BUSINESS AND THE LAW

The major way in which the government intervenes in business activity is through the passing of legislation. There are four key areas of legislation that affect the activities of firms: health and safety legislation, employment protection, consumer protection and competition legislation.

Health and safety legislation

What?
Health and safety legislation places the responsibility for ensuring a healthy and safe workplace on employers.

How are firms affected?
Firms are affected by:
- *Increased bureaucracy.* Firms with more than five employees are expected to have a written health and safety policy.
- *Increased costs.* Partly following from the previous point and also to cover extra expenses involved in ensuring that machinery and equipment are safe and employees are provided with safety equipment.

Who is hit hardest?
Although health and safety legislation may appear to hit manufacturers hard (lots of machinery and heavy equipment), service sector firms should meet the same requirements by law. Arguably, risks may seem less obvious within the service sector and health and safety may be more likely to be ignored.

Employment protection

What?
Employment protection legislation lays out the rights of employees, covering issues such as discrimination, minimum wage, maximum working hours and what constitutes unfair dismissal from a job. Minimum wage is a particularly sensitive issue within the business world. At the time of writing, the government was intending to set minimum wage rates from October 2004 of:

Aged 22+ £4.85 an hour
Aged 18–21 £4.10 an hour

Why a minimum wage?

Arguments for a minimum wage	Arguments against
It is a worker's right to receive 'a fair day's pay'	Pushes up business costs
Should help to meet worker's basic needs and avoid dissatisfaction (N.B. Maslow/Herzberg)	May make it harder for British firms to compete internationally, leading to job losses

Consumer protection

What?
There are a range of laws designed to protect consumers from unscrupulous actions by firms, covering issues such as selling goods that don't do what they claim, or cause harm to the consumer due to poor standards of manufacture.

Consumer protection should have the following effects:
- Enhanced customer satisfaction;
- Increased emphasis on quality control;
- Increased production costs (due to training and introduction of new working practices).

Competition legislation

What?
This type of legislation exists in order to enable the government to promote greater competition within markets. On a fundamental level, the government will use this legislation to strike a balance between 'fair' prices for consumers and 'fair' profits for businesses.

Why?
- *Control of former state owned monopolies.* Unless properly controlled, a supplier with too much power within a market can push up prices to unfair levels or allow service/quality standards to slip to a low level. For this reason, the government has appointed regulators to keep an eye on (or sometimes change) the behaviour of firms that were created by privatising former government-owned firms in industries such as water, gas and electricity supply.

- *Mergers and takeovers*. In a similar way, the Competition Commission was set up to investigate any proposed merger or takeover deals that may lead to the creation of a firm with excessive power within a market, that they could then abuse.
- *Restrictive practices*. This includes any activity deemed to be specifically designed to allow firms to compete unfairly. Examples may include predatory pricing or exclusive distribution deals that deny competitors access to distribution channels.

Application

Birds Eye Walls has been accused of a restrictive practice in its freezer exclusivity deals with small retailers. Birds Eye Walls supplies the retailer with a fridge for ice cream on extremely favourable terms, as long as Birds Eye Walls products are the only ones stocked. Since many small retailers only have space for one fridge, competitors argue that this type of deal represents a restrictive practice.

Are laws necessary?

There are those who argue that businesses do not need to be constrained by laws – the market itself and consumer power should ensure good behaviour. This is known as a 'laissez-faire' approach. The logic here is that if any firm gains a bad reputation for malpractice, consumers will avoid using that firm's products and the firm will be forced to adopt good practice. It should, however, be pointed out that there are many examples where this mechanism has failed to apply, sometimes with tragic consequences.

What types of firm are hardest hit – big or small?

More often than not, it is smaller firms where budgets are tightest that complain loudest about the introduction of new legal constraints. They are concerned about the potential cost increase forced by compliance with new legislation. However, despite the undoubted negative effects of some legislation on small firms, the legislation may be a key factor in ensuring that they are competing on the same 'level playing field' as their larger rivals. In other words, if it was not for legislation, firms might feel forced to lower their own standards to match the low costs of the worst employers within a market.

K Key Terms

Competition Commission – a government-funded organisation whose key role is to investigate possible breaches of competition legislation; if a breach is discovered, the Commission reports its recommendations to the Office of Fair Trading

Office of Fair Trading – the government body set up whose role is to ensure compliance with competition legislation; the OFT can take action against firms found guilty of breaching competition legislation, often the result of investigation by the Competition Commission

E Exam insight

Do not learn long lists of laws and what those laws consist of. This will only demonstrate knowledge. To gain marks for analysis it is important to demonstrate an understanding of the broader effects of government intervention on the way that businesses operate. Terms such as 'a level playing field' and a 'laissez-faire approach' are especially helpful.

S Student howlers

'Competition legislation means that no single firm can have a market share greater than 25%.'
'All legislation acts as a faultless deterrent to illegal behaviour by companies.'

T Test yourself

1. Identify two potential constraints that health and safety laws may present to a train operator. (2)
2. Briefly explain why competition legislation protects consumers. (5)
3. Identify and briefly explain two recent examples of companies that have been found guilty of breaching legislation in some way. (6)
4. Outline the ways in which the minimum wage might be argued to hasten the decline of manufacturing within the UK. (7)

STAKEHOLDING

What?

A stakeholder is a person or group affected by the operations of a business. Social responsibility is the term used to describe what a business should be expected to do to keep each stakeholder satisfied (e.g. a firm has a responsibility to pay its suppliers on time). The diagram below shows a number of stakeholder groups, some of whom are clearly 'part of the business' whereas others are outsiders. All may be affected by the decisions taken by the firm.

Who?

Fig. 5.7A: Internal and external stakeholders

How are they affected?

The table below includes suggestions as to what areas of interest different stakeholder groups may have.

Application to business contexts

- Manufacturing – when producing a complex product such as an airplane, a specialist supplier may be a firm's most important stakeholder.
- Service sector firms may place more focus on trying to keep the customer satisfied, which in turn may make it essential to keep staff motivation high.

Why keep stakeholders happy?

The advantages of satisfying stakeholders can be summarised in three main areas:
- Better relations mean that stakeholders are more willing to deal with the firm in a reasonable and fair way.
- A better public image may encourage sales.

Stakeholder	Area of interest
Managers	Managers will be aiming to achieve their own objectives. This may involve maximising the firm's profit, as the managers may receive some kind of profit-related bonus. Sometimes managers will be more concerned with ensuring their own job security or career propects, perhaps through boosting the importance of their department within the firm.
Shop floor staff/employees	Staff will want to ensure good working conditions, pay and terms of employment. In times of trouble, their primary concern is likely to be protecting their jobs.
Shareholders	Shareholders in private limited companies, especially family firms, may well be happy to see the business growing and retaining profits for future growth. There may be greater pressure from shareholders of public limited companies to maximise profits each year and pay out as much as possible in dividends.
Customers	Firms who accept a responsibility to their customers will be attempting to ensure that customers are happy with the product or service being supplied and following up with good after-sales service.
Suppliers	Suppliers will be concerned with receiving payment for supplies in full and on time. Firms who delay paying suppliers to help their own short-term cash flow may damage their relationship with this group of stakeholders.
Local community	Locals will be concerned with the way the firm treats its local environment and whether the firm is making a positive contribution to the local economy, perhaps by creating new jobs.
Finance providers	The major concern of lenders is whether they receive payments on time – for banks, this means that any loan repayments are made and interest payments covered.

- It is easier to attract potential employees to a firm with a good reputation.

What else?

The stakeholder concept – a way of looking at businesses as having certain responsibilities to each of their stakeholders – is not adhered to by all in business. Many continue to look no further than the traditional 'shareholder concept'. This term is used to describe the idea that businesses exist for one reason only: to serve the needs of their shareholders – in modern terms to maximise shareholder value. Do not underestimate the level to which the shareholder concept remains entrenched throughout the business world. However, the stakeholder concept is increasingly recognised as a valid way of looking at the operation of businesses.

Themes for evaluation

Stakeholder power
This is likely to be the key determinant of how much each stakeholder influences business decision making. Where a firm is reliant upon one major customer for most of its sales, that customer will be acknowledged as a major stakeholder within the business and its needs are likely to be paramount in much of the firm's decision making. On the other hand, some firms may be sufficiently powerful to ignore the needs of certain stakeholders – the UK's major supermarket chains have been regularly accused of forcing their suppliers of fruit and vegetables to sell at unreasonably low prices in order to enhance the supermarkets' profit margins.

Are shareholders *too* important to plcs?
High profile accounting scandals in 2001–2002, such as the collapse of Enron and WorldCom, highlighted this issue – these firms were doing everything in their power to achieve the things that shareholders wanted: high dividend payouts, record quarterly revenues and profits. Other stakeholder groups, such as employees or suppliers, were being ignored as the pursuit of shareholder satisfaction pushed everything else aside. Arguably many plc stakeholders are suffering to keep shareholders happy – often to the detriment of 'the public interest'.

K Key Terms

Shareholder value – the term used to describe giving shareholders what they want, generally maximising the company's share price

Social responsibility – the responsibilities that a company could be argued to have towards their different stakeholders

Stakeholder – a person/group that is affected by, or who has an effect on, the operation of a business

E Exam insight

E grade answers to questions on stakeholders tend to identify what is meant by the term and perhaps identify shareholders and the local community as stakeholders. An A grade answer would be expected, in addition to showing understanding of the term, to pick out the most important stakeholders in the specific case and identify both negative and positive effects of the firm's operations on those stakeholders.

T Test yourself

1. Explain what is meant by the term 'social responsibilities'. (3)
2. Explain what is meant by the term 'stakeholder'. (3)
3. Outline two social responsibilities that a firm may be argued to have towards its:
   a) shareholders;
   b) customers;
   c) local community. (6)
4. Explain the reasons why a firm may choose to ignore the wishes of the following stakeholder groups:
   a) local community;
   b) suppliers;
   c) customers;
   d) employees. (8)

ETHICS

What?

Ethics are the moral principles that may affect decision making. They are a set of beliefs of what is morally right and wrong. Many business decisions have ethical factors that could or should be considered. In many cases, however, managers ignore the ethical dimension to their work. Even if they do consider ethical issues, they may make a judgement that others would disagree with.

How is a firm's ethical stance determined?

Different companies tend to have different perspectives as to what is right or wrong behaviour. Some firms seem to behave in a consistently more ethical way. There are two main factors that will affect the ethics of a company: culture and individuals.

Culture

The organisation's culture (accepted norms of behaviour) will influence the way in which companies approach ethical issues. In some firms, perhaps the Coop Bank, an ethical approach becomes part of the public face and the internal workings of the business. The Coop Bank has announced proudly that it has turned down business worth £4 million, because it did not want to deal with the companies concerned (arms manufacturers etc.). Other companies may have a profit-focused culture that believes that anything within the law is acceptable, even if individuals or other companies suffer.

Individuals

The individuals involved in decision making will have their own personal views of what is and is not ethically correct. Although individuals may be encouraged by the organisational culture to go against their own ethical principles, individuals' own beliefs may lead them to take a principled stance. The term 'whistle-blower' is applied to individuals who warn of wrong-doing within a business. In many cases, such individuals have seen their personal careers harmed by their refusal to accept unethical behaviour.

Why worry about ethics?

The ethical answer to this question is that doing the correct thing morally should be vital for every person's conscience. If you are ashamed of what you do, you should find a different job. A more cynical approach is to say that 'ethics works' – in other words, that firms' long-term profitability and market standing can benefit from being seen as an ethical company.

The benefits of behaving in an ethically correct manner relate to corporate image. An improved image may well lead to:

- increased sales – some customers may only be willing to buy from firms that they believe to be behaving in an ethical way. Cosmetics that are tested on animals are a rarity now, since many firms have chosen, or been forced by consumers' actions, to stop testing on animals. Firms that gain a strong reputation as being the most ethical in their industry may actually attract more customers as a result.
- the ability to charge a price premium – many of the customers that consider the ethical stance of a company when making purchasing decisions are on relatively high incomes and are therefore able, and willing, to pay a price premium for an ethically acceptable product.
- recruiting top quality staff who may be keen to work for an ethical company – the very best staff can pick and choose which firms they work for and some may be unwilling to work for an organisation whose ethical stance contradicts their own personal views.

Why bother?

Some argue that the downside to ethical behaviour is almost always increased costs. Choosing to abandon the use of child labour may mean that a company must pay more for its supplies, whereas fitting pollution filters to factory chimneys would be a substantial one-off cost. Although these cost increases may appear prohibitive to some firms, they would also need to ask themselves what is the cost of not behaving ethically? If competitors are winning their customers as a result of conducting business in a more ethically acceptable way, the cost of ignoring ethics may, in the long run, turn out to be higher than the short-term costs of adopting a more ethically acceptable set of procedures.

Application

The value to a business of ethical behaviour is considered in the table below.

Company	Behaviour	Consequence
Nike	Using Far Eastern suppliers who used low wage, child labour	Dramatic sales decline (in the short term) and more consumer doubt about the high prices charged for Nike products
Ben & Jerry's	Paying 10% of all profits to charity	Making consumers feel warmly towards this 'homely' competitor to Haagen Dazs ice cream (N.B.: today Ben & Jerry's is part of Unilever, the huge, profit-driven multinational)
Coop Retail	Obtaining materials from 'fair trade' sources, e.g. paying higher prices to coffee growers in less developed countries	It is part of a programme to differentiate the Coop from other supermarket retailers. It should help the group survive in the face of fierce competition from Asda and Tesco

E Exam insight

Exam case studies may have quite subtle ethical problems. Examiners will be looking to see a balanced understanding of a potentially unethical decision, with the ability to understand why ethical issues are rarely black and white. Questions that ask you to weigh up the actions of a company from an ethical perspective would expect you to see both sides. Be sure to keep an open mind. If you can only see one side of an argument, i.e. the decision is clearly right or wrong, look harder for the contrasting perspective.

Do remember that individuals have different ethical stances – what you and I consider ethically correct may differ greatly. Therefore, in determining the ethics of a business, it is important to go back to *who* is making key decisions – to identify their own ethical stance, and to consider the prior record of the business in terms of ethics – largely determined by the organisation's culture. Beware of offering your own judgement outside the context of the case study that you have read in your exam. Those of you with strong views on what is and is not morally acceptable may find yourself losing evaluation marks as a result of failing to demonstrate a 'real world' appreciation of the ethics of business.

It is also worth considering that a course of action that seems ethically right in one way may actually have ethical drawbacks. Refusing to buy clothes that have been made by 'exploited', low-paid workers may put them out of a job. Similarly, a firm that makes every effort to act ethically may put its costs up to the point of making the business uncompetitive – in which case every stakeholder loses.

S Student howler

'Businesses that ignore ethics are behaving illegally.'

T Test yourself

1. a) Identify a situation that presents a business with an ethical dilemma. (2)
   b) Explain two possible courses of action open to the firm in this situation and explain why each is morally justifiable. (6)
   c) Outline why one of the courses of action in part b may actually be considered unethical. (3)
2. Outline an example of business behaviour that you believe is legally acceptable but ethically unacceptable. (3)
3. Explain the meaning of the term 'business ethics'. (3)
4. Briefly explain one recent real world example of unethical business behaviour. (3)

TECHNOLOGICAL CHANGE

What?

The natural changes occurring in technology are an external influence on the way that businesses operate. Technological changes may affect the products that firms make, the services they can offer or the way in which products and services are produced.

When?

Now, more than ever before, technological change is an issue that firms must address continually. In global markets, firms can afford to spend vast amounts developing new technologies. This means that one global player can revolutionise the technology on offer within a market place, transforming (virtually overnight) the requirements and expectations of customers in that market.

How?

Examples of technological change as applied to two different business sectors – manufacturing and service – are described below.

Manufacturing sector

New technology can develop new types of product that allow firms to create a whole new market. Apple's I-Pod, that allows thousands of music tracks to be stored on a portable playing device, has carved a significant niche in the personal stereo market as a result of Apple's new technology.

The development of new materials can allow firms to manufacture products more cheaply or to a higher quality than ever before. An innovative approach to production may allow firms to reduce costs and thus cut selling prices to levels that allow customers to buy a type of product that they had not previously been able to afford.

Service sector

New technologies may change the way in which services are offered. Many retailers are now using technology that allows sales data to be monitored by the minute and is also linked with their stock control systems to ensure greater efficiency. Meanwhile, plenty of retailers and other service providers, notably travel firms, have found that the Internet has enabled them to offer their services on-line.

Why adopt new technology?

Technological advances developed in-house can represent a significant competitive advantage. New technology can represent the heart of a firm's future strategy through approaches such as:
- the launch of an innovative product, with the price premiums such products can bring;
- the development of a brand new, far more cost effective, production process.

A technology leader such as Sony can force other firms to be followers, always struggling to keep up.

Why not?

There are a number of reasons why a particular firm may choose not to invest in buying into new technologies:
- *Lack of available finance.* The latest technology is usually expensive and many firms will be in a position where they are unable to afford to buy. Credit from suppliers or bank loans may either be unavailable or the firm may be unwilling to take the risks involved in using either of these sources of finance. The cost of the new technology will also involve installation and training of staff which will add to the initial investment cost.
- *Not crucial part to the corporate strategy.* Firms who are not attempting to produce highly innovative products may feel that new technology is unnecessary for their success. Additionally, firms operating in countries where wage costs are very low may be able to manufacture their products at a comparative cost to rivals who have invested in new production equipment.
- *Avoiding resistance to change.* As detailed in Unit 3.8, any major change is likely to meet resistance from within an organisation. This may result in a lowering of the morale of what may have been a highly motivated workforce and therefore some firms may decide to avoid introducing new production technologies designed to replace

workers, in order to maintain high levels of labour productivity.

As you have read, the introduction of new technology can carry costs as well as benefits. Evaluation may come from weighing up the applicability of the costs and benefits to the firm in question. A firm which is able to benefit significantly from the introduction of new technology may be willing to accept far more drawbacks than one for whom the benefits would be limited. Other firms will experience limited benefits from the introduction of new technology and may therefore be unwilling to take on any of the risks involved in introducing that technology.

K Key Terms

Computer aided design (CAD) – the term given to the process of using computers, rather than pen, paper and models, to design products; using a computer allows a firm to reduce the costs involved in design

Computer aided manufacturing (CAM) – a situation where computers are used to control the machinery on a production line

E Exam insight

Don't overlook the problems involved in implementing new technology. Vodafone spent over £13 billion on licences for 3G mobile phone networks, but it now seems unlikely that they will ever receive a profitable return on their investment. As with every other aspect of business, nothing is clear cut.

S Student howler

'New technology is always the key to success.'

T Test yourself

1. Outline two benefits that may arise from selling a technological breakthrough. (4)
2. Analyse the potential drawbacks of introducing new production technology. (6)
3. Explain two problems involved in launching a brand new piece of technology on the market, such as MP3 players. (6)
4. Outline two ways in which CAD may help to reduce the costs of new product development. (4)

INTEGRATED EXTERNAL INFLUENCES

The AQA specification for this unit says:

This module section comprises external business influences, which affect the decision making process on subject content given in AS modules 1 and 2. Candidates must have an awareness of how the business environment provides opportunities and imposes constraints on the pursuit of short-term and long-term objectives.

Throughout your business studies course you will have been looking at how businesses try to reach their objectives. Marketing and Finance play a big part in this. How firms manage their people and operational issues contributes to the efficiency and therefore profitability of the business. However, you must have noticed that the business does not exist in isolation. A significant impact on marketing effort is the reaction of customers and competitors. Financial issues such as cash flow management are also affected by the behaviour of creditors and debtors. A highly successful production strategy can be ruined if suppliers have problems. A natural disaster can make raw materials unavailable. External issues may influence the workforce. If prices are rising a business will be faced with a demand for higher wages.

This section looks at the background external issues that affect businesses. Although taught separately you will find that they often overlap. Interest rates may be raised or lowered because of what is happening in the economy. This will affect spending levels and so influence demand. It will also affect exchange rates, which will affect international competitiveness and costs of raw materials. The government will not only manage the economy but will also create a climate where there is fair competition and the consumer is protected. Any changes to the social climate or population can have a big impact on a business, providing both opportunities and threats.

An understanding of these external issues will help you to be aware of how these may impact on the business. Business goals can be constrained or aided by what is happening in the external environment. As you look at business problems, try to be aware of these external influences and work them into your consideration of the issues.

T Test yourself (50 marks)

1. What is a market? (2)
2. What are the characteristics of a recession? (4)
3. Who is responsible for setting the level of interest rates? (2)
4. What is the effect on consumers of a rise in interest rates? (3)
5. If the consumer price index was 116 in 2002 and 120 in 2003, what was the annual percentage increase between 2002 and 2003? (3)
6. Why may inflation be a problem for businesses? (3)
7. What laws exist to protect employees? (4)
8. Who are stakeholders? (3)
9. Explain how high unemployment may benefit businesses. (4)
10. What problems might a firm face during a period of deflation? (3)
11. What is the impact on businesses of the trend towards more one-person households? (3)
12. List two advantages and two disadvantages of electronic communication. (4)
13. What is meant by ethical behaviour? (2)
14. If the pound rose on the foreign exchange markets, what is the impact on a UK tyre manufacturer that imports its raw materials? (4)
15. Why does the Competition Commission exist? (2)
16. Explain what an oligopoly is. Give one example. (4)

Now try the following data response questions. Allow yourself 30 minutes for each one.

Data response: Rate freeze wins warm welcome from all sides

On Friday, 5 December 2003 the Bank of England announced that it was not raising interest rates. There was a chorus of approval from the City, industry and the retail sector. The Monetary Policy Committee had been expected to keep the base rate at 3.75% after raising borrowing costs by 0.25% in November.

Although the Bank opted not to play Scrooge in the run-up to Christmas, analysts believed that with the economic outlook improving it would be likely to raise rates in the New Year.

Although parts of the UK economy are growing strongly, with figures showing the service sector expanding at its fastest pace for 6 years, there are signs that growth in the housing market is moderating. The manufacturing recovery is still seen as fragile and consumer confidence is less buoyant in the pre-Christmas period.

'We are looking at very fragile consumer confidence. Consumers are becoming increasingly nervous about the strength of the economy after last month's [rate] rise', said a spokesman for the British Retail Consortium. The BRC released shop price inflation figures yesterday showing a robust 3.1% rise last month compared with the same period a year before, but the spokesman said much of the impetus came from higher food prices due to the severe weather this summer. Industry was equally relieved. The TUC was in full agreement: 'It is premature to talk about more rate rises until we can see a real manufacturing recovery is underway.'

(Source: *The Guardian*, 5 December 2003)

Questions

1. What does it mean when it says that 'manufacturing recovery is still fragile'? (3)
2. Explain how severe weather might have affected the rate of inflation. (4)
3. If the rate of interest had been increased, analyse the effect that this would have on a car retailer. (8)
4. Consumer confidence can adversely affect businesses. Why is this? Suggest and evaluate two ways in which firms could react to low consumer confidence. (10)

Data response: The Grey Pound

The 'grey market' is now seen as an increasingly attractive market, as the population lives longer and has more disposable income. The 2001 national census showed that the UK has an ageing population. For the first time the UK has more people aged over 60 than under 16. By 2020, it is predicted that there will be 25.2 million people in the UK over 50 years of age compared with 19.3 million in 1999. The Department of Trade and Industry (DTI) is encouraging businesses to recognise that the ageing population poses new opportunities and challenges for them. The age shift will open up new opportunities in the shape of extensive new markets for products and services designed to meet the needs of the older consumer. The DTI is concerned that if UK companies neglect the new market opportunities generated by global population ageing, they will run the risk of being outflanked by international competitors.

One person who was not outflanked was Sidney De Haan who set up Saga, the UK's best-known provider of services for the over-50s, in the 1950s. He started the business with a 12-bedroom hotel in Folkestone. Faced with low occupancy during the winter he had the idea of offering off-season breaks to pensioners. These included travel and three meals a day. When he started out, travel agents were not interested as they felt that pensioners had no money so he was forced to do his own marketing. The idea was a huge success. Saga now employs about 2500 people. In addition to holidays, the company offers many different services such as insurance and home shopping. Saga magazine has a readership of 2.5 million and its radio stations are estimated to have 600,000 listeners a week. There is a Saga credit card, a Saga discount telephone service, and a share dealing facility. It has also bought a cruise ship, the Caronia, that used to be owned by Cunard. Initially aimed at the over-65s, Saga now targets the over-50s. This has happened partly because people are retiring early but also because of the huge brand awareness that it has created.

Questions

1. What is meant by disposable income? (2)
2. What are the advantages and disadvantages of an ageing population? (4)
3. How can British firms ensure that international competitors do not outflank them? (5)
4. Outline another external influence on British industry and explain the opportunities and threats that this may provide. (6)
5. Evaluate Saga's success. (8)

BUSINESS START-UPS

What?

Business start-ups vary from one person operating from their bedroom (Bill Gates started Microsoft in that way) to a formal company formation, well-funded by banks and shareholders. Yet the situation facing anyone deciding to start up their own business is never comfortable. A new business faces a range of problems, many of which are common to all.

How?

Sole traders can be started up with no legal requirements. This means that all that is necessary is an entrepreneur who is willing to take the risk of starting up a business and the finance to purchase the assets necessary to commence trading.

The key issues to be considered when starting up a small business include:

- identifying an opportunity and an associated market;
- cash flow;
- sources of finance;
- building a customer base;
- location.

Identifying an opportunity and an associated market

The product or service that the entrepreneur chooses to provide must be in demand. It is crucial to identify exactly who might be interested in the particular product or service on offer and to try to ensure that there are sufficient potential customers within reach to make the idea feasible. The product itself should be differentiated in some way, as a small business attempting to compete head on with an already established firm will struggle unless they are offering something different. Hitting an untapped niche, overlooked by the major players, is frequently the key to success for a small firm.

Cash flow

Cash flow is a focus of great concern in small business start-ups. With plenty of cash needing to be spent before the business opens for trading, there will be a strain on cash flow from day one, with the entrepreneur needing to have secured enough cash to keep the business operating until cash inflows have caught up with running costs.

Sources of finance

Entrepreneurs need to find sources of finance for any small business start-up. The entrepreneur may have finance available already, perhaps through a redundancy payout or an inheritance, but they are more likely to need to find some external source of finance. Forming a private limited company and selling shares to a few associates may raise enough to start the business. Alternatively, banks may be approached with a view to securing loan capital in addition to the owner's capital. Other sources exist, such as venture capitalists or business angels.

In addition to the capital needed to buy any long-term assets necessary for running the business, the entrepreneur will need to ensure there is sufficient finance to cover any working capital requirement in the early stages of the business.

K Key Terms

Business angel – an individual who is sufficiently interested in a small business idea to be willing to invest their own money to help finance the set-up; they will often want some kind of hands-on role within the new business

Entrepreneur – a person who is willing to take the risk of starting up their own business

Venture capitalist – a firm that provides capital for small and medium sized business, usually to finance expansion, but sometimes for larger start-ups

Building a customer base

Satisfied customers are crucial. By returning to use the business over and over again, and by recommending the business to friends, they will reduce the need for marketing expenditure. The first visit from any customer is therefore vital, since the business will need to ensure that the customer is sufficiently impressed to return and perhaps spread positive publicity by word of mouth. Failure to impress customers will make the creation of a solid customer base impossible and the business will fail.

Location

The issue of location usually becomes a trade off between cost and quality. Small business start-ups will want to find a cheap location in order to minimise their fixed costs and therefore keep the break-even point as low as possible. However, cheap locations are usually cheap for a good reason and this is often because the premises are not suitable for running a business. Any start-up that relies on passing trade must ensure that the location offers the potential for picking up these customers. To simply choose the cheapest location possible is often a great mistake.

Application

Some firms need passing trade, as illustrated in the table below.

Businesses that may be able to choose the cheapest location	Businesses who may need to take on expensive premises
Manufacturers	Those reliant on impulse purchases for most of their business (e.g. newsagents)
Specialist firms that people are willing to make a special journey to visit (e.g. fancy dress hirers)	Those attempting to convey an image of high quality – they need a 'classy' location
Businesses that do not need customers to visit (Internet retailers, mail order firms)	Firms whose customers are only found in expensive locations (sandwich shops in the City of London)

Themes for evaluation

It is important to be aware that the majority of small business start-ups are not carefully planned results of feasibility studies undertaken by business graduates. In fact, most entrepreneurs have little or no business education, although they may have plenty of experience. The keys to their success will be the result of instinct. Almost everything that you learn about business studies is an aid to decision making, whether in a small or large business scenario. However, all the business theory does is to increase the chances of success, but that success can never be guaranteed. Entrepreneurs who succeed as a result of instinct and experience may be on their fourth or fifth attempt. In other words they have tried and failed three or four times before.

E Exam insight

Luck and instinct often play a key role in the success of business start-ups. Too frequently students are unwilling to recognise these points, looking hard to find theoretical reasons why small businesses have succeeded. All too often, being in the right place at the right time is the key to small business success. A balanced assessment of the reasons behind small business success or failure will weigh up the extent to which luck played a role against the extent to which traditional business theory was considered, for example the quality of market research conducted, the success of staff recruitment policies and the use of careful cash flow forecasting.

T Test yourself

1. Outline three ways that a small business start-up might have identified an opportunity. (6)
2. Explain why cash flow is so important to small business start-ups. (6)
3. Most small business start-ups have tiny marketing budgets. Identify two methods of promotion that they might use. (2)
4. Identify three common reasons why a small business start-up may fail and, for each, identify one step that can be taken to help to prevent this occurring next time. (6)

BUSINESS ORGANISATIONS

In the eyes of the law, business organisations can be classified in a number of different ways. Perhaps the most crucial feature of these different types of organisation is the liability of the owner for any debts incurred by the business. The owners of sole traders and almost all partnerships have what is known as unlimited liability; owners of both private and public limited companies have limited liability.

What?

Sole traders

A sole trader is a personal business, owned and run by one person. In law, there is no financial separation between the person and the business, so any debts incurred by the business are personal debts of the owner. The owner's personal assets can therefore be lost in order to cover debts run up by the business.

Why be a sole trader?	Why not?
Complete lack of formalities	Unlimited liability
Easy to set up	Big problems if owner is ill or away
Owner in complete control	Lack of finance (and banks may be less willing to lend to a sole trader than larger firms)

Application

Sole traders are characterised by a massive time commitment on behalf of the owner, a shortage of available sources of finance and very often confusion between personal and business issues. Sole traders frequently fail to account for their own wages, so rely on the ability of their business to produce profit in order for them to live. In the event of the business failing the owner may lose personal assets in order to satisfy the creditors of the firm (those to whom money is owed).

Partnerships

A partnership shares a key feature with sole traders – that of unlimited liability for the owners. In the case of a partnership, however, there is more than one owner of the business. The partners draw up a partnership agreement stating who owns how much of the firm, who has invested what and how much of the profit goes to each partner.

Why form a partnership?	Why not?
Extra owners share the risk	Unlimited liability
New partners can bring in extra capital	All partners are bound by one partner's actions on behalf of the business (e.g. if debts are incurred)
New partners may bring specialist skills	Potential for disagreements between partners

What next?

The next step is *incorporation*, which means that the business is given its own legal status, separate from that of its owners. This therefore means that business debts are not the owners' personal debts. As a result, the owners of a company with limited liability can only lose the money they have invested in the business.

Application of limited liability to manufacturing versus service businesses

Limited liability is vital when setting up a manufacturing firm of any size. The investments required for machinery and equipment, along with the cost of buying materials and other supplies, mean that a manufacturer may well build up substantial debts before receiving any revenue. In such cases the ability to limit the risks faced by the owners is critical to encourage them to risk setting up the firm. By contrast, many service firms can be set up relatively cheaply, with little need for substantial investment in plant and machinery.

Another what

Private limited company

A private limited company (with the letters Ltd after its name) is the simplest form of limited liability company. Its key feature, after the limited liability of its owners, is the need for the shareholders to agree to any transfer in ownership of the business' shares. This, in reality, limits the potential shareholders and therefore the potential for a private limited company to generate equity capital.

Why be Ltd?	Why not?
Owners have limited liability	Accounts must be publicly available at Companies' House
Greater scope for raising capital than sole traders/partnerships	Other formalities, such as holding an annual general meeting (AGM) must be observed
Shareholders retain control over who owns shares (unlike plcs)	Still limited potential for raising share capital

Public limited company

Public limited companies (denoted by the letters plc in the name) are companies that are allowed to sell their shares on the stock exchange. This means that these companies have the potential to raise significantly higher sums of capital through the sale of shares, meaning that, generally, plcs are the largest firms within the UK.

Why be plc?	Why not?
Access to vast amounts of capital through the stock market	Stock market demands may cause over-emphasis on short-term objectives
Enhanced reputation	Potential for takeover
Likely to find borrowing easier and cheaper	Greater administration costs, both during and after flotation

Another what next

The phrase 'divorce of ownership and control' is used to indicate that the owners of a business are not the same people that control the business on a day-to-day basis. The problem caused by the divorce of ownership and control is that those in control of the firm may pursue objectives that differ slightly from those of the owners. For example, while owners of a plc may be interested in the long-term stability of the business, the directors may be more concerned with establishing their reputation as business tycoons, by making bold take-over bids for other firms.

S Student howlers

'Johnsons Ltd could raise more money by selling more shares on the stock exchange.'

'Bilston plc will have more share capital because their share price has increased in the last 3 months.'

Risk

Crucial to the concept of limited liability (the major issue in this unit), is the idea of the risks involved in starting up in business. Limiting the liability of company owners allows those owners to take the kinds of risks that allow firms to grow and operate on a large and more efficient scale. However, limiting the liability of owners has a flip side. Companies can be formed that run up huge debts, financing the huge expense accounts of directors before going into liquidation. The result is that shareholders lose only the amount of money they originally invested, whereas creditors are left with bad debts that will never be repaid.

Short-termism in public limited companies

A charge levelled at some firms listed on the stock market is that they take decisions designed to maximise the short-term profits of the firm (thus keeping share prices high), at the cost of the long-term success of the firm.

K Key Terms

Limited liability – the liability of the owners of private and public limited companies is limited to the amount they have invested in the business

Short termism – a tendency to focus on achieving short-term objectives, often at the cost of long-term success

Unlimited liability – a situation where the owner of a business is personally liable for any debts incurred by the business

E Exam insight

Look closely at the name of the company featured in any case study. The name should provide clues as to the type of business – a private limited company features the letters Ltd, a public limited company the letters plc. Having established the type of business you're dealing with, you can then consider the implications. The protection of limited liability should imply a greater willingness to take risks.

T Test yourself

1. Explain three issues that a pair of entrepreneurs may consider when discussing whether to start up as a partnership or a private limited company. (6)
2. Identify three differences between a private and a public limited company. (3)
3. Briefly explain why you may be more likely to be ripped off by a private limited company than a partnership. (3)
4. Outline two benefits of starting up a café as a sole trader. (4)
5. List four reasons why some private limited companies choose not to become public. (4)

BUSINESS PLANNING

What?

A business plan is a document that is designed to provide enough information about a new business or venture to persuade financial backers to invest in the business.

Why?

There are three key purposes for producing a business plan:

1. *To gain finance*: The business plan can help to satisfy the need to provide detailed plans to convince potential backers to part with their cash.

2. *To clarify the idea*: The process of constructing a detailed plan will help to clear up exactly what the business will be offering, what differentiates it, and if anything has been overlooked.

3. *To monitor success*: The business plan should identify objectives and produce fairly detailed financial forecasts. Once the business is up and running, the financial plans can form the basis of a budgeting system, while the firm's success can be measured by referring to its originally stated objectives.

What's in it?

The plan itself is likely to consist of a few, fairly obvious sections, covering:

Application

In the application of business planning to different contexts there will be differences in emphasis when considering business plans for manufacturing as opposed to service sector start-ups:

- Manufacturing start-ups will focus on the details of the production equipment and machinery required. Skills of staff may well be more important than in the service sector and a greater amount of start-up capital is likely to be needed to purchase a significant number of fixed assets.
- A service sector business plan is more likely to focus on marketing elements – in particular in stressing a unique selling point to the service. Although start-up costs for a service sector enterprise are likely to be lower than those for a manufacturer, the financial section of the plan remains crucial.

Section	Content
Introduction	A brief description of the business idea and why it should be a success. This should include a brief account of the market
Personal information	Information about the entrepreneurs' qualifications, experience skills and financial position
Objectives	A statement of what the business should achieve, possibly only in the first year, but perhaps in the medium term
Marketing plan	Should cover the answers to questions such as: Who are the customers? Who are the competitors? How big is our market? What is special about our product/service? What will our marketing strategy be?
Production plan	This should cover the practical aspects of: What do we need? Where can we get it? And who will do which tasks and when, both in the set-up period and once the business has opened
Financial plan	The section of most interest to finance providers is likely to include a cash flow forecast, a break-even calculation and information on the sources of finance and what capital/collateral is being offered by the owners

What it does and doesn't do

A business plan DOES	A business plan DOESN'T
Boost chances of success because of the emphasis on planning for the future	Guarantee success
Involve detailed financial forecasts	Mean that the forecasts will be accurate
Form the basis of a budgeting system	Work as the basis of a budgeting system unless it allows for flexibility
Take a significant amount of time and effort to create	Mean a waste of time – planning may throw up previously unforeseen problems
Mean nothing if financial data is over-optimistically estimated	(Usually) fool a finance provider to fund a bad idea

Application

Banks and venture capitalists are unlikely to even offer an appointment without a business plan, let alone offer finance. Small scale start-ups where friends and family are providing the finance may be far more likely to provide cash without a formal business plan. Start-ups funded by redundancy payouts are also often able to avoid the process of constructing a business plan. Entrepreneurs who do not construct a thorough business plan may find it harder to make the business a success, having not been through the planning process.

Themes for evaluation

Does a business plan guarantee success?
No, there are too many uncontrollable external factors such as competition and changing consumer tastes. The plan is no guarantee, but it increases the chance of success.

Is there any point in spending time constructing a business plan when much of it is based on guesswork?
As suggested above, planning does help to increase the chances of success. A carefully constructed plan will take time, effort and research but should flag up potential problems so that these can be planned for.

K Key Terms

Collateral – assets used to provide security on a loan, e.g. an entrepreneur may use their home as collateral for a business start-up loan

Entrepreneur – a risk taker; the person willing to put in the time, effort and money to set up and run their own business

E Exam insight

Most questions relating to business planning will be evaluative questions requiring some form of judgement as to the merits of the planning process. All too often answers can be one-sided, either concentrating on the positives of planning (e.g. helps to ensure success etc.) or on the limitations of planning. In reality, business planning is a useful process with accepted limitations. Effective judgements will consider the validity of the plan in question. This will be dependent upon a number of factors, including:

- the experience of the person constructing the plan and their market knowledge;
- the time and care that has gone into the research upon which the plan is based;
- the volatility of the market in which the business will be operating.

S Student howlers

'The business plan can ensure that profit will be made once the business has started.'
'The business plan shows how the product is going to be marketed. The main sections will cover price, product, place and promotion.'

T Test yourself

1. Explain two constraints that a business plan might help to overcome and two constraints that a business plan might do little to help with for a small clothes shop. (8)
2. Briefly explain to a friend thinking of starting a small restaurant, why a business plan should be constructed before the restaurant is opened. (5)
3. Identify five key sections of a business plan. (5)
4. Identify two benefits of referring to an original business plan after 1 year's trading. (2)

CORPORATE AIMS, MISSION AND CULTURE

Corporate aims

What?

Corporate aims are the general ambitions of an organisation: what it hopes to achieve in the long term.

Why?

The purpose of a set of corporate aims is to ensure that everyone within the organisation can work together towards achieving the same long-term outcomes. An organisation that is able to instill a shared sense of purpose throughout the workforce is likely to stand a far greater chance of success.

Mission

What?

Mission is the word used to describe the shared sense of purpose within an organisation. A mission fundamentally explains why a business exists. Going beyond a simple notion of making a profit, a sense of mission indicates a desire to do something, such as making the best ice cream in the world, or providing the very highest quality of IT training in the UK. A powerful sense of mission may drive the business on to do extraordinary things.

Why?

Any group of people that wants to achieve the same thing is far more likely to succeed than a group of individuals with differing goals. Mission provides coordination that cannot be actively achieved simply by telling people what to do. Mission implies that staff want to achieve – their motivation to achieve the firm's objectives comes from within, from being part of a group of people all trying to achieve the same aims.

How?

The aims of an organisation are likely to emerge from the mission of the founders. The aims should be a way of clarifying the purpose of the organisation. They may produce a mission statement – a simple, brief statement that sums up the sense of purpose they are trying to instill in the organisation.

Who?

A sense of mission often stems from the founders of an organisation, but as companies expand, the new recruits may dilute the sense of purpose. For example, the sandwich business 'Pret-a-Manger' enjoyed huge success in the 1990s, driven on by a mission to provide freshly made, high-quality food. When the business expanded too rapidly in 2001–2003, it struggled to maintain the commitment among its staff.

Among larger firms it is not always clear whether the mission is a truly shared sense of purpose or a hollow statement made by the senior managers. Careful recruitment, probably placing attitudes above skills in the recruitment decision, may allow a firm to grow while retaining a clearly shared mission. If staff are recruited who already believe in the merits of the firm's existing mission, that sense of purpose will filter down throughout the organisation.

Culture

What?

The accepted behavioural norms found within an organization: 'the way we do things round here'.

How?

An organisation's culture should provide a clear reflection of the firm's mission. If the culture is dominated by a desire to achieve the aims of the organisation, something is working well within that firm. If all staff expect to behave in a way that will help the firm to achieve its mission, the culture of the organisation will be a strong unifying force. However, if the mission has become unclear or if staff fail to 'buy into' the firm's mission, a culture may develop that holds the firm back from achieving its aims.

Fig. 6.4A: How a mission should work

It may seem straightforward for management to instill a shared sense of purpose into their staff, yet few firms seem to succeed. This failing is largely due to diseconomies of scale and ineffective people management. Zeal is far easier to find in smaller organisations, and this helps to explain an increasing desire among large firms to devolve power down to smaller business units. Poor management may mean that staff feel unconcerned with the mission of the whole firm.

E Exam insight

While reading any case study, you should be able to get a feeling for the aims of the business. It should also be possible to form an impression of how effectively the firm has managed to instill its mission in its staff. Try to ensure that you are then able to assess the effect that the resulting culture has on the firm's performance.

S Student howler

'A clearly stated set of aims will ensure that everyone within the business shares the same mission.'

T Test yourself

1. Outline two ways in which company culture may result in increased costs. (4)
2. Analyse the benefits of creating a genuine sense of mission within an organisation. (5)
3. Outline the reasons why staff within a small business are more likely to understand and identify with the firm's mission than those in a larger organisation. (3)
4. Coca-Cola's one-time mission was to ensure that their product was 'within an arm's length of desire', and IBM once declared their mission as being 'to put a PC on every desk'. Evaluate the extent to which such mission statements are likely to enhance the performance of all staff within these organisations. (8)

Objectives

What?

An objective is a specific measurable target that an organisation plans to achieve within a given timescale. To be effective, an objective must be based upon the firm's aims, be challenging and SMART:

Specific, i.e. precisely worded;

Measurable, i.e. have a quantitative target, such as to achieve a 20% market share;

Agreed between senior managers and the executive responsible for achieving the goal;

Realistic, so that the executive and the workforce believe it could be achieved;

Time-specific, e.g. 20% market share *by the end of next year*.

Why?

The objectives should give the organisation a clearer sense of purpose. The key benefits of a set of clear objectives are:
* Everyone working in the same direction;
* Targets to aim for;
* Translate vague targets (aims) into achievable goals for all within the organisation;
* A yardstick against which performance can be measured.

Strategy

What?

A strategy is a medium to long-term plan for achieving a firm's objectives.

How?

Before a strategy can be devised, an audit (examination) of the firm's current position needs to take place. The strategy is the plan for moving from 'where we are' to 'where we need to be' and therefore it is important to firmly establish the firm's current position. Firstly, an external audit should be carried out.

External audit

What?

This involves analysing a range of factors external to the business that will affect its current and future performance. The external audit may follow a three-stage process:

Analysing the broad external environment within which the firm will operate, using a PEST analysis

⇩

Analysing the particular market(s) in which the firm is selling

⇩

Analysing the products within those markets

Fig. 6.5A: **Three steps to external auditing**

Stage 1

* PEST analysis is a framework for analysing the external environment facing an organisation. The letters stand for Political, Economic, Social and Technological.
* Each of the letters acts as a prompt to analyse the external influences affecting the business. Both opportunities and threats are likely to emerge from an analysis of these factors.
* The framework can be used by any organisation. Below is just one possible example of application, using a summary of potential key factors for a leisure centre:

P	Government policies relating to encouraging exercise Increased government support for local authority leisure facilities
E	Increasing disposable incomes Low levels of unemployment
S	Obese population Gyms becoming 'trendier'
T	High tech gym equipment comes onto the market Invention of new slimming foods reduce demand for 'fight the flab' exercise

Stage 2

This involves an analysis of the markets in which the firm is currently operating, including tracking figures for market size, relative market shares and studying market growth rates. Any ongoing trends within the market should also be identified, including a careful study of the performance of any new products recently launched in the market.

Stage 3

The competitive environment should be studied, i.e. direct competitors should be analysed in depth. This analysis will cover the whole range of operating issues for those rivals, from a careful study of their marketing methods, through financial analysis of their strengths (or weaknesses) to an estimation of their productive capabilities.

What's next?

Having conducted a thorough external audit, the firm should link the results of an internal audit of the firm's major strengths and weaknesses to create a SWOT analysis. SWOT is a framework for conducting an overall audit of the company, based on identifying the key corporate Strengths, Weaknesses, Opportunities and Threats. The opportunities and threats identified for the SWOT will be external issues, identified by the process of conducting the external audit.

Why? (for both or rather the whole process)

In order to create a coherent plan that will achieve the firm's stated objectives, managers must understand fully the situation in which they are operating. The process of carefully studying the external factors affecting the strategy will help focus the plan on overcoming potential hazards and making the most of the opportunities available.

The best plans go wrong, for a vast range of different reasons. Whether or not a strategy works is down to implementation. If this is to be right, all functions within the organisation must be working together effectively – the corporate objectives should ensure that everyone is pulling in the right direction. However, it would be foolish to ever suggest that achieving objectives will be straightforward. It should also be remembered that during the lifetime of a strategy both internal and external factors may change dramatically, damaging a company's performance. This may necessitate a change in strategy or a short-term tactical response.

K Key Terms

PEST – a framework used for analysing the external conditions faced by a firm

SWOT – an analytical framework used to carry out a strategic analysis of a firm's current position

Tactics – short-term, immediate measures that did not feature in the original strategy that are used as a swift response to an unexpected (usually external) change

E Exam insight

Many students fail to clarify the meaning of objectives and strategy, treating the two as if they were one word – 'objectivesandstrategy'. Make sure to distinguish clearly between aims and objectives, then again between objectives and strategy.

S Student howler

'A really well-run company will devise a new strategy for each week, to ensure they stay up to date with changes in the market.'

T Test yourself

1. Identify and explain three possible features of a strategy devised by an ice cream manufacturer pursuing an objective of sales growth. (6)
2. Match the objective with the likely strategic measure: (3)

Objective	Strategic measure
Break-even	spend heavily on research and development
Grow	reduce costs to a minimum
Diversify	broaden distribution levels

3. Identify one current example of a firm for whom:
   — Brand image is a strength;
   — Brand image is a weakness;
   — Economic growth represents an opportunity;
   — New laws represent a threat;
   — The arrival of a major new competitor represents a threat;
   — An excellent distribution network is a strength;
   — A lack of available finance is a weakness. (7)
4. Thinking about Rover cars, identify one current issue that belongs under each letter of a PEST analysis. (4)

EXAM SKILLS

The exam is about your ability to use the syllabus (business theory) to answer questions in a way that is applied to the context and shows some judgement.

There are several things that will help you to do this.

1. Read and understand the material

If your exam has a pre-release case study you need to have worked on this in order to give yourself the best chance of success.

When presented with data response or case study material for the first time in the exam, you need to prepare yourself. You should read through the material very carefully, and spend some time analysing any numerical or graphical information. Only then should you read the questions.

If you do not understand the business story you could waste precious marks by failing to apply your answer to the context, or answering the wrong question.

2. Make sure you understand the issues

You need to ask yourself – What sort of business is it?:
* Large or small?
* Plc or private company?
* Manufacturer, retailer or in the service industry?
* What are its objectives?
* Do a quick SWOT analysis. Think about the firm's strengths, weaknesses, opportunities and threats.

In this way you will get a picture of the business and its issues, which will help you to focus your answer on the business (application).

3. Read the questions

Having understood the material, read through the questions.

Identify the key words in the question
* Key '*subject*' words such as price, competitors, and stakeholders are important. This is what the question is about.

* Key '*doing*' words such as describe, analyse, discuss, and evaluate will tell you what you need to do. Anything involving discussion or evaluation or a decision about a situation *always* means that here are marks for *evaluation* in the mark scheme.
* Don't forget the *little* words, such as the difference between 'a business' (you can write about any one) and 'the business', i.e. the one in question. Or the difference between being asked 'how' or 'why' the business is facing problems. These little words are often ignored and often alter the meaning of the question. Look out for clues that relate the question to a point in time or to something that the business has done (before/after).

Look at the marks allocated
* Generally it is fair to assume that 2-mark answers will require a direct response based on knowledge. This is a *content* or *knowledge* mark.
* For a 4-mark answer you will often be expected to show your *knowledge* of the subject but also to put your answer in the context of the case study. This is known as *application*, e.g. you may be asked about sources of finance for the business in the case study. You would give the options available but only those relevant to the business in question. So you might say: 'For a *small business such as this* the options are limited to … etc.'
* For more than 4 marks you are likely to be expected to include *analysis* and *evaluation*.

4. Plan your answers

This is helpful for longer answers as it will help you to keep your answer focused on the question. Students often start off answering the right question but wander off the subject and get lost. Use a spider diagram to stimulate your ideas. Then organise these ideas into a few simple headings. This will remind you of what to say next. Don't worry that it is a waste of time. What really is a waste of time is a long rambling answer that has lost the plot!

5. Plan your time

Try to allocate your time evenly between the marks awarded per answer, e.g. a mark a minute. Spend more time on higher mark answers. If during the exam you find that you are spending a lot of time on one question, the chances are you have started to ramble. So leave that answer, leave some space, go onto the next question and come back to it if you have time.

6. Boost your marks

In most exams you will be awarded more marks for the depth of your answer. AQA papers are marked using a system that awards marks for content, application, analysis and evaluation.

What is content?

Content is about knowledge. Do not be afraid to state the obvious. It often helps to start your answer with a definition. In AQA mark schemes you cannot be awarded any analysis, application or evaluation marks if you have not shown any signs that you know the subject matter. You would be amazed how many students attempt to answer a question without this fundamental basis of knowledge.

What is application?

Application is about applying the knowledge/subject matter to the situation. You need to concentrate on how the subject knowledge is *relevant* to the situation in the case study. If asked about sales promotion think about what would work for *this* business in *its* particular competitive situation. Application is about applying theory to different situations. If all you do is to talk about the theory you will only be awarded content marks.

Another way to demonstrate application is by comparing the situation in the case study to a real life situation.

What is analysis?

Analysis marks will only be awarded if the answer is based on correct and relevant theory used in the context of the question. General answers, say about motivation issues, will get some but not many marks. You need to show which motivation theory is relevant to this business or its present situation and *why*.

Analysis explores the issues. It asks 'why?'. It says 'however' or 'but'. Or you might use 'if' or 'in some cases'. For example:

- 'Cash flow forecasts are a useful business tool – *however* as they are estimates they are only as good as the figures they are based on.'
- 'Just-in-time methods of stock control are good *because*…. *however* they may also cause difficulties for the business such as …'

What is evaluation?

Evaluation is about judgement. If you are asked to compare two possibilities for the business then evaluation is easier. You should *analyse* the two options and then make a judgement about why one is better than the other *for this business*.

Your judgement should be based on the arguments that you have put forward and should always relate to the business in question.

7. Do not forget the QOL

On every A level paper that has a written component, marks are awarded for quality of language (QOL). These few marks should not be ignored! That one extra QOL mark might just tip you into the higher grade. The other reason to give QOL some thought is that well-written work is more likely to make and analyse points with clarity. A level marking is positive marking, which means that the examiner is looking for good points. If your work is clear and easy to follow it will be so much easier to award those marks.

QOL scores can be improved by:

- Using sentences and paragraphs. Try to keep sentences short. Avoid using a lot of 'ands' and 'buts' in a sentence. Use a paragraph to explain one idea.

- Sort out the spelling. If you don't know the difference between 'there' and 'their', that's poor. In Business Studies, though, we care even more about whether you can spell 'lose', 'strategy', 'opportunity' and 'morale'.

AQA BUS 1

This exam is a 60 minute paper consisting of two data response questions, one mainly marketing and one mainly finance. Typically, the data will be a short extract from a newspaper article, perhaps including a table of figures or a graph. Each data response question will start with a question that only tests knowledge, before moving onto questions that also test application, then application and analysis and a final question (worth 9–10 marks) that will additionally test evaluation.

On this paper, 33% of the marks are for your knowledge of business. A further 33% are for your ability to apply your answers to the specific business that the question is about. Most candidates will get most of the marks available for knowledge. Few, however, get as many as half the application marks. Follow the exam rules below, and you will be able to do much better. (Note that the skill of analysis is worth 24% of the marks and evaluation carries 10%.)

Exam rules

- With 50 marks for a 60 minute paper, timing is easy – 1 minute per mark with 5 minutes of reading time for each of the two pieces of data.
- As you read through the data, ask yourself 2 questions:
  1. What is special (or even unique) about this market?
  2. What is special about this company/ business?
  Then jot down your thoughts on the exam paper. Doing this will help you apply your answers to *this particular* business context.
- Be harsh with your timings – no more than two sentences for a 2-mark question – don't fall into the trap of writing half a page for the first little 2-mark question. It is vital that you leave enough time to answer the two large final parts of each question.
- Know the trigger words that will be used and what skills they need you to demonstrate. You only need to evaluate on the final part of each data response question. Don't waste time drawing conclusions to other questions.

Trigger words requiring ANALYSIS (in addition to knowledge and application)	Trigger words requiring EVALUATION (in addition to knowledge, application and analysis)
Analyse	Evaluate
Examine	Discuss
Explain why	To what extent

- If there's a business term in the question, quickly define it at the start of your answer.* With content marks available on every question, they will often be offered for demonstrating a good understanding of the term in the question. Pick up all the content marks in your first line. You can also not be credited with any marks for other skills if you fail to score any content marks on a question.

Calculations

There will be calculations on BUS 1. It is important to prepare effectively for these by practising the types of calculation that may arise, including profit and contribution calculations, calculations involving price and income elasticity, cash flow, budget variances and break-even. These calculations can often bring substantial marks, in the context of a 50-mark paper. However, a warning is needed. If, for some reason, you are struggling with the calculations be strict with your time allocation and move on to the next question.

*The most valuable companion to your studies is the *Complete A–Z Business Studies Handbook*, 4th edn, by Lines, Marcousé and Martin, published by Hodder & Stoughton Educational in 2003. This provides you with short, sharp definitions of terms, clear explanations and revision word lists for each of the Units. For example there is a list of Top 30 Marketing terms for AQA AS level, and Top 20 Finance terms for AQA AS.

In addition make sure to:

- Note down any formulae that you have used in your workings. There are knowledge marks available on these questions simply for showing that you know the formula. So write down the formula for the break-even point – even if you can't do the calculation.
- When calculating, label the figures you are writing down so that the examiner can follow your logic. Business Studies examiners apply the own figure rule (OFR) which allows them to give plenty of marks to a wrong answer if you made just one or two little mistakes.

Example:

Calculate the margin of safety for a firm selling 3000 units, whose variable cost per unit is £5, price is £10 and fixed costs are £10,000. (4 marks)

The mark scheme may look like this:

Content (2 marks)

(2 marks) Good understanding of the concept of break-even (both formulae shown).

(1 mark) Some understanding of the concept of break-even (one formula shown).

Application (2 marks)

(2 marks) Concepts correctly applied in the context (correct safety margin calculated).

(1 mark) Some attempt to apply concepts in the context.

Correct answer (4 marks):

Break-even   = fixed costs/contribution per unit
                = £10,000/(£10 – £5)
                = 2000 units

Safety margin = current output – breakeven output
                = 3000 – 2000 = 1000 units

But this wrong answer would still get 3 marks

Break-even   = fixed costs/contribution per unit
                = £10,000/(£10 – £6)
                = 2500 units

Safety margin = current output – breakeven output
                = 3000 – 2500 = 500 units

However this answer scores zero:

Safety margin = 500 units

With grade boundaries usually 3 marks apart, showing workings could be worth a B rather than a C.

Final advice – Make sure you arrive fully equipped

A ruler, pencil and rubber will be useful if you're required to draw a break-even chart, whereas a calculator will be vital (using your phone will not be allowed). More important than anything else, come prepared with a thorough knowledge of the subject content to be tested on the BUS 1 paper and a working knowledge of the skills that you will be required to demonstrate.

AQA BUS 2 AND BUS 3

The AQA BUS 2 and BUS 3 exams are both based on a pre-issued case study. One case study provides the stimulus material for both BUS 2 and BUS 3 and therefore the case study is a long one covering both people and operations management (Unit 2) and external influences and objectives and strategy (Unit 3). Your exam performance will be dependent on three main factors:

1. Your knowledge of the subject content;
2. Your knowledge of the exam skills tested by all of your business studies exams;
3. Your ability to apply your knowledge to the context of the case study with which you are issued.

Knowledge of the subject content is the groundwork of the whole subject. Using this revision guide, ensure that you understand all the content of the subject's specification. This can be accessed through the AQA website: www.aqa.org.uk. The specification contains a unit-by-unit breakdown of what you need to know for your exams – BUS 2 tests Unit 2, BUS 3 tests Unit 3.

Knowledge of the exam skills to be tested will enable you to understand exactly what you should be showing in the answer to each question. Ensure that you feel confident in understanding what each of the skills is looking for by using Unit 7.1.

Your ability to apply your knowledge to the case study will be largely determined by how well you have prepared for the exam in advance. You should have been given your pre-released copy of the case study in time to spend a couple of weeks working with the case. This will enable you to understand and reflect on the issues faced by the business. You need to be familiar with the firm detailed in the case study in order to avoid wasting time in the exam searching through to check details you need to use in your answers. However, your acquaintance with the business in the case must run deeper than this if you are to succeed in scoring well on application and evaluation marks. You need to understand the firm's current position and the issues it faces as it prepares for the future. Remember that BUS 2 will focus on the people and operations management issues faced by the firm, while BUS 3 will examine the external influences the firm faces along with the strategic choices it has made and now faces.

Techniques for getting to know the firm in the case study

To gain a complete picture of the position in which the firm finds itself, a series of issues need to be examined, that can be best remembered by using the acronym ACCESS.

- *Assets*: What are the firm's major assets? That doesn't just mean physical assets. What are the key areas where this company may have a competitive advantage over its rivals. Examples may include well-trained, experienced staff or a genuine sense of mission throughout the business. An excellent research and development department could represent a strength in terms of operations management, or perhaps the firm has marketing strengths such as an excellent distribution network or a USP. Awareness of these assets will allow you to focus on what the firm does well whenever you are offering advice on what they should do next.

- *Competition*: Is the firm's market highly competitive, with many small firms all competing equally, perhaps using price as a key point of competition? If this is the case, costs of production will be a crucial issue for the firm. However, if the market is less competitive, or the key area for competition is quality rather than price, quality assurance may be more important than reduction of unit costs.

- *Customers*: Consideration of who the firm is selling to will allow you to write sensibly about what the business is trying to achieve. If customers are other businesses, then the firm will operate quite differently from the approach taken by manufacturers of consumer goods. Meanwhile, you should also assess where the power lies in negotiations between this firm and its customers (and indeed suppliers). Is the company so big as to be able to dictate terms to its customers or suppliers? Or are you reading about a small firm at the mercy of a few major customers?

- *Environment*: A thorough analysis of the external factors facing the firm will allow the identification of any major external constraints or opportunities. At this point you should consider carefully the economic data provided in the case study to assess whether economic forecasts represent a source of opportunities or constraints for the firm. Then consider the social and technological factors affecting the business.

- *Stakeholders*: Identify the firm's stakeholders and exactly what they want from the business. Then go on to consider which of the firm's stakeholders seem to have the greatest influence over the firm's decision making. This will allow you to assess whether the firm seems to accept that it should meet wider social responsibilities and, if so, how well the firm is meeting them.
- *Service/product*: Careful consideration of exactly what the firm is selling can allow you to gain an insight that will be helpful in your exam. A firm selling PVC windows is not just selling windows, it is selling the service of installation. So the politeness and efficiency of installation staff may be just as important to customers as the windows themselves. You should also form a judgement on whether the product or service offered by this firm is income elastic and link this to the economic data provided in the case to help make some assessment of what is likely to happen to sales in the future. An estimate of price elasticity will enable you to make effective suggestions relating to the firm's overall strategy. This will help especially on BUS 3.

Format of the exams

You will not be able to take your pre-released copy of the case study into exams. For each paper you will be issued with a clean copy of exactly the same case study.

You have 60 minutes to answer 50 marks' worth of questions. This means you have 10 minutes of thinking time and time to check back to specific details of the case study that you need to help you to answer the questions you have been set.

As with BUS 1, timing is vital, so be strict with yourself to make sure that you have sufficient time to

have a proper go at each of the questions on the paper.

You will be presented with two evaluation questions on each paper, each worth 15 marks, with 3 for knowledge, 3 for application, 4 for analysis and 5 for evaluation. It is therefore crucial that you take care to structure your answer appropriately to enable you to trigger evaluation marks in a conclusion of some kind.

Perhaps surprisingly, candidates struggle to gain application marks on exam papers that relate to a familiar, pre-released case study. Make sure to focus on answering all questions about the company detailed in the case study. Do not write generalised answers applicable to any business.

E Exam insight – a final word of warning

Make sure you do *not*:

- Mix your answers together, putting too much about people in questions about external influences; keep the Unit 2 and Unit 3 material separate in your mind.
- Waffle! Avoid this by starting answers by defining the key term in the question.

Although practice questions based on the case study may provide a useful way of preparing for this exam, do not try to predict what questions are going to come up. The case study is big so that the entire content of the subject's Units 2 and 3 can be tested so you cannot tell from reading the case study what the questions will be – you must revise the whole of each unit. Another trap that some students fall into with pre-released case studies is to guess questions that may come up and then learn their answers. Even if a similar question comes up, the risk is that your answer will not focus well enough on the actual question set. Far better to wait until the exam itself before deciding what your answers will be.

REVISION CHECKLISTS

Revision checklist for Unit 1. Can you?

	Very well	OK	No
Fill in gaps in a cash flow forecast, including cumulative cash, and explain how to improve a poor cash position			
Distinguish between internal and external sources of finance, and identify sources suitable for short-term and long-term needs			
Distinguish between cash flow and profit (if you say yes, you're kidding yourself; Marcouse always says it took him 2 years to really understand it)			
Calculate profit accurately, using revenue, fixed costs and variable costs; also calculate changes in revenue and in profit			
Draw, understand and interpret a break-even chart; indicate the break-even point, the safety margin and profit; calculate the break-even point			
Explain in some detail the purpose of budgets; problems of setting budgets and how to analyse variances between budgeted and actual data			
Explain the meaning and value of zero budgeting			
Explain the value of, and drawbacks to, cost and profit centres			
Distinguish clearly between marketing objectives, strategy and tactics; explain the value of setting clear objectives and strategies			
Calculate, understand and interpret data relating to market size (volume and value), market trends and market share			
Understand the importance of market research in keeping the business in touch with customers; outline the meaning of desk v field, qualitative v quantitative, random v quota; be aware of causes of bias in research			
Show a written understanding of statistical significance, i.e. the desire by research firms to provide data with a 95% confidence level			
Understand product life cycles (including relationship to cash flow and capacity utilisation) and extension strategies; full knowledge of Boston Matrix			
Distinguish between niche and mass marketing and between product differentiation and USPs			
Calculate, understand and write with conviction about price and income elasticities; able to show the effect on demand and profit of a change in price or income; know why products have the elasticities they have			
Full understanding of the marketing mix as a way to implement a firm's marketing strategy			
Good knowledge of pricing strategies, methods and tactics, and the circumstances in which different approaches are relevant			
Understand the importance to firms of the right distribution channels, and the difficulty new firms find in gaining distribution			
Recognise the value of good product design in adding value to a product or brand, thereby increasing its differentiation and lowering price elasticity			
See how marketing problems or opportunities can affect (and be affected by) financial issues such as cash flow			

Revision checklist for Unit 2. Can you?

	Very well	OK	No
Calculate, interpret and explain productivity figures, and their implications for firms		✓	✓
Explain the theories of Taylor, Mayo, Maslow and Herzberg, and use them to analyse the causes and effects of motivation within a workforce		✓	✓
Outline how motivation theory can be put into practice, through job enrichment, enlargement, empowerment and teamworking			✓
Assess the leadership style within a business, using McGregor's theory X and theory Y, and/or the scale from autocratic to laissez-faire styles			✓
Understand the theory and practice of Human Resource Management, especially workforce planning. Relate this to financial incentives and training			✓
Understand the complexities of management hierarchy, and the difficulties of getting the right balance between span of control and layers of hierarchy			✓
Distinguish between: delegation and consultation; functional v matrix management; accountability and responsibility; centralisation and decentralisation			✓
Understand organisational culture, how it differs in large and small firms, and how hard it can be to change an established culture			✓
See the purpose of management by objectives, and the links between MBO and leadership style, plus MBO and financial systems such as profit centres			✓
Distinguish between job, batch and flow production, explaining when each one is appropriate, and the links to productivity, motivation and HRM			✓
Define economies and diseconomies of scale, showing a full understanding of the difficulty of achieving them, e.g. bulk buying means excessive stock levels			✓
Understand how underutilised capacity causes high fixed costs per unit (and therefore average unit costs); explain rationalisation and subcontracting			✓
Full understanding of stock control, both in text and in graphs; can link with working capital and can analyse using the concept of opportunity cost			✓
Full understanding of quality management, whether through the philosophy of TQM, or methods such as quality assurance (BS5750) or inspection			✓
Good understanding of lean production, and how it links with JIT, time-based management and Kaizen			✓
Can see how lean production (and TQM) require excellent underlying people management, i.e. good leadership, trust and a motivated, involved staff			✓
Recognise that time-based management (especially simultaneous engineering) can create competitive advantage by first mover advantage			✓
Understand the philosophy of Kaizen (continuous improvement) from the bottom up, rather than dramatic change imposed from the top			✓
Recognise the benefits and drawbacks of cell production, both in manufacturing and in service business contexts			✓
Acknowledge that effective operations can come from getting the small things right, e.g. stock management in a shop; committed staff can do this			✓

Revision checklist for Unit 3. Can you?

	Very well	OK	No
Distinguish clearly between corporate aims, objectives and strategies; see how they are related to each other; see the need for agreed aims			
See the wide significance of a firm's commitment to long-term or short-term objectives, e.g. the impact on ethical behaviour and decision making			
Understand the implications of the main business objectives: profit, growth, diversification and market standing			
See how a business strategy can be based upon a SWOT analysis to assess internal strengths and weaknesses and external opportunities and threats			
Know the conflicting and common aims of different stakeholders, e.g. owners, managers, employees, customers and suppliers			
Recognise the difficulties and the attractions of starting your own business; the role of the entrepreneur, including the skills and qualities needed			
See how to identify a business opportunity, how to research it, protect it (patents etc.) and market it			
Discuss the suitability of different organisational structures (including implications of limited v unlimited liability)			
Understand problems entrepreneurs have in building a one-person business into a managed company; flotation, and divorce of ownership and control			
Recognise the practical problems in start-ups, especially building a customer base, but also location and raising finance (helped by a good business plan)			
Learn to assess the market in which a firm operates, e.g. fiercely competitive, to judge how the firm should react to different situations			
Distinguish between: excess capacity and capacity shortage; fair v unfair competition			
Understand the impact upon different firms of changes in interest rates (effect on consumer spending; business confidence and business overheads)			
Understand the impact on different firms of changes in the exchange rate, e.g. effect on exporters and importers of £ up or £ down			
Understand the impact on different firms of changes in the rate of inflation (at low levels, the impact may be little or nothing); NB also: deflation and CPI			
Understand the impact on firms (and their impact upon) unemployment; distinguish structural from cyclical unemployment, allowing for local impact			
Recognise that the business cycle means that recessions will happen, though no-one knows quite when; see the implications for business strategy			
Understand why some want government to adopt a minimal, laissez-faire approach to business, while others believe laws and regulations are essential			
Understand that ethics are not a way to make money, but place morality above profit maximisation; see why this approach may not be possible in plcs			
Recognise the way that technological change can transform markets and the businesses that operate within them; see the implications for staff and HRM			

ANSWERS

Section 1: Marketing

UNIT 1.1

Student howlers

1. All companies need marketing. The process is more complicated for large businesses but for all firms it is essential that they know their market and how best to sell their products. 2. Advertising is only part of the process of selling products. For advertising to help to sell the products the business needs to know who to aim the advertising at and what advertising is most effective. This requires market knowledge. Advertising cannot sell the wrong product to the wrong people in the wrong place.

Test yourself

1. Understanding all aspects of the market, the size of the market, the activities of any competitors and the behaviour of customers. 2. If a firm is to sell its products it needs to know about the market that it is operating in. If it does not have this knowledge it may be very difficult to sell the product 3. Marketing will only be successful if it is part of an overall company strategy. Production and distribution need to be fully involved in any marketing campaign to ensure that the product is available. Finance may be required to fund a marketing programme and the commitment of management and workers is essential to ensure the success of marketing activity. 4. It is the goal set for the marketing department. It may be, for example, to increase market share or to expand target markets. 5. It faces fierce competition from rivals such as Nestlé, so it will not be easy. Cadbury's may relaunch the product perhaps with design or packaging modifications. It may target a different market segment. Or it may conduct an aggressive marketing campaign with price reductions or special offers. 6. The unethical aspect is persuading them to buy products that will make them fat, if they buy/eat too many. It is the same issue as advertising alcohol: fun to consume moderately, dangerous if consumed to excess.

UNIT 1.2

Student howlers

1. Marketing objectives cover the whole range of a company's marketing activity, not just capturing market share. The objectives could be to become the best known brand or to introduce the product to a new market segment. 2. Targets and objectives are the same thing so there seems to be some confusion here. The student may have been trying to say that the firm needs good strategies if they are to achieve their objectives. They may also have been trying to say that the objectives must be clear if they are to be achieved.

Test yourself

1. Objectives give the business a clear sense of direction. They spell out what the business is aiming to achieve. 2. Increasing product differentiation, growth, innovation. 3. Making the product stand out from its rivals. This may be by its design or quality or brand recognition. 4. Internal constraints – financial, personnel, market standing; External constraints – competition, customers, the economy. 5. In order to set realistic objectives the firm needs to understand its market. It needs to know its place in that market and how its customers and competitors may react to marketing strategies.

UNIT 1.3

Student howlers

1. Market share is important for the business but it is not the only consideration. The business may be better off selling less and getting a better return from those sales. Some businesses do very well by staying small but focused. Some firms do very well in a small but exclusive market. A local business may serve its local customers and be very profitable. 2. Market research is always important for firms. Every firm needs to understand its market. A successful firm needs to understand why it is successful so that it can ensure that it continues to do the right thing.

Test yourself

1. By volume (quantity of a particular good) and by value (value of sales of those goods). 2. a) Saga Holidays – holidays for the over 50s, the leisure market; b) Volvic Water – the mineral water market, the soft drinks market; c) British Gas – gas supply to industrial and consumer markets, the energy business. 3. Economic growth, social changes, changes in fashion. 4. Sales of Maltesers/all chocolate sales × 100 5. A consumer profile is a statistical breakdown of the people who buy a particular product. It enables the business to target both market research and marketing activity at the particular group.

UNIT 1.4

Student howlers

1. Questionnaires are useful market research tools. They are, however, only appropriate in certain situations. Depending on what the firm needs to know, they may find other methods of research such as desk research or in-depth interviews to be more appropriate.
2. Every firm needs to be aware of its market so market research is essential for all firms. Market research need not be expensive. We have come to associate market research with large agencies conducting surveys. This is only one type of market research. Many businesses – especially small businesses – can find information about their customers in less formal and less expensive ways.

Test yourself

1. Primary research is where the business gathers information for itself, secondary research is where it uses information that has been gathered by others.
2. Quantitative research is statistical information. It shows how many or how much. Qualitative research tries to find out why or how. It looks at the reasons why customers act in a certain way. 3. Random sampling – expensive to carry out properly; only useful if you want a cross-section of the whole population; Quota sampling – requires the consumer profile to be known in advance; still subject to bias, e.g. interviewers selecting people who look friendly or unhurried. 4. Large enough to ensure that the sample is representative of the group being surveyed; the value of the results would affect how large (and therefore expensive) the sample size would be. 5. A good questionnaire will have: • questions that are focused on what the company is trying to find out;
• questions that do not lead towards a particular answer; • questions that are clear and unambiguous;
• questions that have closed answers, i.e. a choice of responses such as yes or no; • basic demographic information to enable a better analysis of the results.

UNIT 1.5

Student howlers

1. Products obviously need to be marketed during the launch and growth phase. The product may need support once it reaches maturity. This will depend on the product and the market conditions. Brands of washing powder such as Ariel, which are at the mature stage of the life cycle, still have huge promotional backing. This is because they are in a highly profitable but competitive market. 2. Cash cows are almost essential to keep a steady revenue coming into the business. However, a business should always have some new products coming into its portfolio. Hopefully some of these will be rising stars. Today's cash cow can be tomorrow's dog as the market changes.

Test yourself

1. Development, introduction, growth, maturity, decline. 2. They may be very successful brands with loyal customers. The business may be supporting them or slightly modifying the product to keep it 'fresh'. (In Coca-Cola's case, Diet Coke now outsells Coke in the UK.) 3. By adding marketing support; by modifying the product; by extending the market either to different groups or to different markets. 4. A product portfolio is the list of products that a business is currently making or selling. 5. Sales of its 400 'core' products may not grow sufficiently to make up for the lost sales elsewhere; withdrawing brands may create gaps that rivals can fill – increasing the level of competition.

UNIT 1.6

Student howlers

1. It is important that the price of mass-market products puts the product within reach of a large number of people. However, that does not mean that the products will be cheap. Once the product brand is established the producer may be able to charge a premium price. The products are unlikely to be 'cheap' in the sense of being poor quality. These would have limited appeal and are unlikely to have a mass market. One advantage for the customer is that mass-produced goods are of consistent quality. 2. A niche product does not have to be expensive although having a smaller market will probably mean that costs will be higher. Some products with very small markets may well be priced higher to make them more exclusive.

Test yourself

1. Selling to a wide market. 2. Lower priced products with consistent quality. 3. Products that are different from other products in the market. They may be innovative or exclusive or just appealing to a small group. 4. To introduce new brands; by breaking down the mass market into smaller segments.
5. i) The company lacks the expertise and the finance to compete with the big, multinational producers;
ii) its marketing proposition is based on being small and exclusive.

UNIT 1.7

Student howlers

1. Cutting prices is a marketing tactic not a strategy. The firm might cut prices to gain more market share, which would be its marketing strategy. Whether or not cutting prices is a good tactic will depend on the market conditions. Is the product price elastic or inelastic? How will competitors react? 2. This implies that manufacturers do not sell their products so do not need to market them. Manufactures may sell to the public through retailers or direct to other firms. In both cases they need to understand their markets and develop plans/strategies for marketing their products.

Test yourself

1. Marketing strategy is a plan for future marketing activity that helps the business achieve its objectives.
2. Strategy is an overall plan; tactics are individual actions that form part of that plan. 3. Making the product different from competitors' products.
4. SWOT analysis is a tool used to audit internal and external business environments. SWOT stands for Strengths, Weaknesses, Opportunities and Threats.

The internal review looks at what the business is doing well (strengths) and what it could do better (weaknesses). The external review looks at the external business environment such as the state of the economy, what competitors are doing, what is happening to technology and at changes in population structure. 5. Market development is finding new markets for existing products; product development is modifying existing products or introducing new products.

UNIT 1.8
Student howlers

1. This statement is incomplete. Demand for a price elastic product will increase if the price is reduced. If the price is increased the demand will fall. 2. This is not true. Luxury goods may continue to sell when the price rises as the customers who are buying them may not care about the price increase (they are price inelastic). However, luxury goods are income elastic. So when household or national income falls, fewer luxury goods will be sold.

Test yourself

1. Demand for the product is price sensitive. Demand will change by a greater percentage than the percentage change in price.

2. Price elasticity = $\dfrac{\% \text{ change in quantity demanded}}{\% \text{ change in price}}$

3. Percentage change in demand = 18,000/120,000 × 100 = 15%
Percentage change in price = 2/20 × 100 = 10%
Price elasticity of demand = 15/10 × 100 = 1.5
Product is price elastic.
4. The demand will fall by a greater percentage than the price increase resulting in lower revenue. 5. a) A price inelastic product – water, gas, designer clothes, specialist hi-fi equipment; b) A price elastic product – standard brands of lager such as Carlsberg, when sold in a supermarket or off-licence; c) A normal good – everyday products such as washing powder and food and clothes; d) An inferior good – supermarket own brands, cheap products such as those found at markets or discount shops. 6. Improve brand awareness, differentiate the product, add value, lessen the competition. 7. Increase in income after the effect of inflation has been deducted. If income rises by 5% and inflation is 5% there is no real increase in income. If income rises by 5% and inflation by 2% real income will have risen by 3%.

UNIT 1.9
Student howlers

1. Advertising is just one way of making the customer aware of the product. What actually sells the product will depend on the product and its market. A new innovative product may sell with little promotional support. For some products such as food, price or the quality of the product may be what the customers base their choice on. 2. Supermarkets make many products readily available to customers. However,

competition for supermarket shelf space is strong. Firms may have problems getting their products on the shelves in supermarkets. Supermarkets will also remove any products that do not have a high enough turnover. In order to sell, the products need to be good and at the right price to attract customers. Some products are also not suitable for selling in supermarkets.

Test yourself

1. Product, price, place and promotion. 2. Probably 'place' would be the hardest to achieve successfully, i.e. obtaining sufficient distribution to give the product a fair chance of building a customer base. 3. Personal visits by sales representatives, to explain the lorries' special features. Direct mail advertising, e.g. posting catalogues to the relevant purchasing decision makers at each company in the target market. 4. A smaller section of a market for a particular product. 5. To make it different from other similar products in the market so that it will stand out in a crowded market. 6. Direct – sales are made directly to the customer; Modern – products go from the manufacturer to the retail outlet; Traditional – products are sold by the manufacturer to a wholesaler who in turn sells the good to the retail outlet.

UNIT 1.10
Student howlers

1. The business will only lose money if its sales rise by less than the price cut, i.e. if the product is price inelastic. If sales increase by more than the percentage price cut the revenue will actually increase. 2. Price is often an important part of the customer's buying decision. However, sometimes other things (e.g. quality, the brand name, exclusivity of the product) are more important to the customer.

Test yourself

1. Products that are readily available will often be priced lower than goods in short supply. 2. Revenue = quantity sold (units) × price. 3. Skimming is used when the product is innovative and there is no competition. The price can be set at a high level allowing the firm to recoup the development costs. Penetration pricing is used when launching a product into an existing market. The price is set lower than that of competitors to gain market share. 4. Firms offer discounted prices for several reasons such as early payment, large quantities purchased, seasonal offers and trade business. 5. A mark-up is added to the average cost. 6. The firm may not recover its costs; customers may think that the product is inferior.

UNIT 1.11
Test yourself

1. Researchers gather information either by using information that already exists (secondary or desk research) or by going out into the market to gather first-hand information (primary or field research). 2. Making the product appear different from other products in the market. 3. Skimming is putting the product on the market at a high price to take

advantage of the exclusivity of the product. Mostly used for innovative products. Penetration pricing is putting the product on the market at a lower price to capture high sales. Often used when there are similar products in the market. **4.** Use extension strategies to boost sales, for example, additional promotion, price reductions, selling to new markets or market segments or developing the product for other uses. **5.** Sales will rise by a smaller percentage than the price reduction. Revenue will be lower. **6.** The share that a product or firm has of the total market for the product can be measured by volume or by sales turnover. **7.** When the product is in the development stage cash flow will be negative to cover development costs. When the product is launched cash flow will continue to be negative to cover launch costs. As sales grow cash flow will turn positive. During maturity cash flow may dip due to the cost of extension strategies. **8.** Market orientation concentrates on customer needs and the activities of competitors; product orientation focuses on the product. **9.** Price reduction is 10% (50p/500p × 100). Percentage change in volume = 20% (2 × 10%). New volume = 120,000 (100,000 + 20%) **10.** A random sample selects the sample participants completely at random ensuring that everyone has an equal chance of being chosen; a quota sample selects participants in proportion to their representation in the target market. **11.** A section of a larger market that has common features. **12.** Selling the product at the market price. **13.** Loss leader, psychological

pricing, special offer pricing, discounting. **14.** Can produce goods cheaper by mass production; spreading of marketing etc. costs over a greater volume; greater opportunity to build brand awareness.
15. Qualitative research looks at why customers behave in a certain way; quantitative research measures customer behaviour. **16.** By describing products as cash cows, rising stars, problem child or dogs it can help to devise a strategy for the future of that product within the product portfolio. Problem children or dogs may be discarded or a strategy might be put in place to change them. **17.** The sales of normal goods will increase as income rises – a positive income elasticity of demand. When income rises the sales of inferior goods will fall – a negative income elasticity of demand.

Questions (The Booze Cruise)

1. Tax is £1.32 less. Company takes a lower profit margin of 4p. Costs will be lower, largely due to the different tax levels. **2.** Store turnover is higher by £0.5 million, i.e. 0.5/1.3 × 100 = 38.5%. **3.** Content (1 mark): Profit margin is difference between revenue and costs. Application (2 marks): Relate answer to the figures in the data given. Analysis (2 marks): Unit profit margin is lower because number of bottles sold is much higher so that total turnover is much higher. As unit costs are lower, total profit will be higher so the business can afford to keep prices lower by taking a lower unit profit margin.

4.

MARKING GRID (out of 6)		
Content	**Application**	**Analysis**
2	2	2
One+ relevant content points explained; or good under-standing of market share	Point(s) made are applied to key business features of the case/ this particular business	Analysis of question set, using relevant theory
1	1	1
One+ relevant content point(s) made, or some understanding shown of market share	Answer shows some application to the case	One or two points applied in a limited way to analyse the question

Possible answers may include: • May encourage bigger, better wine bottlers to supply good wine at good prices and at favourable credit terms. • Growing market share implies more customers who could spread word-of-mouth publicity more widely – helping boost sales further.

5.

MARKING GRID (out of 9)			
Content	**Application**	**Analysis**	**Evaluation**
2	2	2	3
Shows good understanding of the impact of product differentiation	Relevant issues applied in detail to this case	Analysis of question set, using relevant theory	Judgement shown in weighing up the extent to which differentiation is possible
1	1	1	2–1
Shows some understanding of differentiation	Relevant issues applied to this case	One or two points applied in a limited way to analyse the question	Some judgement shown in text or conclusions

Possible answers include: • Depends upon timescale; a company can differentiate itself in the short term, but soon enough competitors will imitate and follow. • A few firms have timeless qualities that cannot be imitated, e.g. Harrods in London or Harvey Nichols in London, Leeds and Edinburgh. • The other way to differentiate yourself is to aim for a market segment small enough to discourage others from imitating you.

Questions (Pearl of the Region)

1. To increase the number of tourists to 10 million by 2010. 2. Setting up of the DTB; integrated programme of international promotions; creating Dubai as a top class tourist destination. 3. Unless there are hotels and airport capacity it will be impossible to bring in the tourists. There is no point in creating demand through marketing if the product is not available in sufficient quantity.

4.

MARKING GRID (out of 8)		
Content	**Application**	**Analysis**
2	2	4–3
One+ relevant content points explained, or good understanding of seasonality	Point(s) made are applied to key business features of the case/ this particular business	Analysis of question set, using relevant theory
1	1	2–1
One+ relevant content point(s) made, or some understanding shown of seasonality	Answer shows some application to the case	One or two points applied in a limited way to analyse the question

Possible answers may include: • Time the advertising campaigns for off-peak periods. • Promote lower, off-peak prices. • Find wider distribution channels for off-peak seasons, e.g. promoting sales through Tesco or Asda. • Devise a product that has all-round-the-year appeal, such as indoor sports and health club facilities.

5.

MARKING GRID (out of 9)			
Content	**Application**	**Analysis**	**Evaluation**
2	2	2	3
Shows good understanding of loss leader pricing	Relevant issues applied in detail to this case	Analysis of question set, using relevant theory	Judgement shown in weighing up the value of loss leaders in the hotel trade
1	1	1	2–1
Shows some understanding of loss leaders	Relevant issues applied to this case	One or two points applied in a limited way to analyse the question	Some judgement shown in text or conclusions

Possible answers include: • May attract off-season visitors who then return in peak times. • The room rates may be low, but other spending in the hotel (e.g. in the restaurant or bar) may generate profits. • BUT low prices may undermine the image and reputation of the hotel, especially if it is attempting to present itself as a luxury destination ... • ... and those who get a cheap room may be reluctant to pay high prices at the bar or restaurant.

Section 2: Accounting and finance

UNIT 2.1

Student howlers

1. Fixed costs do change – rents may increase, salaries may increase, but they are fixed in relation to output.

2. Don't forget that variable costs are usually quoted per unit so a firm's total costs will need to include the variable cost per unit figure multiplied by the firm's output.

Test yourself

1. Variable – car shampoo, sponges. Fixed – staff wages (if paid hourly), maintenance of equipment.

2. Total variable costs = £5 × 1000 = £5000, so with £2000 of profit, the other £5000 of revenue must be fixed costs. 3. Total revenue was £10,000, of which half was profit so total costs must have been £5000, leaving total variable costs of £2000. If 1000 units were sold the variable cost per unit was £2.
4. a) Finding a cheaper supplier, possibly accepting a lower quality of materials, would help to reduce variable costs and therefore increase profit. b) The lower quality of materials will have an effect on the image of the firm's products. Attempts to change the quality of materials are unlikely to go unnoticed by customers who may stop buying from the firm. Alternatively, if the firm comes clean and cuts their selling price this would have an adverse effect on profit.

UNIT 2.2

Student howlers

1. The firm must first *sell* enough units to reach break-even before its costs are covered. Calculating a break-even point does not sell products. 2. Cutting price will change the break-even point. More units will need to be sold in order to break-even since revenue will not rise as rapidly.

Test yourself

1. a) £6000/(£5 − £2) = 2000 units. b) 2500 − 2000 = 500 units. 2. Requires careful forward planning; helps to assess likely cost levels; can indicate the need for a change in strategy, pricing or purchasing. Sales are likely to be quite constant, so the analysis will be useful for quite a period of time. 3. Sales may be hard to predict in such a fast moving market; variable costs may alter significantly as technology advances; competition may hit sales. 4. Sales revenue – the number of customers turning up and paying to use their facilities. This will be complicated by differing charges for different activities. Variable costs will be minimal, but fixed costs such as staffing and maintenance will probably be easier to calculate than revenue.

UNIT 2.3

Student howler

1. Product C is therefore still making a contribution to fixed costs, however small, and therefore its removal will reduce the firm's overall profits since that missing contribution will need to be made up from one of the remaining products.

Test yourself

1. a) £8 − £3 = £5. b) 3000 × £5 = £15,000 − £10,000 = £5000. 2. a) Suppliers charge more for materials – contribution down; b) The firm sells more products – contribution up; c) Selling price is increased due to increased demand – contribution up (the key point being that demand is also up so the increased contribution per unit should also lead to an increased total contribution).
3a) 200 × £12 = £2,400

b) £2,400 − £2,000 = £400
c) New contribution per unit = £15
   Total contribution = £15 × 190 = £2,850
   New profit = £2,850 − £2,000 = £850
   % increase in profit = +112.5%.
4. This information can be used to make decisions relating to product portfolio management – which products to keep selling, which to stop selling, which to plough more time and money into and which may benefit from more management attention.

UNIT 2.4

Student howlers

1. Profit is important if the business is to give a return for its investors. It is also important if the business wants to grow. However, a positive cash flow is necessary to keep the business alive. If the business cannot pay its debts when they are due it may not survive to be profitable. Often having a poor cash flow will be a sign that the business is in difficulty and may eventually mean that the business is unprofitable.
2. A profitable order may seem attractive but the firm should also take care to ensure that the new business does not adversely affect its cash flow situation. If the business has to make payment for raw materials and staff before payment is received for the order it may find itself facing a cash flow crisis.

Test yourself

1. The flow of cash in and out of the business.
2. A management tool that shows the flow of cash in and out of the business and summarises the expected cash balances of the business. 3. If the business does not have sufficient cash to pay its bills it may be faced with bankruptcy or insolvency. 4. In the short term having sufficient cash flow is vital. However, the business needs to be profitable in the long term.
5. To be sure that the business: has enough cash to enable it to survive; will be able to repay the loan; can afford to make the interest payments. 6. They can: speed up cash inflows; delay cash outflows; cut or delay capital expenditure; find additional funding to cover cash shortages.

UNIT 2.5

Student howlers

1. It is true that in the short term not paying a bill will help the cash flow situation. However, suppliers will take a dim view of customers who do not pay their bills on time. They will be less likely to give the firm credit on the next order and may even refuse to trade with the business. In some cases the supplier may go out of business because it has working capital problems made worse by customers not paying their bills on time. 2. It is hard to see what point this student is making. It is true that a debtor is a customer so having lots of debtors means many customers. However, a debtor is a customer who still owes the business money. If total debtors are high then it is likely that the firm could experience working capital problems.

Test yourself

1. The money used in the business for its day-to-day requirements. **2.** Paying suppliers, paying rent, paying staff, paying bills. **3.** Discounting prices; reduce purchases; negotiate more credit; credit control – chase debtors; negotiate additional finance; factor debts; selling assets; sale and leaseback. **4.** The length of the business process; the credit given to purchasers; the credit obtained by suppliers. **5.** Enough to enable the business to be able to pay the bills etc. as they become due. A reserve in case of unforeseen problems is also considered to be useful. Too much working capital could mean that the business is missing opportunities.

UNIT 2.6

Student howlers

1. Selling shares on the stock exchange is only possible for large established businesses. Private limited companies can make private sales of additional shares but cannot sell shares to the public. Sole traders and partnerships cannot sell shares. A plc can only sell more shares if the business circumstances allow it. The business must be successful in order to encourage investors to buy shares. If there is a 'best way' to get finance, it is from making and reinvesting profit. **2.** Revenue is the value of sales made within a trading period. It is not simply 'cash in'. Selling shares effectively means borrowing from investors for an indefinite period of time. This brings in cash, but that should not be confused with revenue from selling to customers.

Test yourself

1. Spending by the business on fixed assets. **2.** Retained profit; sale of assets; from working capital. **3.** Overdrafts – short-term flexible lending; short- and long-term loans. **4.** Business A sells goods to business B and allows business B credit time. The factoring company will give business A a percentage of the outstanding amount. It will then collect the money due from business B when it comes due. It then gives the remaining money to business A less a charge for the service. This allows business A to get cash in sooner and so improve its cash position. **5.** Because it has no history; if it is in difficulty; if it is not profitable; if it already has high debts. **6.** Loans, debentures, sale of shares, venture capital.

UNIT 2.7

Student howlers

1. A favourable variance is one that will boost profit, so higher costs than expected actually represents an adverse variance. **2.** Growing sales are likely to be caused by something – perhaps longer hours from the sales team, and therefore a 25% sales increase that is caused by just a 5% increase in staffing costs is good news for the firm.

Test yourself

1.
2. Focusing management time and attention on areas with significant budget variances. **3.** Helps to control costs that will, by definition, be increasing if the firm is rapidly growing. Can allow delegation of spending power to ensure top bosses are not overburdened at a time of expansion. **4.** Innovation may be hampered with people unwilling to take risks that could lead to budget overspends. Clever budget holders who can negotiate higher budgets may not need to keep their costs as low as necessary. **5.** The ease of budgeting decreases as forecasting gets trickier. Firms manufacturing novelty items are likely to be selling different products for a short time at different times throughout each year and these short bursts of sales will be tough to predict accurately. This also makes it very hard to forecast costs accurately. A washing machine manufacturer may well find a far steadier pattern of sales during the year along with a more stable product portfolio.

UNIT 2.8

Student howler

1. Profit cannot be measured for a cost centre because no revenue can be identified. So any bonus would have to be offered for keeping below a cost target.

Test yourself

1. Financial control, delegation of management power and motivational benefits for managers of cost centres. **2.** The figures for the particular area being managed can be compared with budgeted figures, with the

2.7 Test yourself.

	April			May			June		
	Budgeted	Actual	Variance	Budgeted	Actual	Variance	Budgeted	Actual	Variance
Sales revenue	500	500	–	520	530	**10F**	520	510	10A
Direct costs	200	210	10A	210	220	10A	210	**220**	10A
Indirect costs	200	200	–	200	190	**10F**	200	200	–
Total costs	400	410	10A	410	410	–	410	**420**	**10A**
Profits	100	90	**10A**	110	120	10F	110	90	20A

previous period's figures or with those of other profit centres within the business to identify particular areas of good practice or where improvement may be necessary. **3.** Identification of best practice within the business will allow that practice to be shared throughout the organisation, while identifying underperforming cost centres may allow senior managers to focus their attention on the causes of problems in that particular area. **4. a)** Identifying a profit centre allows staff within that particular area of the business to gain feedback on their performance. Profit centres that are able to generate good levels of profit for their organisation will find that their staff are proud to be a part of this successful little corner of the firm. **b)** The use of profit centres may mean that some firms will develop a tendency to over-focus on the numerical indicators of performance without taking the time to ask why a particular area of the firm is succeeding or struggling. Meanwhile, staff at profit centres that are not performing well may become demotivated as they despair of ways to improve the performance of what may be an inherently unprofitable section of the business. **5. a)** Profit centre: the canteen/café; cost centre: the reception area and staff. **b)** Profit centre: each route; cost centre: in-flight catering; head office advertising (and many, many others).

UNIT 2.9

Test yourself

1. Controlling costs should enable a firm to generate a profit, while cash flow management will be easier if continual and accurate monitoring is taking place. Problems can be identified and prevented early, before they become threatening to the survival of the business. **2.** Financial forecasts will be based on a number of assumptions relating to the future period to which they are related. Both internal and particularly external factors may be impossible to forecast accurately – for example, cost increases from suppliers or unexpected dips in sales caused by the arrival of a new competitor. **3.** Arrange an overdraft to cover the period during which sales are low. Delay payment to suppliers, preferably with their agreement.
4. Expansion implies that costs will be increasing now, in the hope of increasing revenues at some point in the future. This generally means that cash outflows will increase some time before the firm is able to operate at the expanded level of output which would be the time that cash inflows would be expected to catch up with outflows. Of course, during this time lag, bills will still need to be paid and so for the period of expansion, cash will be critical, with profit taking a back seat until the expansion is complete.

5.

Month	January	February	March	April
Cash in	100	110	120	120
Cash out	90	110	130	**100**
Net cash flow	**10**	0	**(10)**	20
Opening balance	10	**20**	20	**10**
Closing balance	**20**	**20**	**10**	**30**

6. Helps to plan for the future; may be needed to secure finance; identifies future cash flow problems early enough to take corrective action. **7.** Factoring means selling a debt to another company who will provide roughly 80% of the value of the debt in cash immediately and a further 15% or so on collection of the debt. **8.** Chasing debtors to pay on time will bring cash into the firm quicker and more predictably, while taking as long as possible to pay suppliers will keep cash in the business for longer. Reducing stock levels keeps more of the firm's working capital in the form of cash. **9.** Trading profit, working capital, asset sales. **10.** Share capital. **11.** Loans, overdraft, mortgage. **12.** Setting budgets to zero each year and requiring budget holders to justify every penny of expenditure they are allocated. **13.** Assumes all output is sold; assumes revenue and variable cost lines are straight; it is only as good as the data used to construct it.

Questions (Celebration Cakes)

1. Overheads are generally indirect, usually fixed costs that do not relate specifically to the production of the firm's product or service, e.g. administration costs.
2. Trading profit may make a contribution if their other business is generating sufficient profit. Any unused assets could be sold off, or even currently used assets could be sold and leased back. Money can be squeezed out of working capital, perhaps by reducing credit terms offered to smaller customers. **3.** 40,000 cakes per month. **4.** Variable costs per unit may fall at higher levels of output as suppliers may be willing to offer bulk buying discounts (an economy of scale). This is especially true given the significant increases in purchasing levels implied by the story of the rapid rise of the Celebration Cake maker. **5.** Possible solutions could include factoring the debts owed by the supermarkets (margins are high enough to cope with the factor's fee), increasing pressure on suppliers to offer more generous credit terms to Robtel (see point made in answer to Q.4 about increased bargaining power) or reducing stock levels in order to free up more cash (this firm's stock may well be at great risk of 'going off' if kept too long. Evaluative themes, such as suggesting that a combination of methods is likely to

be more effective than trying to find one solution would be expected within your answer.

Questions (Nurwoo Noodles)

1. Total revenue is the value of sales made, i.e. the quantity sold multiplied by the price charged. 2. Profit centres provide managers with the opportunity to feel responsible for their part of the business, so each branch manager may be more motivated as a result of a desire to achieve the best results at their branch. 3. Budgeted profit = £4200. Actual loss = £300, variance is adverse = £4500. 4. Closing the Bromley restaurant may be a hasty decision – external factors may have caused the weaker performance. Meanwhile, closing the restaurant will mean that it contributes nothing towards covering the company's total overheads, reducing the overall profit of the business. 5. Tighter budgetary control could have kept variable costs, such as ingredients lower – with lower sales fewer ingredients should be needed. Overheads and wages should have been kept lower with closer monitoring of costs. However, many of the problems stem from disappointing revenues and these are likely to be the result of external factors, such as a very hot summer, opening of competitors or health scares. Budgetary control tends to help on the cost side but revenues tend to be more influenced by factors outside management's control.

Section 3: People and organisations

UNIT 3.1

Student howlers

1. A higher output does not mean higher productivity and in this case it is certainly not true as firm B is getting more out of each worker. 2. Increasing productivity allows the firm to make more units but selling more units does not happen automatically.

Test yourself

1. 40 units per worker per month. 2. Better machinery, more motivated staff, better trained staff, better organised production process. 3. More customers can be dealt with in any given time by an operator, meaning that fewer checkouts need to be open. If the same number of checkouts are open, queues will be shorter meaning happier customers. 4. Some firms may feel that the route to increasing productivity lies in making workers work harder – reducing breaks, imposing output targets, etc. – all of which are likely to be unpopular. Other firms may decide that the only way to increase productivity is to increase the level of automation, replacing people with machines – again rarely popular with those staff being replaced. Finally, any firm that does manage to increase productivity will need to find a use for the extra output being generated, otherwise the increased productivity may simply be the key to laying off a certain proportion of staff.

UNIT 3.2

Student howlers

1. Herzberg said that money was a hygiene factor and, as such, was as important in achieving a motivated workforce as any other aspect identified in his two factor theory. 2. Not correct – Herzberg said that without hygiene needs met, workers would be dissatisfied and you could never motivate them, whilst positive motivation can only be achieved by offering the motivators to people whose hygiene needs have been met. Both are equally important. 3. The Hawthorne effect sounds a lot like that but this student has made the gaffe that may make an examiner chuckle but will not endear you to them – morals and morale are rather different things. 4. A simple spelling problem again – Maslow identified Physiological needs as the most basic type of human need.

Test yourself

1. Paying people commission, Time and motion study as echoed in benchmarking, scientific management – the use of quantitative decision-making techniques in business, such as price elasticity. 2. Accept that your workers are human beings and as such need to have their social needs met – set up a staff social club. Pay attention to your staff, take an active interest in how they are getting on. 3. Physiological – decent pay and working conditions; Security – a permanent contract of employment; Social – Introduce team working; Esteem – appraisal; Self-actualisation – offer opportunities for enhancing skills and achievement by offering regular training in new skills. 4. a) Salary – hygiene b) Recognition for achievement – motivator c) Relationship with supervisor – hygiene.

UNIT 3.3

Student howlers

1. If the company is making losses there will be no profit to share – hardly a great incentive. 2. But customers may be treated rudely at checkouts as operators desperately try to speed up on the number of customers they deal with. 3. Herzberg's policy was job enrichment – a different idea to that of job enlargement

Test yourself

1. Feedback is built into the job, the employee is held responsible for checking the quality of their own work and opportunities for a sense of achievement are built into the job. 2. Teams may be more likely to come up with creative ideas by sharing their thoughts on each job. Teamworking may well help to motivate the staff to work more effectively because their social needs are being met at work. 3. The normal and accepted way of doing things within an organisation will be a key determinant as to the level of productivity achieved within the firm. If everyone expects everyone else to

work to the very best of their ability then the culture is likely to have a beneficial impact on quality levels too. A strong culture would also help new employees to feel that they know what is expected of them when they join the firm. 4. They may have taken the job simply to make money and care little for how much decision making power they have. They may lack the experience and skills required to make the right decisions and may therefore become demotivated if they feel they are doing a poor job. 5. a) shop floor staff in a fashion clothing retailer. Commission may encourage many sales to be made, but some kind of profit sharing based on the branch's profit may produce better overall results for the firm. b) the manager of a branch of a chain of fashion clothing retailers. A salary should be used, possibly with bonuses linked to the performance of their branch – probably profit level if the branch is operated as a profit centre.

UNIT 3.4
Student howlers
1. This common misconception shows that the student is classifying workers, not managers, as being theory X or theory Y. McGregor's theory was a way of classifying managers according to their attitudes. There is, therefore, no such thing as theory X or theory Y workers. 2. Delegation gives authority to staff, therefore it is democratic, not autocratic.

Test yourself
1. These two different types of manager have different assumptions about their staff and will therefore treat their staff differently as a result of those assumptions. *A theory X manager assumes that:* • Employees dislike work and will avoid it if they can. • Employees want to be told what to do, have little desire for improvement and try to avoid responsibility wherever possible. • Employees must be controlled and threatened or bribed to work. *A theory Y manager assumes that:* • Work is as natural as play or rest for humans. • Staff welcome responsibility if rewarded fairly. • Most employees are capable of offering their own ideas when approaching problems. 2. The benefit may be the encouragement of creativity and innovation in methods of delivery and learning. The disadvantage is likely to revolve around an ineffective system of discipline leading to a disrupted working environment. 3. Key issues will include: corporate culture, consequences of mistakes, the type of work being done (standardised or creative), the experience and qualifications of staff, commitment of staff (treat full timers differently from temps). 4. With staff being required to work in a particular way, following clear instructions, the sales method is likely to be standardised, with all sales people selling in a specific way. This may mean that sales are missed as staff are unable to show flexibility in offering deals or offers, but is likely to ensure that no staff present an image or attitude that the company wants to discourage.

UNIT 3.5
Student howlers
1. Confusion over spans of control (can be narrow or wide) and chains of command (can be long or short). 2. Narrow spans of control may well make top-down communication more reliable but often inhibit bottom-up communication since they indicate an autocratic leadership style prevailing within the organisation.

Test yourself
1. a) A manager is responsible for a relatively high number of subordinates – probably more than 6. b) The route from bottom to top of the organisation's structure is long, with a relatively high numbers of layers/intermediaries to pass through. c) An organisation where decision-making power is kept at the top of the structure and not delegated throughout the organisation. 2. Flatter structures encourage delegation – just what tends to be needed in a creative workplace such as an advertising agency. A flat structure should also ensure that even senior managers have fairly regular contact with clients and are therefore able to keep a close eye on trends within the market. 3. Confusion over whose instructions to follow may be the result of having two bosses. The more complex nature of such a structure could breed communication difficulties. 4. All staff know who their boss is and therefore who to go to in the event of needing advice. Clear chains of command ensure that coordination can be achieved.

UNIT 3.6
Student howlers
1. You don't need MBO to set corporate objectives. The novel feature of MBO is the way that all staff have their own working objectives that should match with the firm's corporate objectives. 2. Management by objectives should be a way of empowering workers to decide for themselves how their jobs need doing. MBO simply ensures they are doing the right job.

Test yourself
1. Management by objectives is a system for delegating control within an organisation by devising mutually agreed objectives for each member of staff that flow from the corporate objectives. 2. It can motivate staff who feel trusted to do their work in whatever way they feel is right. This can encourage a positive and innovative approach to problem solving. Coordination should be ensured if all staff's objectives have been agreed with managers. 3. MBO takes up a lot of management time. Within a small firm, managers may not feel they have the time available to go through the full MBO process. Some managers may be unaware of MBO as a technique. Within a small firm, it is likely that all staff are in fairly close contact, including senior managers, so it is more likely that all staff will know what the organisation is hoping to achieve and how their performance can help it achieve its objectives. 4. a) Find a supplier able to

deliver with less than a 0.5% defect rate; reduce the cost of microchip supplies by 20% per unit. **b)** Keep clean sheets in 50% of games this year; improve communication with the other defenders.

UNIT 3.7

Student howler

1. Remind yourself of the advice in the exam insight section here. HRM in itself should not be seen as meaning actions to increase motivation (though some HRM activities may promote 'movement').

Test yourself

1. **a)** Hiring new staff from outside the existing workforce to introduce fresh ideas and attitudes. **b)** Identifying future labour needs within the business and putting in place a plan to ensure that the right people with the right skills will be in place by the time they are needed. **2.** May help to motivate staff if they receive positive feedback from an appraisal. Regular contact with all staff may help management to understand workplace issues more fully. **3.** Planning in advance will allow the firm to identify just what skills will be most useful in the future, once capacity is reduced. Staff with those skills can be encouraged to stay, while shedding staff is easier with more time available since, with time to spare, the reduction in staffing levels may be achieved through relatively painless methods such as 'natural wastage' (not replacing staff who leave of their own accord) or offering early retirement or voluntary redundancy packages. **4.** New roles may mean increased pay and status within the firm. Staff may also feel a sense of motivation as a result of the sense of achievement gained from learning new skills and as a result of feeling sufficiently valued by their employer to be trained in these new skills.

UNIT 3.8

Student howler

1. The second sentence is the problem – no significant change is ever easy to make, even if well managed.

Test yourself

1. Planning, implementation, control and review. **2. a)** A negative reaction would be expected, with staff fearful for their jobs and probably consulting with their trade unions over whether industrial action could help. Many staff may start looking desperately for other jobs, even those that the firm is intending to keep. **b)** The answer must lie in the use of the model for change outlined in the unit. Key features would be explaining to all staff why the firm's current position necessitates change, then encouraging staff to come up with ideas for allowing the firm to regain its competitiveness. Whatever happens, all staff should be not just informed of what is going on but encouraged to take part in implementing the changes planned. **3.** The stronger the culture, the harder it may be to establish a new way to 'do things round here'. Staff

may actively resist change, or may do so passively, by making no real effort to adopt new working methods. But, if the existing culture is progressive, entrepreneurial and optimistic, change may be embraced; in business as in politics, the slogan 'it's time for a change' can ring true.

UNIT 3.9

Test yourself

1. Helps to maintain control and effective coordination and should reduce the possibility of errors occurring. **2.** Wider spans of control will reduce the height of a structure. **3.** A system of matrix management focuses resources on teams that work on individual projects, made up of members drawn from different functional areas within the business. **4.** Should motivate employees; may improve sense of mission. **5.** Passing decision-making power down the organisational structure. **6.** Taylor felt that money motivates people to work and they should therefore be paid piece rate. He felt that the ideal method involves differential piece rates with a higher rate per unit being paid after output targets have been achieved. **7.** The beneficial impact on staff workrate and morale of managers taking an active personal interest in their staff. **8.** Social facilities can be provided; teamworking would also be effective. **9.** Pay, working conditions, company policies, relations with boss, relations with co-workers. **10.** If hygiene needs are met employees will have no reason to be dissatisfied at work. They will not, however, be motivated unless the motivators are also being addressed. **11.** Teamworking will give staff an opportunity to work with colleagues, thereby addressing the need for human interaction at work, as first identified by Mayo. Teamworking should help to address the social needs within Maslow's hierarchy. **12.** Piece rate, performance-related pay, profit sharing, share ownership, fringe benefits, salary. **13.** Workers are lazy; they will try to avoid work if they can; they must be threatened or bribed if you want them to work; they have little imagination or creativity to offer. **14.** An authoritarian leader issues orders which they expect to be followed because they feel those orders are in the best interests of the business. A paternalistic leader will seem very similar yet their orders will be designed to operate in the best interests of the employees – who are perceived as children that need the firm guiding hand of a father figure. **15.** Involves assessing future labour needs in order to begin recruitment or training in time to meet those needs.

Questions (Mainwaring and Werge)

1. The number of subordinates under the direct control of a manager. **2.** High-quality trained staff were available from the moment the business opened in each town. Recruiting plenty of staff helped to ensure that the firm could cope with initial demand from the outset, meaning no disappointed customers. **3.** Internal training is likely to be much cheaper. It also allows the firm to train staff to do things 'the Mainwaring and Werge way' – helping to reinforce

company culture. **4.** Delegating more power to local representatives may motivate them a little more and allow them to make changes to the service to suit the local market. However, mistakes here may be very costly and a centralised structure helps to avoid these. Furthermore, a strength of the business may be the standardised nature of the service that they offer – something that may be lost if power is decentralised.

Questions (Ramsbottom Engineering Ltd)

1. Single status means that all staff enjoy the same working conditions and management receive no special privileges such as a separate staff canteen or reserved parking places. **2.** The democratic style clearly encouraged staff to put forward their own ideas, based on their skills and experience. It was these suggestions that showed Lydia the way through the

tough trading conditions. **3.** Staff would become concerned for the safety of their jobs, which according to Maslow would threaten their security needs. If employees have their job security removed they are likely to work less effectively. **4.** Lydia's approach seems likely to work well when dealing with similar workforces in similarly sized firms. With just four supervisors this firm must be small enough for all staff to feel a genuine commitment to the firm's goals and be committed to the success of the business. By involving staff in decision making, Lydia has enabled them to share their expertise and experience successfully. However, inexperienced staff may have less to offer or be less willing to offer their views. The established culture within a business can be very difficult to change. Meanwhile larger firms may need to retain certain levels of authority to ensure that coordination is effective.

Section 4: Operations management

UNIT 4.1

Student howlers

1. This is a very vague statement. What does 'all the advantages' mean? The suggestion is that large firms are better placed in the market place. That may or may not be true. In some niche markets small firms will have the advantage of being able to fit their customers' needs. Being small may also make them more exclusive. In mass markets the firm may need to be large to be able to produce goods in a quantity and at a price that is acceptable to the buyers. Being large, however, is not always an advantage. Many large firms are inefficient and bureaucratic. **2.** This is a very pessimistic statement. The art of growing successfully is to ensure that economies outweigh diseconomies. If there are particular diseconomies that apply to a business then these should be outlined as support for this statement. 'Diseconomies of scale, *such as the difficulty in recruiting and training new staff in this industry,* mean that *this* firm should *consider if growth is the right option.*'

Test yourself

1. Cost savings due to increased output.
2. Managerial economies, technical economies, financial economies, marketing economies, purchasing economies. **3.** Management problems, employee problems, communication problems. **4.** The level of production at which average costs are at the lowest.
5. Perhaps because diseconomies of scale are also important to large firms. Because small firms have the flexibility and speed of thought to respond more quickly to changes in consumer taste.

UNIT 4.2

Student howler

1. This is a common capacity utilisation howler – confusing capacity with capacity utilisation. A new

factory will increase the capacity of the business but is more likely to decrease the percentage of total capacity that is actually used.

Test yourself

1. $20,000/25,000 \times 100 = 80\%$. **2. a)** £100,000/20,000 = £5 per unit. **b)** £100,000/25,000 = £4 per unit. **3. a)** Machinery unused, with staff standing around doing little and possibly large stocks of materials lying around a quiet factory. **b)** Very low room booking rates with lots of rooms empty most nights, and perhaps an empty restaurant as well.
4. To increase the number of customers using the facility, the leisure centre could run special offers with low entry fees, perhaps encouraging existing users to come more often. A drastic alternative would be to close a part of the centre, perhaps selling off an underused playing field to a housing developer – thus reducing total capacity and, if visitor numbers remained unchanged, increasing capacity utilisation.

UNIT 4.3

Student howlers

1. Batch production is most suited to smaller quantities. However, it can also be used for large-scale production. Instead of moving from one process to another in a continual flow the goods can be manufactured by finishing one part of the production process then moving the batch to another section of the factory for the next stage. **2.** This statement is far too general. It really depends on the situation of the business. The firm may be able to cut costs but may have to invest quite heavily in new machinery if they change their production method.

Test yourself

1. a) Batch (a limited number of identical items); **b)** Job; **c)** Flow. **2. a)** Job – flexible and responsive to consumer demand; tailor-making production adds value. **b)** Batch – more cost efficient than job production; allows more product variety than mass production. **c)** Flow – production is on a large scale so average cost are usually lower; items produced will have consistent content and quality. 3. Products for small niche markets such as designer clothes; hand-made products such as artwork. 4. Mass-produced products that can be individually tailored to customer specifications.

UNIT 4.4

Student howlers

1. Many of the textbook examples focus on lean production in car factories so students could be forgiven for thinking that only large businesses engaging in mass production will be able to take advantage of lean production. Lean production can be used by any organisation, big or small, retail, service or manufacturing. 2. This student is probably confusing lean production with just-in-time. With JIT production the firm will make to order so will in fact only make what it can sell. JIT is one element of lean production.

Test yourself

1. It is a company-wide approach that concentrates on making the production process as efficient as possible. 2. Total quality management, time-based management, just-in-time. 3. Poor quality costs money through wastage and loss of customers; good quality enhances the reputation of the product. 4. Shortage of materials and components if deliveries are missed; lack of stock if demand increases. 5. The reduction in accidents is not only beneficial for workforce morale (eliminating a hygiene factor), but also reassurance that lean production does not simply mean working harder. The reduction in raw materials and finished goods stock will reduce the working capital tied up in the production process and improve the firm's cash flow.

UNIT 4.5

Student howlers

1. One of the criticisms of Kaizen is that it puts pressure on employees to come up with new ideas. A good system will encourage employees to contribute ideas for improvement but will not pressure them. 2. The idea behind Kaizen came from Japan. Many people considered that the reason for the success was not just the idea but also the different attitude of Japanese workers. However, it has been introduced in western companies and has been successful.

Test yourself

1. Kaizen – or continuous improvement – is a method of working that looks for ways of improving business productivity or quality on an ongoing basis. 2. Individual responsibility, teamworking, empowerment, targets. 3. Lack of commitment from managers and workers; insufficient financial support. 4. Little or no threat to job security; small changes enable staff to adjust slowly to new challenges or practices. 5. Nestlé: a better quality of recruit (as people want to feel they are making a difference); recruiting the kind of people who like to be positive and to have their voice heard. GSM Group: reducing

time wastage may help to get new products to the market more quickly (perhaps benefiting from 'first-mover advantage'); focusing efforts on time wastage may make all staff more aware of the ways time can be frittered away in the working day.

UNIT 4.6

Student howlers

1. The term benchmarking is often used for the process of making comparisons between one business and another. However, benchmarking is about more than just comparisons: it is about finding out why one firm is better at an activity and then incorporating some of the methods or activities that make them better. 2. Any business activity that can be measured can be benchmarked. It is just as useful to look at food wastage in restaurants or labour turnover in an office.

Test yourself

1. To improve business efficiency by incorporating ideas used by the best performers. This should help the firm identify its management priorities ('We're fine at stock control, but our quality control is awful!'). 2. a) Lead-time, i.e. how long from customer order to bus delivery; factory labour hours per bus. b) Percentage of items out of stock per day; percentage labour turnover. c) Lessons required per pass; percentage drop-out from customers who start learning with the school. 3. Commitment from management; commitment from workers; adequate funding; best practice information available for comparison. 4. The process or activity being benchmarked cannot be measured; it is not possible to find a best practice company; the best practice company is unable or unwilling to disclose information.

UNIT 4.7

Student howlers

1. This is quite a naïve statement. It is true that all firms should aim to have 100% quality output but in most situations that is not possible. It will depend on the product and the process. If it is a supplier of critical parts for an aircraft, then yes. Generally, it would make products too expensive for the pockets of most customers. The cost of achieving 100% quality has to be balanced with the possible market price for the product. 2. It is difficult to understand what this student was trying to say. Often higher quality is one of the selling points in a niche market. Customers are prepared to pay more for quality products. There may be a confusion with exclusive products or products which are hard to obtain. The key point is that generalising about companies or markets will rarely be successful. Each business is unique.

Test yourself

1. Quality management is the maintenance of consistent levels of quality. 2. A good quality product is: easier to establish in the market; generates repeat purchases; has a longer life cycle; allows brand building and cross marketing; saves advertising costs; allows

a price premium; makes products easier to place. There are also costs associated with poor quality. 3. Inspection of finished goods, for instance at the end of a production line. Self-inspection of work by operatives, at every stage in the production process. 4. Total quality management; continuous improvement; zero defects; quality circles; training; benchmarking. 5. Advantages: Enables staff to feel part of the process of change, and therefore feel committed to it; avoids huge costs on new equipment, staff retraining or replacing staff with those with new skills. Disadvantages: At times, the firm may slip behind rivals that have made more dramatic quality improvements; staff may operate in a 'comfort zone' that needs a sharp rethink from time to time.

UNIT 4.8

Student howlers

1. This is a very general statement and has no validity unless backed by the reasons for the statement. There is no hard and fast rule about buffer stock. Each business will make decisions that will depend on their own circumstances. How often can the supplier deliver? How reliable is the supplier? How much can we afford? How much risk are we prepared to take? 2. Again a very vague and general statement that will not earn any marks. If the student thinks that JIT is best for the particular business then the statement must be backed with reasons why. The student should also address the possible problems. JIT is by no means the best for every business. Some elements of the system can improve stock handing but for many firms the system is unworkable.

Test yourself

1. To minimise the costs involved in stock holding. 2. Raw materials and/or components, work in progress, finished goods. 3. Having stock delivered so that it is available just as it is needed. 4. Advantages: Less space is used for storage, so more shopfloor space can be used for display and selling clothes; minimal buffer stocks mean frequent ordering and deliveries of small quantities of stock – as a result, changes in fashion should not be costly. Disadvantages: A sudden run on a very fashionable item will lead quickly to an out-of-stock position; more orders may mean higher costs for delivery and processing of orders. 5. a) The cost of missing out on other profitable uses of the firm's capital (a retailer with tight stock control may release enough cash to open another outlet). b) The cost of trade lost if a customer does not return after finding goods out of stock.

UNIT 4.9

Test yourself

1. Benchmarking is a management tool that involves comparing business processes with those of other firms and incorporating the ideas that make the other firm better in the business processes. 2. A quality circle is a group of workers that meet to discuss quality issues. It contributes ideas to improve the business processes

in order to improve quality. This in turn reduces costs. It also improves worker morale by increasing involvement. 3. Increase demand; reduce capacity to meet demand; improve production efficiency to make use of available capacity. 4. Increased output reduces average costs by sharing the fixed costs between a larger output. Purchase savings may reduce variable costs. 5. Poor communication, poor coordination, poor motivation. 6. Job production produces small numbers of items individually; batch production produces batches or groups of identical items. 7. Stock may not arrive in time so slowing or stopping the production process, leading to customers having to wait. 8. Length of the production process and the time taken to get deliveries from supplier. 9. Gives the product a good reputation; encourages repeat sales; makes the product easier to place. 10. Average costs = total cost (fixed costs = variable costs)/units produced. Fixed costs are spread over a larger number of units. 11. Any business process that can be measured. 12. Flow production is usually the system used as it produces large quantities of identical products at a lower cost. 13. Kaizen is continuous improvement. If it is to succeed it needs: commitment from management, commitment from workers, empowerment of workers, investment in costs. 14. TQM is a change in attitude that requires everyone working in the business to take responsibility for quality. 15. Reducing the levels of stock held means that less cash is tied up in stock. Just-in-time means that goods go out to customers very soon after material supplies are received, so reducing the time between cash in and cash out. 16. Advantages: Faster production; less human error; output more consistent; quality and consistency improved. Disadvantages: Loss of labour skills; cost of machinery; loss of motivation; machinery breakdown.

Questions (On-line stock management is worth its salt)

1. To provide the service to the public by gritting the road when the weather turns icy. 2. An automated stock management system enables the stock levels to be monitored quickly and easily. This means that reordering can be done on time and at the right level. 3. Content (2 marks): A computerised production process is where some or all of the production process is controlled by computers. This may range from simple computer-aided systems to fully automate production process such as robotics. Analysis (4 marks – 2 for advantages and 2 for disadvantages):
• Advantages: Saves time and labour costs; less human error; process can often be speeded up; may be space saving. • Disadvantages: Loss of worker moral as machines do the job; if there is a breakdown it may be time consuming to resolve; cost of investment in systems and machinery; loss of labour skills.
4. Content (1 mark): Shows an understanding of what is meant by quality. Application and Analysis (4 marks): Quality has both costs and marketing implications for the business. (For full marks answer should include one marketing and one cost

implication.) • In a competitive market poor quality can result in: loss of sales; loss of reputation; may need to reduce prices; may make it difficult to place goods at retailers; loss of goodwill and repeat purchases; may impact on other products in the range. • Costs are increased because of: scrapping of unsuitable products; reworking time to correct faults; lower prices for seconds; warranty and complaints costs. 5. Content (2 marks): Just-in-time system of stock management means getting required stocks of materials or components, as they are needed by the manufacturing process. Application (2 marks): Answer must be focused on the firm in the question and/or related to real life examples that are relevant to the question. Analysis (4 marks – 2 for advantages and 2 for disadvantages): Many of the materials for this firm will be provided just-in-time in any case. Fresh ingredients need to be delivered fresh each day. Other ingredients could be stocked. Reduced stock holding will save on costs. It may be difficult to arrange JIT deliveries of all ingredients depending on the size of the firm and its orders and its relationship with the suppliers. Like any other firm using JIT, if there is a problem with suppliers it could affect the production process.

Questions (Challenge 50)

1. The business is reacting to the situation in the market rather than just producing cars. Production is focused on market demand. 2. Content (1 mark): This is a productivity improvement. Application and Analysis (3 marks): Use the figures in the table to support this, e.g. fewer defects, fewer inspectors, less stock held. 3. To further stimulate demand so that the business could take advantage of economies of scale. 4. Content (1 mark): Benchmarking is a process of comparing against the best in order to improve business processes. Application (2 marks): Relate to the business – both are car manufacturers. Suzuki is a world-class car producer – 'best in class'. Use information given to analyse the benefits. Analysis (4 marks): As well as improving efficiency and reducing costs it has released floor space allowing them to increase capacity by almost 50%. Contributed to other Challenge 50 improvements. 5. Content (1 mark): Kaizen is continuous improvement. Application (2 marks): Answer should relate to the information given or use other practical examples. A general answer gets no application marks. Analysis (3 marks): • Advantages: Worker involvement; improvement in production processes; cost reductions at factory and suppliers. • Disadvantages: Cost of running the scheme; overwhelming number of suggestions. Evaluation (2 marks): A judgement about the system for this factory.

Section 5

UNIT 5.1

Student howlers

1. Perfect competition is very hard to achieve and could actually be wasteful. A baker on every street corner might increase choice but how many people can afford time to go to each one and check out goods and prices. In reality markets break down into smaller units where customers make a few comparisons. They may travel tens of miles to buy a car but will generally choose between the nearest supermarkets. 2. This is far too general. The UK is a mixed economy. This means that free enterprise is mixed with some government involvement. Governments do try to ensure that markets remain competitive and that firms trade in a fair way.

Test yourself

1. Sellers competing against one another to get customers to buy their products. 2. Perfect competition, monopolistic competition, oligopoly, monopoly. 3. Monopolistic competition has more sellers and free entry into the market. The price is determined by the market. Oligopoly has few sellers and more restricted entry into the market. The sellers also tend to set the price in the market. 4. To avoid having a monopoly situation which disadvantages the customer and other firms in the market. 5. Little pressure on them to be innovative; prices can be kept above the real equilibrium level.

UNIT 5.2

Student howlers

1. This is not true. Some firms flourish. The recession may also be confined to a geographical area or an industry, leaving all other business unaffected. 2. If the student had gone on to explain why this particular business will be able to grow then this could have been the beginning of a good answer. On its own it is meaningless. Some businesses will be able to grow during a boom but others may not. There may be problems in finding skilled labour or money for further investment. The product that the firm makes may not experience higher demand.

Test yourself

1. A period of negative growth. Technically two consecutive quarters showing a fall in aggregate demand. 2. Shortage of materials, labour, capital. 3. Declining markets could lead to unprofitability; could result from a knock-on effect of other firms going out of business. 4. Large, well-diversified firms should be able to withstand most shocks; firms with several inferior products may flourish, e.g. Lidl or Aldi retail stores.

UNIT 5.3

Student howlers

1. This seems to be confusion with inflation rates. Higher interest rates may mean that the business has increased costs. However, if demand for the product is

falling as a result of the higher interest rates they will find it very difficult to pass on the cost increases to the consumer. If the firm is importing raw materials costs may go down as the higher interest rates cause the pound to rise so making imports less expensive. **2.** This is usually true but is rather general. As interest rates are increased demand falls. However, this is not true for all products. Customers may shift their buying. Inferior goods could well see an increase.

Test yourself

1. It is the cost of borrowing or the return on money lent. **2.** Generally higher interest rates reduce disposable income. Consumers will have to pay more for credit, and loan and mortgage repayments will increase. However, some consumers who have a high level of savings may be better off as the return on their savings will increase. **3.** Lenders will want to get the best return on their money. If they can get higher returns in safe deposit accounts they will invest less in risky business ventures. The higher interest rates will also mean that the loan will cost more. This will increase business costs and make it harder to get a good return on the money invested. **4.** It may reduce consumer demand, if people choose to save rather than spend. The extra overhead costs may make it harder for marginally profitable firms to stay in business.

UNIT 5.4
Student howlers

1. This is just too vague to merit any marks. What is meant by high exchange rates? What does 'make it easier' mean? If the pound is high against other currencies it will make exporting more difficult as exporters will receive less pounds for their sales. If they then increase prices to cover this they may become uncompetitive. It is true that imports will become cheaper. **2.** Students seem to be very concerned about language barriers. Perhaps this is because of the traditional British reluctance to learn other languages! Language is an important barrier but it is by no means the only one. It is also possible to use agents or to employ people who can bridge the language barrier. The biggest barrier to trade is competitiveness. A firm that is competitive in an overseas market can usually deal with the other problems.

Test yourself

1. International trade is the buying and selling of goods and services between businesses in different countries. **2.** Measures taken by a country to restrict international trade. They may be tariffs or quotas. They are used to protect home industries or to control the balance of trade and avoid a trade deficit. **3.** A fall in the external value of the country's currency; if productivity rises within the country, e.g. due to improved education and training; better government help/advice to firms may help. **4.** It will be cheaper for the firm to import its cocoa and sugar. If it exports the finished product (chocolate bars), it will find it necessary to push its prices up (and suffer a reduction

in sales volume). **5.** Transportation costs, administrative costs, exchange costs, representation costs, product adjustment costs.

UNIT 5.5
Test yourself

1. It is a general rise in prices within an economy. **2.** It is measured in the UK by the retail price index (RPI), i.e. the percentage change in prices since a year ago. RPI is measured by collecting a considerable amount of data on prices of goods and services bought by typical households. **3.** It may become harder to agree on an annual pay rise for staff, as workers will be desperately concerned to avoid a reduction in their living standards, if pay rises by less than the rate of inflation. It may make it hard to export the jeans, if UK prices are rising faster than those abroad; it will help if they have a brand name that people are prepared to pay extra for. **4.** Wastage of resources and the cost of unemployment in terms of benefits, retraining, etc.

UNIT 5.6
Student howlers

1. Although legislation quotes 25% as a guideline, the crucial factor for deciding on whether a monopoly exists and needs to be removed is whether the firm is acting in consumers' best interests. If a large supplier with a 50% market share continues to offer decent value for money and a range of innovative products, the Competition Commission is unlikely to interfere. **2.** If only that were the case, no company would act illegally. Sadly, many firms will cut corners and break the law because they consider either that they will not be caught or that the penalties are worth paying.

Test yourself

1. Increased operating costs caused by added inspection, maintenance work and staff training. **2.** Ensuring competition in a market means that no one firm can get away with doing what they like since consumers should always have an alternative supplier available should they feel that they are being taken for a ride. **3.** Common stories relate to firms found guilty of breaching health and safety regulations after an accident, Competition Commission investigations of potential anti-competitive practices or, on a more personal level, firms that have mistreated staff in some way. **4.** A mimimum wage ensures that all employees are paid at or above a certain rate, e.g. £4.80 per hour. Some UK manufacturers might find that this makes it impossible to compete effectively with countries with far lower wage costs. This might lead to firms moving out of the UK to relocate their manufacturing facilities in lower wage countries – Dyson's move to the Far East is a recent example.

UNIT 5.7
Student howlers

1. Stakeholders are not shareholders – don't confuse the two. **2.** This was taken from a real exam paper.

Social responsibilities in a business exam will not refer to a social life – they will be talking about the responsibilities that a firm or owner has to society.

Test yourself

1. Social responsibility is the term used to describe what a business should be expected to do to keep each stakeholder satisfied, e.g. a firm has a responsibility to pay its suppliers on time. 2. A stakeholder is an individual or group that is affected by the operations of a business. These include external stakeholders such as the local community and the government as well as internal stakeholders such as the owners of the business and its staff. 3. a) Pay a dividend; maintain a healthy share price through sensible decision making. b) Provide a product that does the job it is supposed to do; provide an after-sales service, such as a customer helpline. c) Provide jobs; reduce traffic congestion caused by suppliers. 4. a) Some firms may not accept these responsibilities. b) Some firms may try to 'treat their suppliers mean' because they feel they have many different suppliers they can use. c) Customer needs may be ignored by providing a poor-quality product in order to reduce costs or by failing to charge a reasonable price. d) Employees may be treated poorly, by being offered short-term contracts and expected to work unsociable hours in an unpleasant environment. This may be the result of trying to keep staffing costs low.

UNIT 5.8

Student howler

1. The law does not necessarily cover all areas of unethical behaviour. Just because something is unethical does not mean that it is illegal.

Test yourself

1. a) Should a pharmaceutical manufacturer that has spent millions of pounds developing a new drug for treating AIDS sell the drug at a low price that makes it accessible to everyone suffering from AIDS worldwide? b) The firm may decide to sell the drug for whatever customers (likely to be governments) can afford to pay, based on the idea that it is morally wrong to deny access to such a product on the basis of income levels. Alternatively the company may charge a very high price in order to recover its development costs, justifying this by saying that if the firm is unable to make a profit, it will be unable to fund the research and development necessary to continue developing new drugs. c) The second course of action has placed the firm in a position where it could save the lives of thousands if not millions of people but is unwilling to do so due to its desire to make a profit. 2. Using pictures of scantily clad women (or men) to advertise products such as cars is not illegal but is hard to justify ethically. 3. Ethics are the moral principles that affect decision making. They are a set of beliefs of what is and is not morally right and wrong. 4. Answers to this will vary based on what you consider to be morally right or wrong. You may have in mind an example relating to the abuse of workers in less economically developed countries, or some kind of poor treatment of staff or customers by a business. Perhaps you are aware of examples of firms that have used highly pressurised selling techniques to persuade customers to buy products that they don't actually need.

UNIT 5.9

Student howler

1. Never overlook the problems of introducing new technology. If it can't be introduced successfully it certainly won't be the key to success. Some firms are able to operate perfectly successfully without keeping abreast of the latest technological developments, perhaps by offering a low-cost alternative or by offering a traditional 'hand-made' image.

Test yourself

1. A price premium can be charged as the product is likely to be unique. The benefit to a firm's image that can arise from being perceived as the original and therefore the best – the classic example being the benefits enjoyed by Sony as producers of the very first ever personal stereo, the Walkman. 2. Workers may fear for their jobs – this could lead to lower levels of motivation and possible higher labour turnover levels. 3. One problem may arise from the need to educate consumers as to what the technology actually does (they may be unaware of the uses of the product) – what benefits does MP3 bring over and above traditional CDs? In addition, it may be hard to gain distribution for the new product – how eager will retailers be to stock the product if consumers don't know what it can do? 4. CAD can produce more accurate designs than traditional methods of design. The key benefit lies in CAD's ability to dispense with the need for many prototypes. The design can be tested using computer simulations, perhaps a car design can be tested in a simulated wind tunnel rather than needing to meet the costs of building a prototype and hiring time in a wind tunnel. Designs can also be devised and realised faster, reducing the time taken to develop products and therefore the ongoing development costs.

UNIT 5.10

Test yourself

1. A place where buyers and sellers meet. 2. Two consecutive quarters when the economic activity is lower than the previous quarter, characterised by low demand and high unemployment; often low interest rates and lower inflation. 3. The Bank of England's Monetary Policy Committee. 4. The cost of borrowing will rise so customers may have less disposable income. 5. Increase is 4. This is an increase of $4/116 \times 100 = 3.4\%$. 6. Prices of input may rise; businesses become uncompetitive internationally; wage inflation will make labour costs higher; price rises will be a cost; spending power is reduced so demand will be lower. 7. Equal Pay Act, Sex Discrimination Act, Race Relations Act, Disability Discrimination Act, Health and Safety at Work Act. 8. Individuals or

groups that are affected by the business or who can have an impact on the business, e.g. employees and customers. **9.** If unemployment is high there should be more labour available and there will be less pressure for wage increases. However this only works if the labour available has the required skills. **10.** Falling demand may lead to inefficient production. Loss of economies of scale may mean unit costs rise. If demand goes below break-even the firm will start to make losses and may go out of business. **11.** Sales of household goods may increase. Housing units will become smaller and there will be more demand. Goods may need to be sold in smaller packet sizes. **12.** Advantages: Speed of transfer of information; much more information can be gathered; costs are lower. Disadvantages: Information may be lost or intercepted and misused; employees waste time; loss of personal contact between employees. **13.** Actions carried out by the company which take into account the social and moral impact of the activity. **14.** If the pound rises imported goods will become cheaper and therefore the costs of production for the tyre manufacturer will be lower. However, they will face competition from cheaper imports of ready-made tyres by overseas producers. **15.** To ensure that no company has excessive power in the market; to prevent monopoly situations arising. **16.** A market where there are few sellers who tend not to compete on price but on product differentiation, e.g. chocolate makers in the UK, washing powder manufacturers.

Questions (Rate freeze wins warm welcome from all sides)

1. It would suggest that there are signs of a recovery in manufacturing but that it is not yet certain and may be patchy. **2.** Content (1 mark): Inflation is a general rise in prices. Application (1 mark): In this case the very hot summer weather has made vegetables more expensive. Analysis (2 marks): The RPI is measured by taking a basket of goods and services. The total price is compared to the price for the previous month. If any component of the basket goes up in price it will affect the average. Severe weather will affect the price and availability of raw materials, especially items such as fruit and vegetables. **3.** Content (2 marks): The rate of interest is the cost of borrowing. Application (2 marks): Answer should focus on a car retailer. A general answer will not get application marks. Analysis (4 marks): If the rate of interest is increased the cost of borrowing will rise. This will make it more expensive to borrow money for a car loan. Also customers may have less disposable income if they have mortgages and other loans. Both of these will make it less likely that people will buy cars, which are a luxury item. They

may buy second hand rather than new. There may be some customers who have savings so will have more disposable income. **4.** Content (2 marks): Consumer confidence is the expectation that consumers have about what will happen in the economy. Application (2 marks): It affects how customers behave. If confidence is low they may be expecting higher interest rates so may spend less to avoid building up debts that will cost them more in the future. Analysis (3 marks): Businesses may increase promotional activity. This may be expensive and may not encourage consumers to buy. Interest-free loans will allay the consumer's fears of increased interest rates. Lower prices may attract more sales but this will depend on price elasticity and may reduce revenue. Evaluation (3 marks): Show judgement in weighing up your argument, e.g. by suggesting which of the two ways is more likely to be effective.

Questions (The Grey Pound)

1. The money that is available to individuals to spend after paying for the necessities such as housing costs. **2.** Changing population trend may open up new markets such as the grey market in this case. It may, however, shrink existing markets. A reduction in the number of young people may mean that there are fewer workers available in the employment market, which may force up labour costs. **3.** Content (1 mark): International competitors are firms operating in other countries. Application (1 mark): Answer should relate to international competitors. Analysis (3 marks): British firms need to recognise changing trends and take action to take advantage of them. They need to ensure that they enter the market at the earliest opportunity. They need to ensure that costs are kept low so that they are competitive with international firms. If costs are too high overseas firms may be able to undercut the prices. **4.** Content (2 marks): Description of an external influence – this may be government (law changes); the economy (rises in inflation or exchange rate movement); stakeholder influence (pressure group influence on firm's activities). Analysis (4 marks): 2 marks for opportunities explained, 2 marks for threats outlined. **5.** Content (1 mark): Saga's target market is the over 50s. Application (2 marks): Answer should relate to Saga. Analysis (3 marks): Recognised the possibilities of the market segment when others were ignoring it; the market has grown as population trends have changed; good idea helped by changing demographics. Recognised target market and has focused activities on this market. Has not tried to move into other market segments but has developed products to suit this market. Evaluation (2 marks): Make judgement about Saga's success based on analysis.

Section 6

UNIT 6.1

Test yourself

1. Analysing gaps in the local market; innovative idea based on knowledge of a particular product market; buying a franchise; turning a hobby or interest into a business idea. 2. No small business start-up ever has as much money as they would like. At the start of the business there are many demands on the limited finance available. Generally this finance will be used up before the business actually starts trading, through the purchase of assets and stock. Once the business begins to trade, their running costs (e.g. wages and bills) will need to be paid, with cash. It is therefore critical that they are able to generate sufficient cash inflows from trading to cover these outflows. However, unless the business is able to open in a blaze of publicity and build up a strong base or regular customers quickly, cash inflows may start to arrive slowly and in small quantities. There will therefore be huge pressure on cash flow for a small business start-up. 3. Advertising in the yellow pages; direct mail shots or flyers to targeted potential customers and word of mouth; personal selling by the entrepreneur. 4. Shortage of cash meaning that bills cannot be paid: *Help by*: arranging enough finance to cover working capital requirement for first few months of trading; careful financial monitoring and cost control. Insufficient customers: *Help by*: Choosing the right location and improving the effectiveness of launch marketing. Poor organisational skills or entrepreneurship from the boss: *Help by*: Seeking plenty of advice from experts in this area.

UNIT 6.2

Student howlers

1. The LTD in the name means Johnsons are a private limited company who therefore cannot offer shares for sale on the stock market. 2. Firms only receive money from selling shares when they are first sold. Any increase or decrease in the price of the shares will not affect the firm's own finances.

Test yourself

1. Whether they will need limited liability. Whether they want to be the only owners or would they benefit from raising more money by selling shares to other shareholders. If they expect the business to grow in the near future they may well then need to take advantage of the limited liability offered by Ltd status.
2. Different initials in the name of the firm (Ltd is private PLC is public). Only the PLC can offer shares for sale to the public through the stock market. Ltds are likely to have shareholders who are more understanding of long term policies than PLC shareholders, who are likely to be demanding a return on their investment immediately. 3. If owners have limited liability they cannot lose personal assets as a result of their business being sued for malpractice or wrongdoing. Suing a partnership means suing the owners themselves. 4. There is no need to follow any legal formalities, thus reducing legal fees and possibly allowing the start up to happen faster. As a cafe is unlikely to run up significant debts, the need for limited liability is less than would be found in, say a manufacturing start up. 5. Family firms may wish to retain full control over the business. Some firms do not welcome the short-termist pressure that often comes from a stock market listing. Some firms may not be willing or able to find the money required to float on the stock market. If there is no need for extra capital, there is little to be gained from a flotation.

UNIT 6.3

Student howlers

1. No plan can ensure that a profit is generated. Profit will result from effective operations – these may be aided by forward planning. 2. This student is describing a marketing plan, and even then only one section of the marketing plan will contain the four Ps.

Test yourself

1. Will help to tackle: lack of finance, lack of forward planning. May not help to: increase number of customers; add extra skills to the business. 2. The planning process will help you to think through your ideas for the business very carefully. It should help you to gain finance from providers such as banks. It should also be useful once your restaurant is up and running – you can use the plan as a way of measuring whether performance is below expectations and therefore changes need to be made. 3. Personal information, objectives, marketing plan, production plan, financial plan. 4. Allows an objective assessment of success; could identify the major areas where the business failed during the year.

UNIT 6.4

Student howler

1. This is by no means true, since the aims of the organisation may be clearly stated, yet those within the organisation may be uncommitted to achieving those aims unless they were involved in the process of setting them in the first place. Telling people what their aims are will not ensure their commitment.

Test yourself

1. A highly bureaucratic culture may result in increased administration costs with extra paperwork to be completed. Bureaucratic cultures may also require more managerial costs since most decisions will need to be checked with managers. A more informal culture where staff are expected to 'go their own way' may lead to poor coordination resulting in the doubling up of certain tasks, leading to wasted time. 2. A sense of mission implies that everyone within the organisation is committed to the same goals. This means that all staff are likely to be highly motivated and more productive, specifically in achieving the goals the firm sets out to achieve. 3. The immediacy involved in a small firm, where everyone is clearly working for one organisation and has regular contact with the

most senior management tends to lead to a clearer understanding of the mission that the organisation's bosses are trying to achieve. In a larger organisation, some staff will feel isolated from the rest of the firm and a 'them and us' divide between management and workers may well lead to staff feeling uncommitted to the organisation's mission, since they neither care, nor genuinely understand what the organisation is trying to achieve. 4. A mission statement does have the benefit of allowing all staff to understand clearly the general goals of the firm. In this sense, staff will be clear on what it is they are trying to achieve. However, especially in larger organisations, staff are unlikely to have played any significant role in creating the mission statement and will therefore not be committed to achieving a goal that they may well feel has little or nothing to do with their own working lives. Overall, a mission statement is often a hollow, top-down exercise that brings little to the firm, yet a mission statement that has had genuine input from most within the organisation can provide a sense of unity of purpose that can drive the organisation towards success.

UNIT 6.5

Student howler

1. Strategy concerns the medium to long term – not the next week. A firm that wishes to change operational plans on a regular basis will do so, but will seek to ensure that any changes still fit in with their longer-term strategy.

Test yourself

1. If the strategy is designed to sell more of the same products in existing markets, price reductions may be used to boost sales levels, whilst aggressive promotion may also be needed. Strategies involving launching new products in existing markets will need investment in new product development and fairly expensive launch marketing campaigns, while attempts to break into new markets may well involve a process of education of new consumers unfamiliar with the firm's brands. Certainly marketing strategy will have a key role to play. HR strategy may involve recruiting extra staff to cope with the expected growth, and extra production and delivery equipment and machinery may be needed to cope with higher volumes of manufacturing. 2. Break-even – reduce costs to a minimum; Grow – broaden distribution levels; Diversify – spend heavily on research and development. 3. Brand image is a strength – Calvin Klein; Brand image is a weakness – most rail companies; Economic growth represents an opportunity – luxury goods manufacturers; New laws represent a threat – tobacco firms now that advertising is banned; The arrival of a major new competitor represents a threat – could be local firm pressurised by a new branch of a major national chain; An excellent distribution network is a strength – Amazon.co.uk; A lack of available finance is a weakness – MyTravel PLC (formerly Airtours). 4. Political – government transport policy relating to road transport. Economic – economic uncertainty may undermine sales, yet continued credit boom is an opportunity for most car manufacturers with many people willing to use credit to buy their new cars. Social – attitudes to car use may suggest possible long-term problems for many car manufacturers. Technological – significant technological advances in the car industry are the result of heavy research and development expenditure, something that a smaller player such as Rover may find hard to achieve.

INDEX